DICKENS ON LITERATURE

"HOUSEHOLD WORDS" OFFICE,
No. 16 Wellington Street, Strand.

DICKENS ON LITERATURE

A Continuing Study of His Aesthetic

RICHARD LETTIS

AMS Press
New York

Library of Congress Cataloging-in-Publication Data

Lettis, Richard
    Dickens on Literature: a continuing study of his aesthetic/by
Richard Lettis.
       p.   cm. — (AMS studies in the nineteenth century; no. 8)
    Includes bibliographical references.
    ISBN 0-404-61488-4
    1. Dickens, Charles, 1812-1870—Knowledge—Literature.
2. Dickens, Charles, 1812-1870—Aesthetics. 3. English fiction—19th
century—History and criticism—Theory, etc.
4. Aesthetics, British—19th century. I. Title. II. Series.
PR4592.L5L48 1990
823'.8—dc20

                                          89-45850
                                             CIP

All AMS books are printed on acid-free paper that meets the
guidelines for performance and durability of the Committee on
Production Guidelines for Book Longevity of the Council on Library
Resources.

AMS Press, Inc.
56 East 13th Street
New York, N.Y. 10003

Manufactured in the United States of America

Table of Contents

To Larae, Rebecca, Ritchie, Stephen, and Kimberly I.

Acknowledgements

I wish to thank the Faculty Research Committee of the C. W. Post Campus of Long Island University for granting me released time from teaching to facilitate the completion of this book. I also wish to thank Mrs. Dorothy Cole of the C. W. Post Computer Center for her tireless assistance in preparing the book for publication.

1

Criticism: A Nervous Dread

A study of Dickens' comments on literature must begin with the reminder that he hardly ever wrote at length about his profession. We have little more than briefly-expressed thoughts, a few delivered to friends and colleagues in moments of reflection, but most hastily written in conjunction with some practical concern. Dickens rarely undertook as much as a paragraph on abstract literary topics; much of what we glean from his writings comes in no more than a sentence or even a phrase, rendering a private judgment of a writer, making a point about good writing, or--far more infrequently--suggesting a theoretical concept or implying a principle of criticism. Often the reader is left to infer what he can from offhand comment, and must be constantly on guard against the dangers of putting together what Dickens would not have united, or of finding in a casual remark more than he intended to convey.

Why did an author of Dickens' stature not say more about literature? The answer has usually been that he had no interest in abstract statement; it has even been said that he had little interest in fiction beyond the practice of it. But the evidence of his nonfictional writing suggests a different conclusion. He says enough about other writers, about the craft of fiction, and about literary principles to indicate that he cared a great deal--certainly enough to show that his intelligence, far from being merely "animal," as George Henry Lewes called it, was capable of handling general literary concepts on a sophisticated level. But the writing also gives evidence of three convictions that, along with a real reluctance to hurt anyone by negative criticism, almost prohibited him from writing critical essays: he was embarrassed by what seemed to him pretentious professional discussion; he believed that literature should not be written about but should explain itself; and he seems to have had a real diffidence about making literary pronouncements. As I have shown in another work, he repeatedly demonstrated the first of these convictions in his commentary on painting: self-conscious orations on color and line seemed to him pretentious and unnecessary, and his comments on literature show a similar avoidance of "literary" language. The worst thing a writer could do, he felt, was explain his own work. "It is not for an author," he said in his Address in the Cheap Edition of *Pickwick Papers* in 1847, "to describe his own books. If they cannot speak for themselves, he is likely to do little service by speaking for them." "If the object an author has had, in writing a book," he said in his Preface to the third volume of *Master Humphrey's Clock* "cannot be discovered from its perusal, the probability is that it is very deep, or very shallow." And he felt the reading audience shared his feeling about prefaces: that which he wrote for the Second Series of *Sketches by Boz* might as well be short, he said, "because nine hundred and ninety-nine people out of a thousand never read a preface at all."[1]

Such statements leave little doubt that there is considerable difference between Dickens, who said very little in his prefaces, and such a novelist as Henry James, who said a great deal, but the difference is not that one author cared nothing for abstract literary concepts while the other cared much. Dickens was convinced that fiction should stand alone, that good writing was intelligible to most readers (if not to all on all levels, to nearly all on some level that would make the novel worth reading), and that commentary was offensive to his audience, a kind of patronizing "Let me tell you what you missed." He discouraged Richard Henry Horne from writing a long preface to a volume of poems:

> I would reduce it by five-sixths of its present amount. It is a strong impression, even with the discerning portion of the public, that a man makes a weak case when he tries to explain his writing. His writing should explain itself; rest manfully and calmly on its knowledge of itself; and express

whatever purpose and intention are in him.[2]

The man who writes this will probably not have his prefaces collected in a book entitled *The Art of the Novel*, but he still may have strong aesthetic convictions.

Dickens did not oppose critical commentary in general. He wrote many such comments in his private correspondence, published a few critical articles, and edited others for his journals. Still, though he said nothing against literary criticism, he would not have been in favor of the industry of exegesis that has developed in the twentieth century. Brief pieces of criticism in magazines could help readers to improve their skill in reading, and could guide public opinion about writers, helping good ones to acquire the larger audience they deserved. But I doubt that Dickens would have liked books of extended critical analysis (to say nothing of present efforts to elevate criticism to the level of literature). He did not think it right to direct readers, who he felt should make their own way, so that received writing would not become, as to some extent it is today, the result of professional guidance concerning what one should read and what one should not, but would instead remain a process of natural selection, with each reader coming to and enjoying what he or she was capable of understanding, the success or failure of writing therefore being determined by the whole, not merely the top, of the literate world. He refused to be a party to influential, prejudicial, pronouncement. He admired Samuel Johnson, but had no desire to be a Cham. Refusing to allow H. G. Adams to publish his "Appreciation" of John Overs' "Legend of Canterbury" in the *Kentish Coronal*, he said "I have a nervous dread of being supposed to direct the judgements of people who can judge very well for themselves. . . ." He told Overs that he was reluctant but willing to offer criticism of his work, and accompanied his subsequent commentary with the statement that he was "by no means satisfied, nor do I wish you to be, that my conclusions are infallible; and I scarcely expect, and certainly do not desire, that you should attach any weight to them, whatever."[3] This, from the greatest writer of his age, to one of the humblest.

"I entertain a very strong objection to seeing my opinion of any Book in print," he wrote, "as it does seem a kind of presumption and a dictating to people's taste." He wrote George H. Lewes that he had "a most accursed diffidence about writing to men concerning their own books, as though I were setting myself up for a kind of literary special pleader, and sending out my opinions with grave importance." In part, his modesty may have been owing to experience. "I have always found, as yet," he wrote, "that however much 'the trade' [book publishers] may care for my writings, they are by no means deferential to my opinion of other mens' [sic]--indeed that they rather doubt, and look with distrust upon it. . . ."[4] But perhaps the silence was not merely humility on Dickens' part; perhaps in good measure it was in keeping with his desire for privacy. Reluctantly granting to G. H. Lewes permission to quote a privately-written note, he said, ". . . No one save yourself can imagine the full extent of the grounds I have for never stepping out of my picture-frame to address the spectators. . . ." One does not have to be Lewes to guess that preservation of his private life was one of them. Commentary on writing, by the writer or another, led to commentary on writers: Dickens greatly disliked the pursuit of literature through study of the lives of its authors. He burned his own correspondence to cut off any such indirect study of his own work, and said of Shakespeare,

> It is a great comfort, to my thinking, that so little
> is known concerning the poet. It is a fine
> mystery; and I tremble every day lest something
> should come out. If he had had a Boswell, society
> wouldn't have respected his grave, but would
> calmly have had his skull in the phrenological
> shop-windows

--just as, we might note, society failed to respect Dickens' wishes concerning his own burial, placing him in Westminster Abbey instead of in the private grave he desired. (Dickens wrote the above, it is important to note, in 1847, well before he had cause to conceal details of his private life.) He also objected to the kind of critical writing in which he saw a divisive potential threatening that literary world to which he labored to bring dignity and union. He disliked Thackeray's series entitled "Punch's Prize Novelists," begun in April of 1847, which parodied contemporary novelists, thinking it "a great pity to take advantage of the means our calling gives us with such accursed readiness, of at all depreciating or vulgarizing each other--but this seems to me to be one of the main reasons why we are generally more divided among ourselves than artists who have not those means at their command."[5]

The convoluted paths of twentieth-century literature have make extended literary criticism necessary: when we read *Finnegans Wake*, we must agree that literature needs elucidation, and may sometimes even wish the author himself would, like Byron's wish for Coleridge, explain his explanation. But Dickens saw another possible path for literature, one in which great novels would be comprehensible on some level to all who read them, and so would not require extended analysis. There are fascinating similarities between Dickens and modern literature, but nothing so separates him from the age of Joyce as his belief in the kind of audience for whom he was to write.

Still, none of this completely accounts for Dickens' minimal discussion of literary theory. The assertions of his friends and followers that he cared little for abstract speculation cannot be entirely wrong; nevertheless, the fact that he did upon occasion write about the theory and principles of literature suggests that they are not entirely right, either: more than an indifference to the abstract--more than we have seen so far--is needed for us to understand the infrequency of Dickens' aesthetic pronouncements.

To begin with, it would seem that in good part Dickens had not the pressing need other novelists have had to talk about literature. Fielding had to explain, no doubt as much to himself as to others, the new genre his age was developing. Flaubert struggled and suffered with his art, and needed to record the process. James' writing was so much from the head, and his practice of it was so fastidious-- Blackmur said that he "enjoyed an excess of intelligence and he suffered . . . from an excessive effort to communicate it"--that exhaustive exploration of its theory was essential. But Dickens knew his fiction and (some deconstructionists to the contrary notwithstanding) trusted it; though he thought about it all his life and, when good reason presented itself, wrote about it, he felt no pressure to put it all into words for himself, to fix it with a formulative phrase.   The long journey of his novels from *Pickwick* to *Edwin Drood* demonstrates well enough that he found no Trollopian ease in the concept of the novel which he inherited: he sought always to stretch its potential beyond those who preceded him, to leave it something other than he had found it.   I have suggested elsewhere that in his illustrations and his dramatic readings he tried to go beyond the bounds of prose fiction.   But while much that he said showed writing to be for him a birth-giving agony, little he wrote suggested a need to fight his way to a new understanding or acceptance of the novel.   As Johnson put it, "He felt, . . . as a writer, no troubled areas that he needed to explore."[6]

We may add one simple additional reason for Dickens' limited critical commentary: few novelists of his time ever did discuss literature at length.   Accustomed as we are to thinking of the novelist in terms of Flaubert, Moore, James, and their followers, we have come to consider such writers the rule, and to wonder what is wrong with a novelist who does not talk or write about his fiction.   Certainly it is a mistake, as Richard Stang has shown, to believe that "criticism of the novel and discussions of the theory of the novel somehow began *ex nihilo* with Flaubert in France, and that England remained remarkably insulated from these theories until infected or fertilized (depending on one's point of view) by either Henry James or George Moore in the eighties."   But while Stang demonstrates that criticism was alive as early as the first half of the eighteenth century, he also shows that it was neither very extensive nor very good, and that though it became more plentiful in the middle of the nineteenth century, relatively little of it was carefully formulated theory worked out in detail in scholarly studies-- and when it was, it was done much more often by critics such as Leslie Stephen, R. H. Hutton, and G. H. Lewes than by major novelists: when Stang lists those who offer "brilliant discussions" of the novel, he includes only that novelist we will expect: George Eliot. If some novelists of the nineteenth century--for example, such "followers" of Dickens as Collins and Reade--were willing to say more about the novel than he did, it was not because they were more capable of considering the abstract, or were more interested, but because unlike him they were eager in their prefaces to defend their work against hostile reviewers, and got involved in arguing about what a novel should be in order to demonstrate that their works fit the defined desideratum. In his limited critical commentary, Dickens was not behind his time. "The most trenchant discussions" of literature of the time, Stang says, "are not those published in books. . . ." True, Stang calls Bulwer's "Art in Fiction" "one of the most important critical documents of the period."[7] But Bulwer's importance lay in his arguing for the seriousness of the novel in a time not yet willing to accept it, not in the formulation of new or even particularly valuable critical principles.

Dickens wrote nothing like "Art in Fiction," but in speeches, letters, and articles he argued no less strongly for the importance of literature, which "as a profession," he said, had "no distinct status" in his time. The effort by no means originated with him and Bulwer: since the beginning of the century Isaac D'Israeli and others had been fighting for "the dignity of literature." Angus Wilson says that "Dickens revered Scott, not only for his novels but for the dignity, the dedication and the industry with which he followed his profession of writing," though he rightly guesses that Dickens "must have had reservations about Scott's tendency to decry his professionalism. . . ."[8] In the middle of the century, the Dickens circle carried on the cause. John Forster struck several blows for literature in his study of eighteenth-century writers; Dickens called him "the gallant champion of the dignity of literature," and told him that in his work on Richard Steele "the assertion of the claims of literature throughout is of the noblest and most gallant kind." Dickens praised such champions wherever he found them. "When literary men shall begin to feel the honor and worth of their pursuit, as you would teach them to," he wrote to Lewes, "Literature will be a happier calling. . . ."[9]

The one friend who clearly diverged from this course was Thackeray; no doubt the rift that widened between him and Dickens, though caused by several things, was deepened by their different attitudes.   Even in his "In Memoriam: William Makepeace Thackeray," Dickens mentioned the disagreement: "We had our own differences of opinion.   I thought that he too much feigned a want of earnestness, and that he made a pretence of undervaluing his art, which was not good for the art that he held in trust."[10]

In his letters and speeches, Dickens insisted again and again on the high position art should hold, and objected when other things were placed above it.   Speaking at a soiree of the Mechanics Institution in Liverpool, he praised the accomplishments of science, but spoke too "of those gentler works of art which, though achieved in perishable stone, by yet more perishable hands of dust, are in their influence immortal."   Repeatedly he declared, as he did in a reply to Lord Houghton's remonstrance against his refusal to seek political office, that "when he took literature for his profession he intended it to be his sole profession," and that "literature was a dignified calling on which any man might stand or fall. . . ."   He wrote of his profession to James A. Manson that "I have never allowed it to be patronized, or tolerated, or treated like a good child or a bad child.   In simply doing my plain duty by it, I am always animated by the hope of leaving it, a little better understood by the thoughtless than I found it."[11]

He chafed at the inadequate protection the law gave to the literary man; concerning a "case" in law he wrote to S. W. Fellom that "I cannot doubt that any author is justified in asserting his own literary rights.   They are at the best, shabbily enough secured to him."   He lamented in his "Nobody's Story" that Nobody was able to find among the honored people of society those "whose wise fancy had opened a new and high existence to the humblest. . . ."   He was critical of anything--whether done by writer, publisher, or anyone else--that he thought potentially damaging to the reputation of literature: when a good publisher printed a bad book, he wrote that ". . . we must, for the honor of Literature, plainly express our great surprise and regret that [the writer] comes arm-in-arm with such good company as Messrs. Longman and Company." "I hope I shall never fall off," he said, "from my duty of assisting the claims of literature and of its professors." About many serious things Dickens could be light-hearted, but he never joked about this: we have no text of the speech he made at the Artist's Benevolent Society annual dinner in 1844, but the Reverend W. H. Brookfield assures us that it had "Not a jot of humour in it."[12]

On the other hand, Dickens never tolerated pretentious pumping of the dignity of art, nor trading on it for unearned advantage or profit. "I find that to make no exacting assertion of its claims, on the one hand--and steadily to take my stand by it, on the other, as a worthy calling, and my sole fortune--is to do right, and to take sufficient rank." He despised the cliché of the unappreciated writer, and when he wrote an introduction to a small collection of poems by the workingman John Overs, he made it clear that he did not intend to

> charge mankind in general, with having entered into a conspiracy to neglect the author of this volume, or to leave him pining in obscurity. . . . I see no reason to be hot, or bitter, or lowering, or sarcastic, or indignant, or fierce, or sour, or sharp, in his behalf. . . . I have nothing to exalt; nothing to flourish in the face of a stony-hearted world. . . .

That the world could be hard on a writer, Dickens knew, but it was the world's contempt for his profession that he fought most vigorously, not its treatment of individual authors. He thought that those who sought unearned advantage by invoking the sacredness of literature only damaged it the more. Writing of the biography of the poet John Clare, he said,

> Did you ever see such preposterous exaggeration of

small claims? And isn't it expressive, the perpetual prating of him as the poet. So another Incompetent used to write to the Literary Fund when I was on the committee. "This leaves the Poet at his divine mission in a corner of the room. The Poet's mother is weaving."

He disliked what he considered pretentious tributes to writers. He was an inveterate opponent of memorials, even one for so admired a friend as Thomas Hood: "I have the greatest tenderness for the memory of Hood, as I had for himself. But I am not very favorable to posthumous memorials in the monument way . . ." and therefore he declined to support John Watkins' effort so to perpetuate the memory of the poet. One's work should be one's monument; all else was puffery, and would ultimately hurt literature. Dickens did quietly contribute three guineas to a fund for a statue "for Wilson," while refusing to serve on the memorial committee. "These posthumous honors of committee, subscriptions, and Westminster Abbey," he said two years before his death, "are so profoundly unsatisfactory in my eyes that--plainly--I would rather have nothing to do with them in any case," and added that he hoped to be "quietly buried without any memorial but such as I have set up in my lifetime."[13] His time loved him too much to grant anything but the very last part of his wish: Dickens was buried in Westminster Abbey, and must take his eternal consolation only from the fact that the stone in the floor bears nothing more than his last name.

For unpretentious struggling artists Dickens had considerable sympathy: his money and his time were frequently at their service. In 1848 he wrote to friends about "a plan I have for getting the general mass of authors and artists to ensure their lives . . ." by means of a National Provident Institution. But the idea was for writers to help themselves, not to be helped by others. While he supported organizations for the relief of the indigent artist, he did not like anything which furthered the popular notion that most artists shamefully failed to support themselves. In speeches at the General Theatrical Fund he took issue with "the sweeping charge of improvidence" leveled against actors "and other not dissimilar pursuits." True, he was also a member of the Royal Literary Fund Society, formed to assist the needy writer, but part of his work in that organization was, first, to put the control of the Society "entirely in the hands of literary and scientific men," because "no other human being had any business there whatsoever," and second, "to consider the feasibility of making the Literary Fund Society an Institution serviceable and creditable to the followers of Literature as a liberal profession, and not wholly restricted to the temporary relief of writers in distress."[14] Dickens and his friends (principally John Forster and C. W. Dilke) were defeated in their efforts to change the nature of the organization, but their attempt makes it clear that Dickens held the dignity of his profession even above the needs of its poorer members, humanely concerned as he was for their welfare. (I admittedly restrict my consideration to but a corner of the battle Dickens and his friends waged; the entire question is more complex. As K. J. Fielding says: "Their exact objections to the management of the Literary Fund are not easy to define," though he agrees that "above all, they had the positive ideal of reorganizing the society so that it should be run by authors, for authors, and should help to make authorship a respected profession instead of a precarious branch of journalism. Time after time they insisted that they wanted to raise the status of the whole literary profession; for although they were rebels and reformers they not only wanted respect, but respectability.") A few years later, Dickens effected a similar change in the Guild of Literature and Art: ". . . All assistance hitherto, has been so much in the way of alms-giving that we purposely make the merit, rather than the means of the applicant, our test"--for future grants. The needy must be helped--Dickens played an important role in getting a pension of 100 pounds for John Poole, for example[15]--but it must be, *contra* Mr. Doolittle, the deserving poor: scribblers need not apply.

Dickens found one cause of the inferior status of literature to be that ancient form of support for the writer, patronage. Our age is gravely concerned with the potential damage to literature of writers and publishers who seek only to please the masses, but Dickens saw that in his time the average reader was a far better influence upon fiction than the wealthy and titled patron. In a speech at Birmingham he said,

> To the great phalanx of the people . . . literature had turned happily from individual patrons, sometimes munificent, often sordid, always few, and has found there at once its highest purpose, its natural range of action, and its best reward. . . . From the shame of the purchased dedication, from the scurrilous and dirty work of Grub Street, from the dependent seat or sufferance at my Lord Duke's table today, and from the sponging-house and Marshalsea tomorrow, . . . from all such evils the people have set Literature free. . . . Literature . . . cannot too ardently advocate the cause of their advancement, happiness, and prosperity.

At a banquet celebrating the laying of the foundation of the Southwark Literary and Scientific Institution, he said,

> Had institutions similar to this existed long since, that one disgraceful leaf of dedication which formed the blot upon the literature of past ages, would have been torn from its pages. That huckstering, peddling, pandering to patronage for the sale of a book, the offspring of intellect and genius, would not now remain a stain upon their most brilliant productions. Oh! it was sickening to see a man whom God had made a poet, crouching to those whose only title to eminence was derived from the achievements of the great great grandfather of those sons. The poet--for it was his natural avocation--was entitled to worship the stars; but when they contemplated him paying his adoration to stars and garters too, that was indeed a very different thing.

The great body of readers, he believed, would judge

literature far better than the condescending aristocrat; freed from patronage, writing would succeed or fail as it did its job: "I hold the opinion that there is a great deal too much patronage in England. The better the design [a literary venture has], the less (as I think) should it seek such adventitious aid, and the more composedly should it rest on its own merits." Dickens, Forster tells us, was "intolerant of every magnificent proposal that should render the literary man independent of the bookseller. . . ."[16] Not even royal patronage was acceptable: ". . . The three great keys to the royal palace (after rank and politics) are Science, Literature, Art. I don't approve of this myself. I think it ungenteel and barbarous, and quite un-English. . . . But so it is." Writers who toadied to rank infuriated him: he detested the man who "would rather exchange nods in the Park with a semi-idiotic Dowager, than fraternize with another Shakespeare." But he was even angrier with Important People who offended his profession, and wrote wrathfully of an incident in which "the accredited representatives of our arts and sciences are disdainfully slighted by our Ambassador in the French capital. . . ." At times Dickens was too sensitive: Forster tells of an incident in which Dickens was invited by the Lord Mayor to a Mansion House dinner which he was giving in honor of literature and art. Expressing himself, for Dickens' taste, a bit too much to the effect that he and his colleagues were "in the habit of having princes, dukes, ministers, and what not for our guests," and that it was a delight to have ordinary people like writers and artists for a change--"In other words, what could possibly be pleasanter than for people satiated with greatness to get for a while by way of change into the butler's pantry"--, the Lord Mayor drew upon himself a reply of thanks by Dickens for his interest in literature, "which was not lessened by the fact of its being unusual in that hall." All this, as K. J. Fielding remarks, was unfair: "Dickens and most of his fellow authors . . . were all alike in complaining of lack of recognition when it was withheld, and rejecting it as patronage when it was offered."[17]

But if Dickens was over-sensitive to fancied slight from outside the profession, he was also meticulous in his own actions within it: he would do nothing that might render it vulnerable to insult. Forster says that of paramount importance in the consideration of whether Dickens should give public readings of his novels was "the question of respect for his calling as a writer . . ."; Dickens announced himself ready to read only after having "satisfied myself that it can involve no possible compromise of the credit and independence of literature." Some years after the Mansion House dinner, he declined an invitation to another such, explaining to the artist David Roberts that he must do so since he had recently criticized the "City Corporation" in *Household Words*:

> I do not think it consistent with my respect for myself, or for the art I profess, to blow hot and cold in the same breath; and to laugh at the institution in print, and accept the hospitality of its representative while the ink is staring us all in the face. There is a great deal too much of this among us, and it does not elevate the earnestness or delicacy of literature.[18]

Enough has been quoted to make it clear that Dickens took literature seriously, however reluctant he might be, for what he saw as good reasons, to write at length about it. As we sift through what he did find occasion to say--first as we examine his work as editor, then as we see his comments on prose fiction--we will find that he thought seriously, as well, and that he could, had he desired to do so, have made a solid contribution to the developing literary concepts of his time.

2
Journalism: Indispensable to Civilization

If journalism is the poor relation of the arts, it nevertheless occupies a room in the same dwelling, and Dickens' experiences in it reveal and confirm important aspects of his aesthetic. Angus Wilson says that "in his letters to contributors [to Dickens' journals] we have a collection of his views on the writing of fiction that up to a point illuminates his own practice--the craftsmanship, rather than the deeper aspects of his art. . . ." For the most part the qualification is valid, but a careful reading of some comments reveals deeper concerns than craft. It is no bad beginning of our task to study the work of the man whom Lord Northcliffe, founder of several nineteenth-century English journals, called "the greatest magazine editor of his or any other age,"[1] for his work as editor not only reveals his appraisal of journalism and his standards as editor, but also tells us much about his principles of fiction and of composition in general.

Dickens was both critical and supportive of journalism. He thought it too often just short of patriotism as the last refuge of scoundrels, who used its power to attack and vilify. He was critical of many of the papers of his time, finding them to be commonplace in their approach, trite in their language, and inaccurate in their reporting. But he was one of the first to realize that newspapers would be indispensable to civilization--a public safeguard, a record and teacher of life's changes and uncertainties. He took pride in his own skills as reporter, felt they contributed to his talent as author, and clearly enjoyed his experiences in journalism. As editor, he showed that same delicate sense of what would affect the reader that he displayed when considering how a play would affect its audience. As editor of stories, he worked for the same kind of reality in dialogue, scene, and character that he looked for as truth to nature in paintings, and for the same reason: he felt that it was the only way of

penetrating to a deeper truth (one that few realists ever
concede to be there). He strongly supported originality in
writing submitted to him, and detested the trite, the
ordinary--he hated, for example, language which had the
common story-telling tone. Suspense, liveliness, the striking
effect, were qualities he preferred, and he always opted,
when he could, for the positive ending--not, I believe, merely
to make the reader happy, or for any puerile preference for
the pleasant, but because he believed that literature should
find something to affirm. He liked the technique of contrast,
scene with scene, and character with character. Finally, he
liked a story in which the narrative voice played as small a
role as possible, leaving the story to, as Howells said of
Dickens' own novels, "somehow make the thing transact
itself."

Despite the great amount of time he spent in the
newspaper room, Dickens did not think too highly of the
abode; it contained, he said,

> Every dirty speck on the fair face of the
> Almighty's creation, . . . every rotten-hearted
> pander who has been beaten, kicked, and rolled in
> the kennel, yet struts it in the editorial "We" once
> a week; every vagabond that an honest man's
> gorge must rise at; every live emetic in that
> noxious drug-shop the press. . . .

Usually an advocate of free speech, Dickens felt so strongly
about the abuses of the press that he favored a stamp duty
as "some protection against the rash and hasty launching of
blackguard newspapers." When the servant of his friend Miss
Coutts mistakenly informed her that Dickens needed a
courier, he wrote, "I cannot understand how your man got
such information--unless he derived it from a newspaper. I
see almost daily, in these sources of intelligence, the most
prodigious accounts of my occupations, intentions, &c. &c.,
which are all so new to me that they make my hair stand on
end." Not only was Dickens not fond of its practitioners,
but he at times disliked the very practice of journalism--
"an occupation which is sufficiently irksome in itself. . . ."[2]

Dickens commented fairly often on the poor quality of newspaper reporting, especially when it affected his own life. Writing to his sister-in-law Georgina from Edinburgh while on a reading tour, he said, "I have not sent up any newspapers, as they are generally so poorly written, that you may know beforehand all the commonplaces that they will write." An exception was the *Scotsman*, which he did send. Telling Miss Coutts of his presiding at a soiree in Glasgow, he wrote, "I would send you a newspaper of this morning with an account of the proceedings, but my speech is so dismally done in the report, that I can't make up my mind to send it." His wife Catherine had not attended the above function because she had a miscarriage on the train; Dickens said that "In one of the Glasgow papers, she is elaborately described."[3]

Dickens did not comment at length upon the writing style of newspapers; he seems to have been more concerned with inaccuracies and downright misrepresentation than with aesthetics. But in a few places in his writing he did poke fun at the verbiage, pomposity, and clichés of journalism, as in the piece "It is Not Generally Known," in which he works overused phrases to death. Long before Frank Sullivan, of *New Yorker* fame, he made fun of the journalistic cliché expert: speaking of the strong winds at Walworth, he wrote,

> I have read of more chimney-stacks and house-copings coming down with terrific smashes at Walworth, and of more sacred edifices being nearly (not quite) blown out to sea from the same accursed locality, than I have read of practiced thieves with the appearance and manners of gentlemen--a popular phenomenon which never existed on earth out of fiction and a police report. Again: I wonder why people are always blown into the Surrey Canal, and into no other piece of water! Why do people get up early and go out in groups, to be blown into the Surrey Canal? Do they say to one another, "Welcome death, so that we get into the newspapers"?[4]

But his objections are otherwise confined to content, like that in which he complains that the "Court Newsman" gives other countries false ideas about England through his recounting "the dull slipslop" of court news about Royalty riding horses, having lunch, and exercising their infants, or that in his article on the London reporter of the *Tattlesnivel Bleater*, who sends honest facts home to his paper only to find them fiendishly changed by people out to damage his reputation.[5]

American newspapers, which earned his disgust and hatred during his first trip to the United States, largely by their angry reaction to his appeal for international copyright, but also by their very real scurrilousness, came in for scads of criticism in *American Notes*. Missing the street entertainments of London, Dickens asked himself if there were no amusements in New York and, among other things, found them in the newspapers,

> dealing in round abuse and blackguard names; pulling off the roofs of private houses, as the Halting Devil did in Spain; primping and pandering for all degrees of vicious taste, and gorging with coined lies the most voracious maw; imputing to every man in public life the coarsest and the vilest motives; scaring away from the stabbed and prostrate body-politic, every Samaritan of clear conscience and good deeds; and setting on, with yell and whistle and the clapping of fool hands, the vilest vermin and worst birds of prey.

Church and education might thrive in America, he said, but "while the newspaper press of America is in, or near, its present abject state, high moral improvement in that country is hopeless." Perhaps by his second visit he felt the state of the press to have improved to some extent; the New York Press gave him a public dinner, which he seems to have attended with some pleasure.[6]

But obviously Dickens was attracted to the world of newspapers and magazines, the profession which gave him his first literary employment, and in which he intermittently labored until his death.   At a speech of the Newsvender's Benevolent Institution he praised "that great power which had become the axis on which the moral world turned. . . . [It was] a fountain of knowledge to all men. . . . [The presses] were felt in their faintest throb throughout the civilized world."   "He could not forget that his first entry into life, his first success in life, his first view of the heavings of life around him, were in connexion with a London daily newspaper. . . ."   At another meeting of the same organization, he said that ". . . The daily press is the portal through which men of great ability, intelligence, and energy pass to win their way to distinction in every quarter of the world. . . ."   It was "the great public safeguard," an asset of the modern world greatly improved from earlier days when, as he wrote in a poem, "the Press was seldom known to snarl and bark, / But sweetly sang of men in power, like any tuneful lark."   Chairing the anniversary festival of the Printer's Pension Society, he toasted the Press, "which has impelled [the world] onward in the path of knowledge, of mercy, and of human improvement. . . .[7]

Newspapers taught reality.   "I think the lesson we can learn from the newsman is some new illustration of the uncertainty of life, some illustration of its vicissitudes and fluctuations."   Such illustrations, of course, were not always pleasant: to read the newspaper "from the whimsical point of view" is the reading "that most promotes digestion."   We should be grateful too, Dickens said, for the things the press does *not* tell us: he suggested "how much we the public owe to the reporters, if it were only for their skill in the two great successes of condensation and rejection.   Conceive what our sufferings, under an Imperial Parliament however popularly constituted, under however glorious a constitution, would be if the reporters could not skip."[8]

Perhaps Dickens was the first ever to make public fun of advertising. In the newspaper, he said,

> I am offered every kind of house, lodging, clerk,
> servant, situation, that I can possibly or impossibly
> want, with everything to eat, drink, wear, and use.
> I learn to my intense gratification--for I begin to

have some doubts upon the subject myself--that I
need never grow old; that I may preserve the
juvenile bloom of my complexion to any period of
life; that I need never more have any grey hairs;
that if I ever cough again it is entirely my own
fault; that I need never be ill of any complaint;
that if I want brown cod liver oil I know where to
find it; that if I want a Turkish bath I know
where to get it; and that if I want an income of
seven pounds a week for life for 2s 6d down, I
have only to send the postage stamps and there it
is.[9]

In some respects, Dickens' age sounds much like ours.

It is of interest, in passing, that Dickens did not like
the idea of a magazine especially for children. "I have no
faith," he said, "in the prospering of any periodical addressed
to the young ones. The greater should include the less, and
a good miscellany for grown people, should have much in it
of interest to growing people."[10]   As always for Dickens,
the best writing was that which could reach many audiences.

There were good newspapers, as well as bad. If some
papers could not cover meetings well, others could: the
Birmingham Journal was "The newspaper with the best report"
of the proceedings of the Birmingham Institution at which
Dickens had been guest of honor. Of coverage of the
Sanitorium dinner which he chaired in 1844, he said, "The
Sanitorium was exceedingly well done in the Herald. . . ."
On other grounds, he greatly approved of the *Morning
Chronicle*, on which he had worked; he wrote to Forster that

There never was any body connected with
newspapers who, in the same space of time, had so
much express and post-chaise experience as I. And
what gentlemen they were to serve, in such things,
at the old Morning Chronicle! Great or small it
did not matter. I have had to charge for half-a-
dozen break-downs in half-a-dozen times as many
miles. I have had to charge for the damage of a
great-coat for the droppings of a blazing wax-

candle, in writing through the smallest hours of the night in a swift-flying carriage and pair. I have had to charge for all sorts of breakages fifty times in a journey without question, such being the ordinary results of the pace which we went at. I have charged for broken hats, broken luggage, broken chaises, broken harness--everthing but a broken head, which is the only thing they would have grumbled to pay for.

Another of the papers for which he had worked, the *Examiner*, was also good--"one of the most able, original, useful, upright, and honorable journals in the world."[11]   And again, he liked the *Scotsman* of Edinburgh: "It is really a good newspaper, well written, and well managed."   Close friends with several members of the staff of *Punch*, he "lauded" that magazine, according to one source; in 1844 he found it "better than ever," and in 1845 he reported that "Punch's Almanac [published at Christmas] is brilliant. . . ." He commented favorably upon issues of other journals: he wrote that he was "perfectly charmed" with the October 1841 number of the *Edinburgh Review.*   He even liked one American newspaper.   He informed the New York editor Lewis Gaylord Clark that his paper *The Knickerbocker* was "as good as ever--and that is saying a good deal."[12]   But he had nothing good to say about *Chambers' Journal*, "that somewhat cast-iron and utilitarian publication (as congenial to me, generally, as the brown paper packages in which Ironmongers keep nails). . . ."   And he was not fond of the *Gentlemen's Magazine*: in one of his pieces a talking raven says, "If I contributed, in my natural state, to any Periodical, it would be the *Gentleman's Magazine.* [sic] I have a passion for amassing things that are of no use to me, and burying them."[13]

Dickens never forgot the satisfactions of his own work as a reporter; one wonders if this was not in part responsible, along with his fear that his novels might some day lose their appeal, for his sacrifice of so much time he might have given to creative work for the lesser achievement of editing.   He had been a good reporter: "There never was such a shorthand writer!" a colleague exclaimed, and added that Dickens "was the *Chronicle's* star reporter. . . ."[14]--no slight honor, for the *Morning Chronicle* was the only important rival of its day to the *Times*. Near the close of a long account of the trials he experienced as a young reporter, Dickens said that "The pleasure that I used to feel in the rapidity and dexterity of its exercise has never faded out of my heart," and he ended by saying that "my feeling for the vocation of my youth is not a sentiment taken up tonight to be thrown away tomorrow but is a faithful sympathy which is a part of myself." He believed his first efforts in fiction to be founded in good part upon his work as reporter: "To the wholesome training of severe newspaper work, when I was a very young man, I constantly refer my first successes. . . ." Dickens was one for paying debts, and he supported his first profession all his life, attending and chairing many meetings of professional and benevolent groups, serving as officer of several (e. g., he was Vice-President of the Newspaper Press Fund), and by working as one of the best editors of his time. "In *Household Words* Dickens demanded a care, a control, and a vision beyond all editorial precedent. . . ." Gerald Grubb adds that "nothing better illustrates his indomitable energy, and the boundless capacity for taking pains which distinguished him [sic] than the strenuous manner in which editorial duties were discharged,"[15] though some of the things his sub-editor Wills says in their correspondence suggest that in his role as editor Dickens occasionally put in something less than a full day: with all the other work he was involved in, it would seem to be impossible for him to have given the job his entire attention. He admitted as much to Macready in a letter announcing that a hunting accident to Wills had left him without help, so that "all the business and money details of 'All the Year Round' devolve upon me. And I have had to get them up, for I have never had experience of them." But get them up he did, and kept the magazine going until Wills recovered: the tremendous amount of work he undertook might have spread even the energies of Dickens thin at times, but he never balked at taking on work for others, and his contribution to journalism in his own time, as others have shown, was considerable. This large fact is supported, among other pieces of evidence, by an interesting small one: Dickens' preference for blue ink (because it dried faster, and he disliked blotting) set a fashion for London journalists for several years.[16]

As editor, Dickens labored unceasingly to improve the quality of his magazines, and while much of his work was necessarily in the area of style--extending to the minutiae of grammar, punctuation, and spelling--he also revealed many of his ideas about all facets of writing. Dickens had no tolerance for writers who turned out so much work that they became careless. He warned one of his regular contributors, Percy Fitzgerald, that

> You make me very uneasy on the subject of your new long story here, by sowing your name broadcast in so many fields at once, and undertaking such an impossible amount of fiction at one time. Just as you are coming on with us, you have another story in progress in "The Gentleman's Magazine," and another announced in "Once a Week." And so far as I know the art we both profess, it cannot be reasonably pursued in this way. I think the short story you are now finishing in these pages obviously marked by traces of great haste and small consideration; and a long story similarly blemished would really do the publication irreparable harm.
>
>   . . . Take a little more into account the necessity of care and preparation, and some self-denial in the quantity done.

Fitzgerald must have informed Dickens that he was prepared to care, for two days later Dickens accepted the long story, and assured him that their "engagement" would continue.[17] Fitzgerald did not, as he could have, remind Dickens of a young author who, nearly forty years before, had undertaken to write so many novels at one time that he almost had to go to law to extricate himself from his obligations, but who nevertheless became the greatest novelist in the English language.

In his biography Forster offers a picture of Dickens as giving free rein to his writers:

> It was said in a newspaper after his death, evidently by one of his contributors, that he always brought the best out of a man by encouragement and appreciation; that he liked his writers to feel unfettered, and that his last reply to a proposition for a series of articles had been: "Whatever you see your way to, I will see mine to."

Encouraging and appreciative he certainly was, but a reading of his letters indicates that he often brought out the best in a man or woman by either insisting upon extensive revision according to his instructions, or by rewriting articles on his own, sometimes to the point of virtually making the story or article his own in deed. Marion Troughton tells us that Dickens "developed a habit of writing and improving the work of his various contributors, and it mattered not to him whether they were established authors or newcomers to writing; all were liable to have their work tailored to suit his magazine." This is not entirely true: Dickens did not revise the contributions of his friend Bulwer (though he did offer advice), and he learned to alter the work of Elizabeth Gaskell only after obtaining her approval. Forster quotes him as saying of the more famous contributors to *All the Year Round* that

> When one of my literary brothers does me the honour to undertake such a task, I hold that he executes it on his own personal responsibility, and for the attainment of his own reputation; and I do not consider myself at liberty to exercise that control over his text which I claim as to other contributions.[18]

But on his less famous contributors he rode herd to such an extent that Forster's source might better have said,

"Whatever I see my way to, you will see yours to."

As early as *Bentley's Miscellany* we find Dickens insisting upon extensive revision. Of Dr. John Gideon Millinger's paper, "The Last Portrait Gallery," in the very first issue, he said, ". . . he must re-write the last half of it; it has cost me three hours this morning, and I can make nothing of it." Frequently, his comments express the vexation of the great artist who knows he could do a better job with an article or story than his contributor has, and is constantly tempted to do so. He thought a story by Catherine Crowe "horribly dismal; but with an alteration in that part about the sister's madness (which must not on any account remain) I should not be afraid of it. I could alter it my self in ten minutes." Only occasionally did he find something sent on by Wills to be so bad that he could not doctor it:

> The introduction to "Soldiers' Wives" [HW 9/61/51] must be entirely rewritten, and should be a plain and earnest representation of an obvious impropriety. Pray take out of the correspondent's part the message about "quivering at the smell of gin"-which makes *me* shudder from head to foot, in its unspeakable badness.
> "The Whitsuntide Festival" is so horribly maudlin and washy, that nothing can be done with it.

Sometimes he settled for a partial improvement: "Nothing can improve the design of Miss Lynn's story ["Marie's Fever," HW 7/30/53] (which I think very bad), but I have altered the wording of it, to avoid its looking, as it did, exactly like an indifferent translation." And sometimes he liked a piece very much, but still could not resist touching it. He told Wills that of "Four Stories" [AYR 9/14/61] "The first (by far the best) is a remarkably good and original one. I nearly rewrote them all."[19]

But since he could not rewrite everything, and since he did not receive enough good material to make up every issue, Dickens as editor learned the ugly lesson of compromise. A constant theme of the letters is the reluctant acceptance of inferior writing because, in the absence of anything better, something must be printed: the Dickens who as author only occasionally found himself obliged to shape his art to the exigencies of publication now faced the realities of editorship, and again and again groaned over poor stuff, but let it go in. He wrote to his subeditor Wills that he could not "conceive what 'Hope, an Epigram' [HW 6/12/52] meant, and I declare to you I have not the least idea now! Having nothing to put in its place, I could not disturb the Make-up by taking it out." "The Right One" was for *Household Words* [8/9/51] "poor--but I think just passable." He suffered over work submitted for the Christmas number for 1855:

> "The Actor" is altogether out of the question. By Miss Lynn, I suppose. By whomever--unmitigated Rot.
>   "The Question of Identity" I can make do, by cancelling at least a page. (I suppose it to be Sidney's.)
>   Do. [ditto], "The Landlady," by cancelling about half a column.
>   I trust in our good stars that we shall get better matter than this, or by Heaven we shall come poorly off!

(One notes that Dickens seems to have been able to recognize the style of several of his regular contributors.)[20] Of two pieces for the November 22, 1862, issue of *All the Year Round*, "The Shamrock" and "Under the Black and Yellow," he wrote Wills that the first was "just nothing at all, and really not worth inserting," and that the second "will just do, but will not more than just do, because the writer always does the same thing and rides somewhere to save somebody. When it goes in, observe (beside looking it well over for pointing) that 'venturino' in the fourth paragraph, ought to be 'venturini'; and that 'Ingleso' at the bottom of the same slip, ought to be 'Inglesi.'" A piece submitted the next year--"What a bad Hand"--was so horrible that it was not only to be rejected but "to be remorselessly distributed, and given to any of the four winds of Heaven that will accept it." Still worse, apparently, was an unidentified piece rejected by *Household Words*:

> If my mind could have been materialized, and drawn along the tops of all the spikes on the outside of the Queen's Bench prison, it could not have been more agonized than by ____; which for imbecility, carelessness, slovenly composition, relatives without antecedents, universal chaos, and one absorbing whirlpool of jolter-headedness, beats anything in print and paper I have ever "gone at" in my life.

But though at times Dickens' exasperation produces such Twainian-tempered letters, rarely is a contributor allowed to see one: though on a few occasions Dickens could lambaste a writer, the few rejections he wrote himself (most, apparently, were written by Wills) were of that polite but chillingly impersonal style affected by modern editors: "it is not suited to the requirements of All the Year Round." Perhaps Dickens originated that time-honored (or cursed) phrase. Certainly he was as little pleased with unsolicited material as are most editors: he wrote to his publisher Richard Bentley complaining of "voluntary contributions for the Miscellany" which were "the most appalling nonsense I ever had the ill fortune to peruse."[21]

Fortunately, not everything contributed to Dickens' journals was slovenly composition and appalling nonsense. A number of the good, and a few of the best writers of his time appeared in the pages of *Household Words* and *All the Year Round.* Such friends as Edward Bulwer, Wilkie Collins, and Leigh Hunt made contributions; so did Elizabeth Gaskell, Anthony Trollope and his mother, George Meredith, and Charles Reade. Writers less known today but popular in their time were also well represented: George Augustus Sala, Harriet Martineau (whose portrait may be seen in the Peabody museum in Salem, Massachusetts), Emily Jolly, Holme Lee (Harriet Parr), Walter Thornbury, Marguerite Power, and Edmund Yates. Dickens may be said to have discovered or at least materially to have assisted the early rise of several of these writers, including Elizabeth Gaskell.

Unlike some novelists, Dickens never felt threatened by the appearance of possible rivals: his comments on his contemporaries constantly demonstrate a generous delight in real talent. When unknown writers sent him promising material, his appreciation was great, no doubt all the more so because he found such wheat only by poring through the hills of chaff we have heard him lamenting. Probably such labor was part of what caused him to react so sharply to writers who moaned that good writing could not find a market; to one woman he wrote that

> You make an absurd, though common mistake, in supposing any human creature can help you to be an authoress, if you cannot become one in virtue of your own powers. I know nothing about "impenetrable barriers," "outsiders," and "charmed circles." I know that anyone who can write what is suitable to the requirements of my own journal-- for instance--is a person I am heartily glad to discover and do not very often find. And I believe this to be no rare case in periodical literature.

Not all of his finds proved to be major writers, and some were later disappointments to him, but his liking for such young writers as George Augustus Sala and Edmund Yates was justified by later achievement. When John Hollingshead submitted his first article, called "Poor Tom" [HW 10/17/57], Dickens called it "a pretty little paper of a good deal of merit," and added, "I am inclined to hope that the writer may be very serviceable to us."[22] Hollingshead never achieved literary fame, but he did become a regular contributor, and later was the lessee of the Gaiety Theatre.

Dickens also thought one Mrs. Blacker would prove to be a useful contributor. Her first piece accepted for *Household Words* was "The Clergyman's Wife" (1/22 & 1/29/59). "I have rather a strong hope she may turn out a very useful contributor," Dickens said. "I have read several of her papers, and have generally advised her how to make them better. . . . She has an excellent knowledge of a poor country parish, some very pretty womanly humour, some very good womanly observation, and a decided faculty for writing." Four months later he was trying to decide whether to include another story by her--"very good . . . exceedingly well done"--or to replace it with one by Thornbury.[23]   But no further mention of her is made, either positively or negatively, which suggests that Dickens' hope for her may have been frustrated not by his mistaken judgment of her talent, but by some event that terminated her writing for him.

One of Dickens' stars, until they had a falling out over his attack on industrialism in *Hard Times*, was Harriet Matineau.   Well before the division between them, he could be critical--in 1850 he said of her "The Sickness and Health of the People of Bleaburn" [HW (5/25/50)] that "It is heavy"--but most comments were favorable.   Of a contribution by her to the Christmas number for 1852, he wrote, "I have not a shadow of a doubt about Miss Martineau's story.   It is certain to tell.   I think it very affecting--admirably done--a fine plain purpose in it--quite a singular novelty.   For the last story in the Xmas No. it will be great.   I couldn't wish for a better."   After their disagreement, his comments became far less enthusiastic.[24] But with all contributors, male and female, he showed the same eagerness to find good work, and the same patient effort to improve it.   "It is at least as much a pleasure to me as it is to my interest," Dickens wrote to Mary Nichols, a would-be writer, "to find new contributors who hit the mark."   The comment accompanied a rejection of two papers by her, but Dickens proved his assertion by continuing to receive and comment on work from her, until he was able to accept something, a "condensed and altered story" (unidentified), though he rejected several other things, the last of record being a story for which "there appears to me no reason for its being a story.   The incidents are so worn and trite" that only "ingenuity" could save it, and there was no ingenuity.   One senses in such correspondence an effort on the part of the editor to hang in with any writer of minimal promise in hope that the mark might be reached, but for poor Miss Nichols it was not to be.   At other times, Dickens could be impressed by a first effort, yet foresee no great future for the writer.   A piece entitled "Now!" which appeared in *All the Year Round* (8/15/68) was described as "a highly remarkable piece of description.   It is done by a new man from whom I have accepted another article, but he will never do anything so good again."[25]

The   neophyte   who   seems   most   to   have   impressed Dickens was Emily Jolly.

> There is no doubt whatever, that the "Wife's Story" is written by a very remarkable woman.   I am quite clear that there is a strong reason to believe that a great writer is coming up in this person, whoever it is.
>
> . . . .
>
> . . . I assume the writer to be a lady. . . .   I think there is a surprising knowledge of one dark phase of human nature throughout this composition; and that it is expressed, generally, with uncommon passion and power.

There was one qualification: he found "the catastrophe to be altogether wrong.   That part must be rewritten if I accept it."   But clearly he was impressed; he wrote to her of "The Wife's Story" [HW (9/1-22/55)] that "I recognize in it such great merit and unusual promise, and I think it displays so much power and knowledge of the human heart, that I feel a strong interest in you as its writer," and concluded, "I have never been so much surprised and struck by any manuscript I have read. . . ."   Soon he was comparing her, to her advantage, to Miss Lynn, whose work he had published but who was not a favorite: a story by Miss Jolly "is more wholesome and more powerful, because it hits the target, which Miss Lynn goes a little about, with a rifle-shot in the centre of the Bull's eye, and knocks it clean over."[26]   Miss Jolly did not turn out to be a great writer, though she did go on to write *Mr. Arle* and other novels.   A writer of some talent must have seemed a writer of huge talent among the reams of worthless stuff that Dickens was obliged to plow through.

His early prediction of greatness for Emily Jolly was tempered by her later work. Two years after the above, he found himself reluctantly disapproving of a story by her, in a long comment that reaffirms several of his principles of fiction:

> it appears to me that the story is one that cannot possibly be told within the compass to which you have limited yourself. The three principle [sic] people are, every one of them, in the wrong with the reader, and you cannot put any of them right, without making the story extend over a longer space of time, and without anatomizing the souls of the actors more slowly and carefully. . . .
>
> The whole idea of the story is sufficiently difficult to require the most exact truth and the greatest knowledge and skill in the colouring throughout. In this respect I have no doubt of its being extremely defective. The people do not talk as such people would, and the little subtle touches of description which, by making the country house and the general scene real, would give an air of reality to the people (much to be desired) are altogether wanting. The more you set yourself to the illustration of your heroine's passionate nature, the more indispensible this attendant atmosphere of truth becomes. It would, in a manner, oblige the reader to believe in her. Whereas, for ever exploding like a great firework without any background, she glares and wheels and hisses, and goes out, and has lighted nothing.
>
> Lastly, I fear she is too convulsive from beginning to end. Pray reconsider, from this point of view, her brow, and her eyes, and her drawing herself up to her full height, and her being a perfumed presence, and her floating into rooms, also her asking people how they are, and the like,

on small provocation. When she hears music being
played, I think she is particularly objectionable.

He suggested that if Jolly kept the story by her for three or
four years, she would come to agree with his judgment, and
he urged patience and restraint, concluding with advice that
is positively Jamesian:

> When one is impelled to write this or that, one
> has still to consider: How much of this will tell
> for what I mean? How much of it is my own wild
> emotion and superfluous energy--how much remains
> that is truly belonging to this ideal character and
> these ideal circumstances? It is this laborious
> struggle to make this distinction, and in the
> distinction to try for it, that the road to the
> correction of faults lies.

He himself is impulsive, he concludes, but for years he has
tried to practice what he here preaches to her.[27]

Here are basic tenets of Dickens' craft: the finding of a
proper length for the kind of story to be told--especially
room for the necessary presentation of character; the careful
building of a realistic background so that otherwise
improbable characters may be accepted; the dislike of
theatrical (instead of dramatic) figures; and the stern
restriction of the story to *its* needs instead of to the desires
of the author. Perhaps only one or two critical writers
before Edmund Wilson would have believed that Dickens could
have made that last statement.

Following this letter, Dickens rarely wrote again to the
woman for whom he had predicted greatness. In 1865,
apparently in response to a request for help, he advised her
that he could not influence the publishers Chapman and Hall
to accept a work of hers, but suggested that she offer the
manuscript to them and mention her earlier work in *All the
Year Round*: "I think you would do so, with a very fair
chance of success." In the year before his death, he was
almost as pleased by her "An Experience" as he had been by
her first story: "I read it with extraordinary interest, and

was surprised by its uncommon merit," he wrote.

> . . . I accept it with more than readiness. . . . I
> think so very highly of it that I will have special
> attention called to it in a separate advertisement.
> I congratulate you most sincerely and heartily on
> having done a very special thing. It will always
> stand apart in my mind from any other story I
> ever read.

This was the "remarkable story" which he mentioned in a
letter to his daughter Mary (8/3/69); in a later letter to
Fitzgerald he called it "one of the most remarkable pieces I
ever saw."   Dickens must have been pleased to have
something of his early admiration justified.   But later that
year she apparently complained to him about the hardships of
the author's life, and with his characteristic tough-
mindedness on such a subject, Dickens would not sympathize:
he told her she had "not sufficiently considered what you
have to bear, if you publish a book. There is no help for it
but to bear, or forswear authorship."[28]
     In the same month that Dickens was so impressed by
Miss Jolly's "The Wife's Story," he was equally overwhelmed
by the work of another woman whose pen name was Holme
Lee, and real name was Harriet Parr.   The work was called
"Gilbert Massinger," and though Dickens was obliged to reject
it for *Household Words* because of its length and his fear of
exposing his readers to its painful subject (hereditary
madness, which he had rejected as a topic for an article
when Wilkie Collins proposed it in 1853), he declared himself
"so very much affected by [it] . . . that I am scarcely fit for
a business letter." He directed Wills to return it with his
praise and--in another exception to his usual rule--an offer
to send her a letter which "might, perhaps, help soften a
publisher."   Again poor Miss Lynn was used as an
unfavorable comparison: her "Sentiment and Action" [HW
(11/3 to 11/24/55)] "shews to considerable disadvantage, after
such writing. But it is what she represented it in her draft,
and it is very clever."[29]
     Dickens wrote directly to Miss Lee to express his

admiration. He had read "Gilbert Massinger," he said, "with the strongest emotion--and with a very exalted admiration of the great power displayed in it. Both in sincerity and tenderness I thought it masterly. It moved me more than I can express to you. . . . I felt the highest respect for the mind that had produced it." He complimented her upon "the vigor and pathos of the beautiful tale," and then accorded her his highest praise: "You had no existence, as to me when I read it. The actions and sufferings of the characters affected me by their own force and truth. . . ."[30] If the narrator is not refined out of existence, the authorial presence should be.

There is but one subsequent reference to Holme Lee, but it shows that she continued to write for Dickens. Seven years later, he wrote to Wills that a story by her (unidentified) was "very pretty, and *decidedly accepted*. . . ." It is curious that he wrote so little to or about these two women, whose first works so greatly impressed him. Perhaps the simple explanation is that a busy editor writes much more to and about writers who give him trouble--either by their poor work or their temperament--than about those whose writing and nature offer little need for written comment. In any case, Dickens had much more to say about the unappreciated Eliza Lynn, who later became Mrs. Lynn-Linton, from whom Dickens bought his last home, Gad's Hill. We have already seen his comment that "nothing can improve the design" of her first story, an unpromising beginning. Her next story, "Faithful Margaret," [HW (8/19/54)] is treated with equal disfavor: required to reduce the size of the number, Dickens told Wills that "*Whatever you want to take out, you can take from Miss Lynn.* The punctuation and dashing of whose story require particular attention." A year later he criticized her sense of reality: "Miss Lynn's notions of a criminal trial are of the Nightmarest description. The prisoner makes statements on oath, and is examined besides!"[31]

The next reference to Miss Lynn, however, is complimentary: Dickens thought her "Winifred's Vow" [HW (9/29/55)] "a very pretty story indeed." But while rejecting stories considered by Wills for the Christmas number of that year, he called one "unmitigated rot" and, as we have seen, assumed it was by Miss Lynn; one wonders what she would have charged for Gad's Hill if she had seen that comment. Still, he continued to accept work from her for several years, and so must have thought her at least minimally capable; G. S. Layard reported his saying that she was "Good for anything, and thoroughly reliable." His last reference to her, long after she, as Mrs. Lynn-Linton, had sold him the house, was again complimentary: he called her account of a book by Mrs. Gordon "most admirable," and asked Wills to explain to her at length why he had deleted a detail.[32]

A number of other writers can be followed with interest through Dickens' editorial commentary--Marguerite Power, George Sala, James Payn, Edmund Yates, Walter Thornbury, and Wills himself as writer, for example--but we must confine ourselves to more famous names. Some of these are mentioned only briefly: of Charles Reade Dickens said no more than "He seems to me, to be the best man for our purpose." To Adolphus Trollope he wrote, "I cried over the proof of Mrs. Trollope's last paper . . ." and added that she had "a gift of observation and tenderness. . . ." Of Anthony Trollope he wrote to Wills that a submitted story was "*exceedingly good*; highly picturesque and full of interest. But he mars the end by over-anticipating it, and I have changed it there a good deal." His only editorial comment on Leigh Hunt was that "'Gore House' is very poor. Page 591, first column. Stop at the Graces, and dele the rest of that paragraph. It is Skimpole, you know--the whole passage. I couldn't write it more like him."[33]

Though Bulwer wrote very little for Dickens, the comment is more extensive, though in letters not to Wills but to Bulwer himself. In 1860 Dickens wrote to ask if his friend could write something for *All the Year Round* and letters exchanged in November and December of that year led to the inclusion of *A Strange Story* in that journal, beginning in August of 1861 and ending in March of the following year. Dickens looked forward to it by saying that he had "never been so pleased at heart in all my literary life, as I am in the proud thought of standing side by side with you before this great audience. . . . I have perfect

faith in such a master-hand as yours. . . ."   And when he
received the first proofs four months later he wrote, "I could
not lay them aside, but was obliged to go on with them in
my bedroom until I got into a very ghostly state indeed. . . .
Of the beauty and power of the writing I say not a word, or
of its originality and boldness, or of its quite extraordinary
constructive skill."   Instead,   he   responded   to   Bulwer's
concern that readers would not believe in its psychological
"wonders" and assured him there was no cause for alarm.
Then he added modest criticism:

> Occasionally   in   the   dialogue   I   see   an
> expression here and there which might--always
> solely with a reference to your misgiving--be
> better away; and I think the vision . . . in the
> museum, should be made a little less abstruse. . . .
> I would also suggest that after the title we put
> the two words--a romance.
>   . . . .
>   . . . I think the story a very fine one, one that no
> other man could write. . . .

Four days later, another letter summed up the changes to be
made:

> --In shortening the conversations, to bring out the
> immediate   human   interest,   particularly   through
> Isabel.
> --to [sic] make the vision in the Museum less
> abstruse, and perhaps to shadow out in Margrave's
> brain, his part of wickedness in the story.
> --Greatly to condense the MS. read by Fenwick at
> Derval Court.
> --To substitute some other terror for the raising
> of the dead from the Mausoleum.[34]

The overall intention seems to have been to tighten the
story, provide a greater degree of reality and clarity, and to
avoid what Dickens may have felt to be too great a horror
for some of his readers--all in keeping with Dickens'

standards for fiction.

Three months later, when sales figures were coming in for *All the Year Round*, Dickens had good news for Bulwer: in terms of profits, at least, all was well. "We certainly have not in the least lost ground since Great Expectations [which Dickens had serialized in the journal to revive sales] finished; and to the best of our belief we have risen a thousand. . . . Under any other circumstances, we should unquestionably have dropped." In the following month, he was still happy: "it could not have taken a better hold.

". . . The exquisite art with which you have charged it, and have overcome the difficulties of the mode of publication, has fairly staggered me." Two months later, he wrote to approve of new material introduced into Numbers 19 and 20: "It is at once very sensitive and very new to have these various points of view presented to the reader's mind." His only qualification was to urge Bulwer to avoid notes, which he said the readers "invariably regard as interruptions of the text, not as strengtheners or elucidators of it. . . ." In the next month, the praise continued: "most masterly and most admirable! It is impossible to lay the sheets down without finishing them. . . . There cannot be a doubt of the beauty, power, and artistic excellence of the whole." And thus the correspondence and Bulwer's contribution to *All the Year Round* ended; about three years later Dickens asked for another story of one volume for the journal,[35] but nothing more by Bulwer was included before Dickens' death.

Another close friend with and about whom Dickens had a still longer correspondence in his role as editor was Wilkie Collins. His first letter to Collins about work for *Household Words* (that I have found) was in 1855; responding to Collins' idea for a piece entitled "The Ostler," to be included in *The Holly Tree*, the Christmas number for that year, Dickens said,

> The Ostler shall be yours, and I think the sketch involves an extremely good and startling idea. I am not, however, sure but that it trails off in the sudden disappearance of the woman without any result or explanation, and that some such thing

may not be wanted for the purpose--unless her never being heard of any more could be so very strikingly described as to supply the place of other culmination to the story. Will you consider that part again?

Collins did, and Dickens liked the revision: "I thought your Christmas Story *immensely improved* in the working out." Later, he called "The Ostler" "a charming paper. . . . Nothing can be more pleasant, easy, gay and unaffected."[36] Publication of Collins' "A Rogue's Life" began in *Household Words* on March 3, 1856, and finished on the twenty-ninth; as Collins was sending in instalments in February, Dickens wrote that the story "so far, is *admirable* . . . " and presumably was happy with the whole, though no further written commment was made. "A Petition to the Novel Writers," accepted a few months later, was "uncommonly droll, and shrewdly true." A short story, "The Diary of Anne Rodney," published in *Household Words* in July of 1856, also seems to have required no revision; Dickens wrote that it "possesses great merit and real pathos." "I cannot tell you what a high opinion I have of Anne Rodney," he also wrote. "I think it excellent, feel a personal pride and pleasure in it, which is a delightful sensation, and I know no one else who could have done it." To another correspondent he wrote that the story "possesses very remarkable merit--especially in the close of it." Two years later Collins' "The Unknown Public" was judged "very funny. Just what we want," and was printed in *Household Words* on August 21, 1858. Dickens took exception to remarks in Collins' "Highly Proper," [HW (10/2/58)] fearing they would unnecessarily offend the middle class; he asked Wills to check the article carefully, adding, "He has always a tendency to overdo that. . . ." By April of 1859, though, Dickens wrote Wills that Collins "has done a few very good paragraphs for the 'Register.'" (The "Occasional Register" was a regular feature of *All the Year Round* which offered paragraphs on matters of current interest.) A slight note of dissatisfaction crept back in a year later, when Dickens wrote to Georgina that

Wilkie brought the beginning of his part of the
Christmas No. to dinner yesterday. I hope it will
be good. But is it not a most extraordinary thing
that it began: "I have undertaken to take pen in
hand, to set down in writing & &" like the W in
W narratives? Of course, I at once pointed out
the necessity of cancelling that,--"off," as Carlyle
would say, "for evermore from the face of this
teeming earth where the universal Dayvle stalks at
large."[37]

This is the total of Dickens' editorial commentary (in
writing) upon Collins; it hardly seems enough to justify the
assertion by that other writer for Dickens, Elizabeth Lynn-
Linton, that

To Wilkie Collins he was a literary Mentor to a
young Telemachus, and he certainly counted for
much in Wilkie's future as a *litterateur*. I was
told by one who knew, that he took unheard-of
pains with his younger friend's first productions,
and went over them line by line, correcting,
deleting, adding to, carefully as a conscientious
schoolmaster dealing with the first essay of a
promising scholar.[38]

Either Mrs. Lynn-Linton had in mind the help Dickens also
gave Collins with his plays and novels, or she knew of
editorial advice to which we no longer have access (at least,
that I have not found).

Dickens' most interesting correspondence regarding one
of his contributors is that which he held with Elizabeth
Gaskell. Dickens' correspondence with Wills refers more
often to Gaskell than to any other writer, a fact owing more
perhaps to the difficulties he had with her than to his
admiration of her work, though admiration there certainly
was. She was one of the first authors he invited to write
for *Household Words*:

there is no living English writer whose aid I would
desire to enlist in preference to the authoress of
'Mary Barton' (a book that most profoundly
affected and impressed me). . . .
        I should set a value on your help, which your
modesty can hardly imagine; and I am perfectly
sure that the least result of your reflection or
observation in respect of the life around you,
would attract attention and do good.

He ended the letter with his expression of "unaffected and
great admiration of your book." A few days later, when she
had agreed to send him a story, and apparently inquired
about possible length, he told her that three pages of *Mary
Barton* would make one page of *Household Words*, and added,
"I would rather that you occupy just as many pages as you
think your design wants than that I should put any
constraint upon you."[39]   It was, as we shall see, an addition
replete with ironic foreboding.
        Mrs. Gaskell sent him a short story, "Lizzie Leigh"
(printed in the first three numbers of *Household Words*).
Dickens' initial comment--to Wills--approved in general but
offered the first of what was to be a series of objections to
the length of her submitted fiction: "It is very good, but
long."   However, at this point he still assured Gaskell that
length was not a problem: "*Let me particularly beg you not
to put the least constraint upon yourself as to space.*"   It
was the last time he offered her elbow room: a story
accepted two years later was also called "long," and we will
soon see length as a concern in the serialization of *North
and South*.   A letter to Wills the following month defended
"Lizzie Leigh" against an objection by Wills which cannot
quite be made out: "I don't feel your objection to "Lizzie
Leigh" so much, for this reason.   She had seen and watched
Susan, before she deserted the child; and she has yet to give
her own account of that transaction."   Wills seems to have
been complaining of an improbability in the character of
Lizzie, as she responds to the fact that her daughter Susan
has abandoned her child; Dickens did not agree.   But in his
correspondence with Gaskell, he did--circumspectly at first,

then with increasing directness--advise her on points in the story. When he received the first part, he wrote,

> Do not let me interfere with any idea you may have in your mind when I ask if you propose to make Lizzie dead at this time. I seem to see through that means, a forcible lesson on the postponement of forgiveness, and the way we have of only leaving that legacy when we are obliged to leave all legacies--at the point of Death. . . . But I earnestly conjure you not to let me interfere with any idea you may have formed.

The suggestion is again ironic, for though Dickens was soon complaining that Gaskell visited disasters upon too many of her characters, she did not kill off Lizzie Leigh. She might have replied to Dickens here that, in putting his idea into her head, he had already interfered. Dickens' next suggestion about plot is more forceful: he urged upon Gaskell a change which he thought would more strongly bring out the themes of mother-love and desertion:

> I am strongly of opinion that as Lizzie is not to die, she ought to put that child in Susan's own arms, and not lay it down at the door. Observe!-- The more forcefully and strongly and affectionately, you exhibit her mother's love for her, the more cruel you will make this crime of desertion in her. [The "her's" refer to the daughter, Susan.] The same sentiment which animates the matter, will have been done violence to by the daughter; and you cannot set up the one, without pulling down the other.

Contrast of character with character, or background with character, is a technique Dickens constantly urges upon writers. Mrs. Gaskell made the recommended changes in Chapter 2. But in general, apparently she did not respond well to suggestion: in later correspondence Dickens offers very little, and that discreetly. Still, he must have been happy with "Lizzie Leigh": within four months of the above letter he was begging for more: "Can't you--won't you--don't you ever mean to write me another story?"[40]

"Another story" turned out to be "The Well of Pen-Morfin"; after reading it, Dickens wrote her, "I shall be delighted to have it." Following that story came "The Hearty John Middleton" [HW (12/28/50)], which Dickens again both praised and criticized--to Wills:

> The Story is very clever--I think the best thing of hers I have seen, not excepting Mary Barton--and if it had ended happily (which is the whole meaning of it) would have been a great success. As it is, it had better go into the next No., but will not do much, and will link itself painfully, with the girl who fell down at the Well, and the child who tumbled down stairs. I wish to Heaven her people would keep a little firmer on their legs.

In the first two stories, a child had fallen down stairs and a girl had fallen down a well; in the present story, the wife dies. As we will see, Dickens did not like an unhappy ending unless the story absolutely required it (as he thought it did in "Lizzie Leigh"); Gaskell, he felt, had a penchant for terminal misery. To her he wrote, "I think it . . . a story of extraordinary power, worked out with a vigor and truthfulness very few people can reach." But he added, "I wished you had not killed the wife. . . . I thought it an unnecessary infliction of pain upon the reader, not justified by the necessities of the story." Gaskell agreed to change the ending, but too late: Dickens informed her that copies were already in print. "Never mind," he said. "It is a very fine story, nobly written--and you can put a pleasanter end to the next one."[41]

Early on Dickens seems to have understood that the kind of extensive rewriting he did with other writers--for example, Harriet Martineau--was not possible with Elizabeth Gaskell. He wrote that he had made only "two or three slight corrections" in "The Hearty John Middleton." Two days later he wrote to Wills of a proposed change, that "I could not think of making so important an alteration in Mrs. Gaskell's story without her consent.   It must therefore stand as it is."   He did make an unauthorized change in the first part of her *Cranford* series [HW (12/13/51)].   Gaskell had mentioned that a character was reading *Pickwick Papers*; wishing not to see himself puffed up in his own journal, Dickens changed the title to "Hood's Own."   Gaskell asked that it be changed back, but again he had to tell her that the story was already in print.   He apologized: "I would do anything rather than cause you a moment's vexation."   He loved the next part of *Cranford* and had no need to suggest a change: "I thought it masterly."   Writing to her of her "The Old Nurse's Story" [HW, Extra Christmas Number, 1852] he tried, with that charm of which he boasted to his wife that he could get his illustrators to change their work, to persuade Mrs. Gaskell to alter a part of the story.   It was "A very fine ghost-story indeed," he said.   "Nobly told, and wonderfully managed.

> But it strikes me (fresh from the reading) that it would be very new and very awful, if, when the narrator goes down into the parlor on that last occasion, she took up her sleeping charge in her arms, and carried it down--if the child awoke when the noise began--if they all heard the noise--but *only the child* saw the spectral figures, except that they all see the phantom child.

He finished with a compliment--"It is a grand story"--but it didn't work: she rejected the proposed change, and Dickens gracefully gave in: "I don't claim for my ending of 'The Nurse's Story' that it would have made it a bit better.   All I can urge in its behalf is, that it is what I should have done myself.   But there is no doubt of the story being admirable as it stands. . . ."   While this conclusion was being reached, he had written to assure her than no one else would touch the rest of her story: "of course if you wish to enlarge, explain, or re-alter, you will do it."[42]

Trying to divide a later story, "Half a Life Time Ago" [HW (10/6 to 10/20/55)], for serial publication, he wrote

Wills, "I have marked a place at page 235 where the effect would be obviously served by making a new chapter: Is such a thing to be done with that lady?" But his letters to her indicate perfect approval of her work, and his desire to continue the professional relationship; in 1853 he wrote to say "I have joyfully sent the Cranford last received, to the Printers, as I shall joyfully send its successors yet to come. As to future work, I do assure you that you cannot write too much for Household Words, and have never yet written half enough." Returning from Switzerland during the next year, he wrote to her, "I want to thank you, cordially, simply, and affectionately, for your valuable aid to Household Words during my absence abroad." And about a month later he wrote to tell her "how much I liked The Modern Greek songs," and even treated lightly the constant problem of division:

> Don't put yourself out at all as to the division of the story into parts; I think you had better write it in your own way. When we come to get a little of it into type, I have no doubt of being able to make such little suggestions as to breaks of chapters as will carry us over all that easily.[43]

But both division and length returned as sizeable problems in the serialization of Gaskell's novel, *North and South*, in *Household Words*. Dickens wrote to her expressing considerable appreciation of the material for the first six numbers but trying quietly to get her to let him divide the material: "It opens an admirable story, is full of character and power, has a strong suspended interest in it (the end of which, I don't in the least foresee), and has the very best marks of your hand upon it." It would have to be divided according to the needs of "the weekly space available," he points out; it would be "mortally injured" by any other division. If she will let him, he will be glad to do the dividing, adding here and there at the end of his divisions "a word or two of conclusion." Only one place "seems to me to flag unmanageably without an amount of excision that I dare scarcely hint at. . . ." The place is "between Nos. 2 and 8"--where Margaret learns that the family is moving to Milton--"where the dialogue is long--is on a difficult and dangerous subject--and where . . . I think there is a necessity for forcing two Nos. into one." He ends by repeating the importance of "its dividing well. . . . If it did not, the story would be wasted--would miss its effect as it went on--and would not recover it when published complete."[44]

The next letter to Mrs. Gaskell, a bit more than a month later, offered advice on the division of the next portion of the manuscript into five numbers, and added that the first part, up to the conversation between Margaret, Hale, and Thornton about the strike, "is unnecessarily lengthy," and should be cut. By this time Mrs. Gaskell may have complained about changes made without her consent, for the next letter promised her that Dickens would merely divide it into chapters. "If I ever have a suggestion to make, I will intimate it on the proof in pencil. You will take no notice of it, if you don't approve of it." In the next month, as early numbers of the novel went to proof, Gaskell had apparently not followed his suggestions: he wrote to urge her to do so, especially "to make the scene between Margaret and her father relative to his leaving the church and their destination being Milton-Northern, as short as you can find it in your heart to make it." Perhaps in part to smooth any ruffled feelings (Mrs. Gaskell sometimes thought his praise of her work to be "soft sawder"), he added thanks "for the Edwin Chadwick story, which appears to me to be the most wonderful story in the world."[45]

The correspondence with Wills during this time showed Dickens to be more troubled than he had let Gaskell know. It began confidently enough, with Dickens telling him that there was "far less difficulty about Mrs. Gaskell's story than you suppose." But he also indicated that she was late in returning proof, and said, "You must tell Mrs. Gaskell, in so many words, when you *must have* the proof back, or go to press without it." From there on things got worse. "I am alarmed by the quantity of 'North and South,'" he wrote Wills almost at once upon receiving numbers. "It is not objectionable for a beginning, but would become so in the progress of a not compactly written and artfully devised story." He also mentioned notes he had been making "concerning the divisions of Mrs. Gaskell's story." Length and division continued to be sore points to the end of the novel's serialization. On the very next day Dickens wrote that "It is perfectly plain to me that if we put in more, every week, of 'North and South' than we did of 'Hard Times,' we shall ruin Household Words. Therefore it must at all hazards be kept down." "She can't take out too much,"[46] he wrote three days later (an ironic reversal of his earlier assurance that she couldn't write too much for him), and the following day returned to the problem of division: "When I read the beginning of this story of Mrs. Gaskell's, I felt that its means of being of service or disservice to us, mainly lay in its capacity of being divided at such points of interest as it possesses." A later criticism switched to another problem, and implied that Mrs. Gaskell was indeed sensitive about revisions: "Some of Mrs. Gaskell's dialogue open to criticism, but I will not bring a correspondence upon you by touching it." In the next month, he professed himself not surprised to hear that the sales of *Household Words* were dropping: "Mrs. Gaskell's story, so divided, is wearisome in the last degree. It would have scant attraction enough if [the division were well done]; but thus wire-drawn it is a dreary business."[47] "Dreary" probably appears more often in Dickens' editorial correspondence than any other words excepting conjunctions: the absence of liveliness was the fault he seems most to have abhorred.

Meanwhile, Gaskell had objected to editorial liberties Dickens had attempted. In 1855, when proofs of *North and South* were going to print, Dickens wrote to Wilkie Collins that Gaskell had written to his subeditor Wills,

> saying she must particularly stipulate not to have her proofs touched, "even by Mr. Dickens." That immortal creature had gone over the proofs with great pains--had of course taken out the stiflings--hard-plungings, lungeings, and other convulsions--and had also taken out her

weakenings and damagings of her own effects.
"Very well," said the gifted Man, "she shall have
her own way.   But after it's published shew her
this Proof, and ask her to consider whether her
story would have been the better or the worse for
it."

On her side of the matter, Mrs. Gaskell believed that
Dickens' constant pressure upon her to condense had hurt
North and South:

> . . . The story is huddled and hurried up;
> especially in the rapidity with which the sudden
> death of Mr Bell, succeeds to the sudden death of
> Mr Hale. But what could I do?   Every page was
> grudged me. . . .   At the very last don't feel quite
> certain that I dislike the end as it now stands.[48]

The hurried end might be all right, she felt, because the
lovers in the story would indeed get together quickly, once
the wall of differing ideas between them began to crumble.
    Both parties, then, had found something to be unhappy
about.   But as the novel came down to its last numbers, each
wrote to the other in conciliatory fashion.   Gaskell professed
herself

> very much gratified by your note the other day;
> very much indeed.   I dare say I shall like my
> story, when I am a little further from it;   at
> present I can only feel depressed about it, I meant
> it to have been so much better.   I send what I am
> afraid you will think too large a batch of it by
> this post. . . .
>   . . . I have tried to shorten & compress it,
> both because it was a dull piece, & to get it into
> reasonable length, but there were [sic] a whole
> catalogue of events to be got over. . . .   *If you
> will keep the MS for me, & shorten it as you
> think best for HW*, I shall be very glad.   Shortened
> I see it must be.

Such a letter suggests that despite her stern adjuration to Wills and her complaint about pressure, Gaskell got on fairly well with her editor. Knowing that, whatever faults she may have possessed, Elizabeth Gaskell was his star writer, Dickens tried to close any possible rifts.

> Let me congratulate you on the conclusion of your story; not because it is the end of a task to which you had conceived a dislike (for I imagine you to have got the better of that delusion by this time), but because it is the vigorous and powerful accomplishment of an anxious labor. It seems to me that you have felt the ground thoroughly firm under your feet, and have strided on with a force and purpose that must now give you pleasure.
> You will not, I hope, allow that not-lucid interval of dissatisfaction with yourself (and me?) which beset you for a minute or two once upon a time, to linger in the shape of any disagreeable association with Household Words. I shall still look forward to the large sides of paper, and shall soon feel disappointed if they don't begin to reappear.

They did: Gaskell wrote several more stories for *Household Words* and *All the Year Round*, and though Marion Troughton and others have suggested (on the basis of a letter in which Gaskell said that a story of hers was not good enough for *Cornhill Magazine* but "might be good enough for H. W.")[49] that she reserved her best work for other magazines, Angus Easson points out that her "two major contributions to *All the Year Round*, 'The Grey Woman' and 'A Dark Night's Work', [were] both written after the establishment of the *Cornhill* and amongst her best work," and concludes that we should "abandon . . . the popular idea that Gaskell gave him only her inferior work in the 1860's." Easson might also have cited the letter in which Gaskell declined a "proposal of writing for a new weekly periodical. I am not in the habit of writing for periodicals, except occasionaly [sic] (as a personal mark of respect and regard to Mr. Dickens) in *Household Words*." Dumping her poorer stuff on Dickens would hardly have been a personal mark of respect and regard. We find Dickens, in 1859, confidently asking for a story "of about 400 pages of your usual manuscript," and offering two hundred guineas. He did not, however, reconcile himself to what he considered her faults, and perhaps the memory of their unpleasantness concerning *North and South* remained with him as it did with her: he wrote Georgina that he could not put Gaskell into the Christmas number for 1861 because she was "much too long for the purpose . . ." and in 1868 he wrote to Mrs. Field that a Mrs. Clifford would fill Gaskell's place in *All the Year Round*.[50]

There was one other occasion for difference between the two. In 1862 Gaskell sent Dickens the first part of a story she ultimately called "A Night's Work," understanding that the ending would not be required for some time because publication was not imminent. When Dickens unexpectedly called for the story's completion, Gaskell, busy with another story for *Cornhill*, hastily finished the story for Dickens, and sent it in with a title. Not aware of the circumstances, Dickens wrote to Wills, "I see that Mrs. Gaskell *has* put a name to her story--at the end, instead of the beginning--which is characteristic. The addition of one word will make it a striking name."[51] And he changed the title to "A Dark Night's Work," [AYR (1/24/ to 3/21/63)] providing a title more to his liking and nature in its hint of melodrama, but impairing the subtlety of Gaskell's story.

Because Dickens has been rated (on all too convincing evidence) a male chauvinist, it may not be amiss to point out here that he frequently solicited contributions from most of the better female writers of his time. To Ann Marsh--later Marsh-Caldwell--for instance, who he said had given him "much heartfelt pleasure by your writing," he wrote seeking contributions, telling her (he did not stint on what Gaskell had called "soft sawder" when he solicited material) that she was "one of the most original, earnest, and delightful writers that have ever graced our language." With another novelist, Geraldine Jewsbury, he was more restrained, merely begging

her aid because "I estimate it very highly."[52]   Elsewhere he
said, and often, that woman's place was in the home, but he
seems to have felt she belonged in his journals, too.

Dickens' correspondence with famous writers is
interesting, but perhaps we learn more about his critical
principles from his letters to and about the lesser
contributors to his journals, simply because he often needed
to guide them more.   Again, Dickens seldom paused for
leisurely contemplation of an aesthetic problem: when he
talked about literature, he did so for the practical purpose of
improving a specific work before him.   We have seen the
despair that sometimes came over him at the poor quality of
much of the writing he was forced to print, and have noted
how diligently he worked to improve it; we might also
remember, in addition to his disgust with the inability of
some of his contributors, his warm human concern for them,
his desire that their work be as good as it could be, not
only for his sake or the sake of his readers, but for theirs.
On several occasions he rejected material not only because
he thought it not right for his journal, but because he
thought his journal not right for the material.   Of a work
called "Uncle Sam's Peculiarities," by G. P. Payne, he wrote
to Wills:

> I have looked over Uncle Sam, and am still of
> the opinion I originally formed, that we could not
> use it for the Miscellany without great injury to
> the Author.   It contains a great deal of matter;
> and if I took a few pages here and there,
> occasionally, it would neither, I am convinced,
> serve his purpose nor ours. . . .

He added that he wished "by no means to be considered as
expressing my unfavorable opinion of the MS   itself."[53]
Concern for the writer was also a part of his decision not to
print "Gilbert Massinger," and other works.

At times this concern pushed him beyond the routine
notice of refusal: he saw the poor writer, with no hope of
ever getting into print, suffering repeatedly the pain of
rejection, and could not refrain from advising him or her to

avoid it.   Along with his return of a contribution by a Miss Reynolds went the urge to give up "the exercise of your pen. You cannot conceive the store of troubles and vexations you are preparing for yourself by entering upon the trade of authorship--constant harassing and annoyances which will embitter [your] life. . . ."   It was advice he often gave to those who wrote to him for guidance and support; one such (J. H. Carleton, an American officer), he urged

> to consider well before you mistake your future
> course in life and struggle through a troublesome
> and thorny track in which the tombs of many
> great and adventurous spirits like the stone-
> stricken adventurers in the Eastern Tale warn you
> to recede--to remind you how many men who have
> gone before, have confounded thoughts and
> impulses with the power of realizing them, and
> languished in helpless obscurity and chilling
> neglect. . . ."[54]

No doubt some of this advice was owing to the impulse we all have to warn people away from the unpleasant aspects of our professions: the exotic tone of the last quotation suggests something of this.   On the other hand, not even the young Dickens (and the above quotations are from letters written before 1840) ever experienced much if any helpless obscurity and chilling neglect as a writer, however he may have felt such suffering in childhood; his concern for untalented writers seems genuine.   As in the above quotation, he was constantly struck by the idea that all men and women have the "thoughts and impulses" from which literature comes, and by the fact that it was easy to confuse the impulse with the ability to create.   No man knew better than this man, with the reputation for writing quickly and easily, that good writing comes only through hard work, and for some never comes at all.

What Dickens was concerned with in his pointing out the error of confusing "impulse" with "power," I believe, was the distinction he felt between content and form: we all have something of the former (queens and costermongers, he wrote, have the same dreams), but few of us can achieve the latter in which to express it.   Our century has agreed that content and form are one, and of course they are, but of course they also are not.   Perhaps they are most completely so at the upper reaches of writing: the mind capable of producing a great thought no doubt is able to formulate it greatly.   But many a thinker of good or mediocre thoughts and emotions has found it a devilish business to put them into words that convey them successfully.   Dickens constantly distinguished in submitted articles and stories between good subject and bad style, or good style and poor subject.   A paper by one Dixon was "admirably told, but nothing new in it"; a piece on the Crystal Palace was "very well done, but" was after all but part of "the great Forge-bellows of puffery at work" on the popular subject (Dickens disliked what he considered the excessive attention given to the Great Exhibition), and so Wills was advised to "cancel this article altogether."   An article by Fitzgerald was "not very original, but still good."[55]

In general, originality was an important test for Dickens: effective execution could not overcome material that was derivative.   He rejected a piece by a friend of Henry Austin: "It is very neatly done indeed, but as it is a mere versification of the prose description of the Chess-Player, I do not think it would do either the author or the Miscellany any good. . . ."   When R. H. Bonham proposed for the *Miscellany* a serial based on *The Rake's Progress*, Dickens responded, "I don't like the notion and would not touch it on any account.   I feel asssured it would never do." (It never did: the idea was soon abandoned.)   For Dickens the derivative was the trite: a piece by Henry Mayhew entitled "Mr. Peter Punctilio" which he was obliged to print in the *Miscellany* contained a hero of whom he said, "all our readers who have ever seen a dreary face will have known him for many years. . . ."   He wished that "Hannay would not imitate Carlyle,"[56] and found imitation of himself neither flattering nor amusing: he accepted a piece by one Miss Craik for "one of our ordinary Nos." but commented, "Her imitation of me is too glaring--I never saw anything so curious.   She takes the very words in which Esther

[Summerson, of *Bleak House*] speaks, without seeming to know it." Part of his reason for rejecting a piece submitted by the Reverend Edward Taggart for a friend was that in some of the characters and action he detected echoes of *The Chimes*. Looking over articles submitted to *Household Words*, he commented on "how extremely dreary they were--all with a drone of imitation of myself in them. . . ."[57] (Conversely, as we shall see, some of his writers criticized him for trying to make them all write like him.)

Only once, when a friend both imitated him and openly confessed it, did he approve: Fitzgerald's "Autobiography of a Small Boy" [AYR (8/15 & 22/68)] "is 'serviley founded' (he writes me) on me. But it goes on well enough. . . ." And one idea by Walter Thornbury to write a series of stories based on traditional tales was also approved: "the idea of old stories retold is decidedly a good one. I greatly like the notion of that series." But most work based on or in the style of previous fiction was disapproved: he kept a story by Wilkie Collins' brother Charles, but criticized it because (among other things) it was "greatly too much in the manner of the stories of about the time of the Essayists. . . ." He liked very much a story by the Hon. Robert Lytton called "The Disappearance of John Ackland," and began serialization until he discovered that the action upon which the story turned had been done before; then he insisted that it be wound up as quickly as possible (though he suspected the author of no plagiarism: "In the case of a good story--as this is--liable for years to be told at table--as this was-- there is nothing wonderful in such a mischance").[58]

Important among the grounds for selecting writing for the journals was originality of topic: if original writers could not always be found, perhaps original subject matter could, and Dickens was not above accepting a piece if it was at least topical. He sent Wills an article "from Lord Normanby's brother at Florence. There is not much in it, but the subject--the Bible prisoners, man and wife--attracts so much attention, just now, that I think it worth a push to get it into this Number." (The article was "An Interview with the Madial" [HW (11/20/52)], about a couple imprisoned in Tuscany for possessing a Bible.) But usually Dickens distinguished carefully between the topical and the merely sensational: when Walter Thornbury sent him an article on a notorious criminal he replied,

> I am very doubtful about "Vaux," and have kept it out of the number in consequence. The mere details of such a rascal's proceedings, whether recorded by himself or set down by the Reverend Ordinary, are not wholesome for a large audience, and are scarcely justifiable (I think) as claiming to be a piece of literature. I can understand Barrington to be a good subject, as involving the representation of a period, a style of manners, an order of dress, certain habits of street life, assembly-room life, and coffee-room life, etc.; but there is a very broad distinction between this and mere Newgate Calendar. . . .[59]

With but a few exceptions, then, Dickens as editor was always on the lookout for the new and the unusual. He advised a Mr. Hardy to turn a sketch of his into a story because in that form "its oddity and humour would be much more apparent to general readers." Several letters proposed lists of new and different subjects for writers who could or did not come up with anything on their own. Dickens was perhaps the first editor who thought that the "bridges of London in general--would be a fine subject. . . ." Consulting with Thomasina Ross about a proposed topic, he said, "It should be interesting, of course; if somewhat romantic, so much the better; we can't be too wise, but we must be very agreeable." All writing, whether in magazine or novel--all art--should be agreeable if possible, and certainly interesting.[60]

For Dickens an important part of interest for the reader lay in suspense. He took a passage out of a story by one Mr. Spicer "*Because it tells his story.* His main incident is gone--disclosed to any sharp reader--the moment that passage is read." He liked Robert Lytton's story about the murder of John Ackland, but wrote, "I think you let the story out too much--prematurely," and suggested the title be changed to "The Disappearance of . . .": "This will leave the reader in doubt whether he really *was* murdered, until the end." Part of his admiration for Gaskell's *North and South* lay in its "strong suspended interest . . . (the end of which, I don't in the least foresee). . . ." Suspense has never been high on the critical list of virtues in fiction, but Dickens never disdained anything because it was simple, no doubt partly because he knew how effective the simple could be, partly because he never disdained to please the simple reader. When Charles Knight disparaged such readers, Dickens quietly came to their rescue:

> the English are, so far as I know, the hardest-worked people on whom the sun shines. Be content if, in their wretched intervals of pleasure, they read for amusement and do no worse. They are born at the oar, and they live and die at it. Good God, what would we have of them!"[61]

It was no small emotion that caused Charles Dickens to call upon the Deity.

Upon just a few occasions, one can suspect that Dickens himself accepted work for his journal not for its artistic merit nor for its general interest, nor even to fill space, but because he found it personally appealing. Remembering Mary Hogarth and Little Nell and a number of other expiring maidens, we may suspect that Dickens thought T. J. Ouseley's poem, "Dream of the Dying Girl," to be a "beautiful little poem" simply because its content appealed to him. But such instances are of course conjectural, and they are rare. In almost all cases in which content is mentioned as distinct from quality of form, it is the appeal to the reader that is uppermost in Dickens' mind. Commenting on "several articles by Major Pryce Gordon," he said, "Although they would possess considerable interest for military or naval gentlemen, I fear that to the public generally--*our* public at all events--they would present few attractions. . . ." And despite his own great love of music, he returned an article to one James Hine, saying, "I am afraid the inclosed is too exclusively musical to suit the Miscellany. . . ."[62]

By and large, Dickens tried in his journals to supply his readers with the same things he gave them in his novels. The great force behind both is life--full, pulsing, and vibrant. He did not care for seriousness which threatened to become dull, for scholarship which tended to be merely technical (he urged Bulwer to refrain from using notes in *A Strange Story*, we remember), for restraint which was likely to squeeze its subject dry.   Of an article probably submitted by Charles Mackay he wrote, "I think you have treated it too seriously, and am sure you could do it much better in another vein." He complimented the Countess of Blessington on her contribution to the "On Dits" column of the *Daily News*, saying, "I wonder how you make so much of such a dull time."   He chided Charles Collins for not exercising his ability to be humorous: "You have such an excellent humour-- of your own--and such a correct and delicate observation-- that it is a great pity not to give the quality more play in such a narrative."   His compliments are all for the lively, the vigorous, the emotional: "uncommon passion and power,"[63] writing which brings "those tears it is good to shed," "good touches of character, passion, and natural emotion," "great power . . . sincerity and tenderness,"--and on, and on.   The negative criticisms are often of the reverse: "a little too dry and didactic for Household Words," "in the last degree flat and poor," "there is little fancy in it," "It is dreadfully heavy," "Very weak.   A kind of imbecile thing that seems to want crutches."[64]

In his journals length was, for this writer of huge novels, an enemy, both because of the limitations of space and because he considered it in most cases another detriment to lively fiction and good writing.   Mrs. Gaskell did not suffer alone: probably no direction for change of stories and articles is made more frequently than that of cutting.   "I have gone through Mr. Sala's paper," Dickens wrote of "The Foreign Invasion," [HW (10/11/51)] and have cut a great deal out, and made it compact and telling. . . ."   "Morely," he said, "always wants a little screwing up and tightening.   It is his habit to write in a loose way."   An unidentified paper "wanders about when it should get straight to the point. . . . I think it might be reduced by at least one third. . . ."

Lever's *A Day's Ride* began well, though "we ought to get to the action of the story, in the first No. . . ."[65] Dickens was always disturbed by fiction in which the reader could not discern a developing plot almost at once; several of Gaskell's stories troubled him for this reason.   Leisurely setting of scene or establishing of character before action began was, he felt, not the way to catch the attention.   But, as we have seen in his comment on Emily Jolly's first story, he was capable of urging greater length in the middle of a novel if development of character required it.   Other elements of style also received attention, though the comments are far fewer than on length.   Dickens liked an easy, graceful style, charming and agreeable, though as we have seen he wanted plainness and simplicity when content required it.   He did not often comment on poor sentence construction or word choice or style inappropriate to content, though he did on occasion object to things such as so much "huddling up of sentences, that I really cannot understand it."   But most often we find him commenting that a piece wants "more grace of handling" or complimenting a style that is "particularly easy and agreeable" or objecting to one that has no "charm of expression. . . ."   "Pleasant" and "pretty" are two of his more frequent compliments: articles by Dudley Costello are "Two most pleasant productions," and a story in the *Miscellany* is "a pretty little tale. . . ."[66]

The editorial commentary represented in this chapter illuminates much of Dickens' literary concerns, though of course we cannot be certain that other literary problems were not also addressed in conversations with the authors and his editor, or in writing that has been lost.   But on the basis of what we have, Dickens' attention focused largely on the ability of an article or story to reach its reader--to raise his interest, involve his emotions, offer him clear and succinct information, and leave him entertained and fulfilled. Dickens had to fit each work to the needs of his journal, but usually he felt that this could be done without injury to the artistic integrity of the piece--and often felt it improved the work.   He took care of his reader, and would include nothing he considered potentially harmful; neither in his novels nor his journals did he seem to feel any need to sacrifice art to the interests of his audience, or his audience to the requirements of art. Above all, the lively and, for the most part, positive rendering of the human condition was the very core of his editorial intention. In most evaluations made in his time he was, as Lord Northcliffe said, a superlative editor.

3

Literary Judgments: Scratches in the Sand

It is disappointing to find among Dickens' writings no more than a handful of comments upon famous writers, but if we remember the relatively modest role he assigned to criticism, and how he disliked imposing his opinion, we will not be surprised by the scarcity. During Hans Christian Andersen's visit to Dickens, he confessed himself much hurt by an *Athenaeum* review of his novel, *To Be or Not to Be.* Dickens consoled him by saying that he never read newspaper notices of his novels: "They are forgotten in a week, but your book will live!" As they walked together up Gad's Hill, Andersen tells us, Dickens scratched the sand with his foot. "'That is criticism,' he said, and stroked it with his foot: 'Gone!--But that which God has given you, that will remain!.'"[1]

When he had reason to do so, Dickens wrote perceptive criticism, but something had to impel him to offer judgment, or he would not use his pen. Furthermore, since most occasions offered were in connection with minor writers of his own time--the majority of whom are of relatively little interest to us, and some of whom we know not at all--what is left as comment upon major figures is scanty indeed. Since Dickens' judgments of virtual unknowns can be of interest only to a small number of scholars, we confine ourselves mostly to the comments upon well-known writers and familiar figures. Because of his editorial work and because his opinion was valuable to publishers and writers, much of Dickens' reading was rather forced upon than chosen by him: despite the disclaimer concerning the influence of his opinion, he was sent books by publishers from both England and America, with requests for his reaction, and he seems tirelessly to have responded to most such importunities. To his credit, he never used his influence either to inflate the reputation of a friend nor to crush that of an enemy (in a time when such misuse was routine); as for the kind of professional jealousy which the comments of some of his literary contemporaries show they possessed in regard to him, he seems, as Forster said of him, to have been perfectly free: ". . . Nothing interested him more than success won honestly in his own field. . . . In his large and open nature there was no hiding-place for little jealousies."[2]

Despite the limited comment, we learn much about Dickens' literary aesthetic from the opinions he expressed about other writers. The first thing we learn, obviously, is that he had and could express literary judgments, contrary to the long-standing idea that he thought little about such matters. Coming, as always, in brief and often off-hand spurts, the comments are subject to hastiness and mood and other influences of the moment, yet one must be impressed by the general common sense, sound judgment, and consistent application of aesthetic principle that many of them display. If at times Dickens shows himself influenced by content more than by artistry, if occasionally he is too enthusiastic too soon, still the passage of time and the opportunity for objective reflection usually bring him to respectable, measured judgment.

A major current running through the comments is Dickens' liking of qualities of fiction closely associated with the dramatic. He preferred writing which could create the magic spell he felt in a play: writing which could make scene and character come alive as they did for him upon the stage. A style tending toward stiffness and formality put him off, as did narrative without pace or movement; he looked for that which had the power (one of his favorite words) to move the reader, to express and evoke passion and tenderness--though he was always wary of violent extremes, of straining for effect, and approved of delicate treatment of a subject (caustic satire, for example, disturbed him). Above all, he thought that writing should enable the reader to see the essential affirmative "truth" of life--this was for him the best that writing could achieve. He disliked the obvious, and approved always of subtlety, but knew that judicious use of the commonplace, of carefully-selected detail, could bring reality to a story--but it must always be the kind of reality he found in drama: "wonderful reality"--the world as we know it, but "polished by art" until it assumed values not felt in the dull settled world itself. For him reality was not what it was to the realists; it was neither commonplace as in Howells nor sordid as in so many others. Yet the polish that art lent must be carefully controlled: much that Howells said about real heroes instead of ideal ones would have been agreeable to Dickens. He did not care for psychological fiction: it was the secret processes not of the mind but of the heart that he thought fiction should seek out. Finally, he was quite in agreement with his time that fiction should instruct the reader in virtue, but he detested any strict moral preachment; the idea was to make the reader love virtue, not be imprisoned in it. In this chapter's comments on other writers, and in the gathered comments on craft and on literary theory of the following chapters, these opinions will be plentifully seen.

Dickens admitted that he did not read everything sent to him--at least, like Samuel Johnson, did not read everything "through." Polite letters acknowledging the receipt of a book (or books) often say no more than that he is grateful for the gift, and looks forward to a pleasant perusal. Of "books" sent him by publishers Wiley and Putnam of New York, he wrote, "I have only had time to glance at them, but have been much pleased, and hope to be more so." He told Milnes that he thought it "a poor compliment to thank an author for his book, without having first read it," but this may have been merely an excuse for his tardy thanks for Milnes' gift of a book of poems, not a credo acted upon for every piece of writing sent him. When the sender asked for an opinion, however, he usually responded. Such requests, along with his position as editor of journals and his generous availability to, it seems, almost any hack in the world who courted his judgment, were the occasions which brought forth most of the critical statements we have in his writings; would that more correspondents had sought his opinion of the great eighteenth-century novelists, or of the eminent Victorians. We will begin with the seventeenth century, pausing only to note that Dickens had read many earlier poets and playwrights, including "brave old Chaucer," and, of course, Shakespeare. But even of his master, Dickens had little to say other than the few remarks which I have recorded elsewhere. Shakespeare, of course, was "the great master who knew everthing. . . ."[3] As dramatist, he does not in narrow terms fit in to our present interest in prose fiction, but in view of his great influence on Dickens, it is interesting to note that, despite Dickens' slight regard for critical commentary on literature, he read books about Shakespeare: he called John Campbell's *Shakespeare* a "very curious and interesting little work. . . . Apart from the knowledge and ingenuity it evinces, it is so exceedingly graceful and pleasant, that I read it with uncommon satisfaction." And he referred to an essay by one Morgann "on the character of Falstaff, a delicate combination of fancy, whim, good heart, good sense, and good taste. . . ." When he purchased the Gad's Hill house, he had a speech of Falstaff's from *Henry IV* illuminated and placed on the first floor landing, so that it greeted every visitor. His letters are dotted with quotations from the plays, many of which are not the most familiar ones. Of prose of the sixteenth century, though, Dickens mentioned only Cervantes and Le Sage; he called *Don Quixote* "without doubt" the greatest work of fiction, and said that *Gil Blas* would have been the greatest except for Cervantes.[4]

Except for dramatists, only a few writers of the seventeenth century are mentioned. James I "wrote some of the most wearisome treatises ever read. . . ." Bunyan's *Pilgrim's Progress* is also decried: "I question the propriety of putting the Pilgrim's Progress in the hands of moral people, unless upon the homeopathic principle of alleviating a disease with a medicine that very often caused it." Izaak Walton is criticized: "Izaak Walton hadn't pace--look at his book and you'll find it slow."[5] But Pepys is admired; his *Diary* is "a favorite book of mine . . ." which "remains to this day the most honest diary known to print . . ."--because, says Dickens, Pepys wrote it in shorthand which he never thought anyone could make out. It hardly need be added that the King James Bible is much admired by Dickens, though the comments mainly concern themselves with its spiritual, not its aesthetic nature. But though occasional allusions to the

Old Testament in his letters indicate that he had at least read in it, it was only the New Testament that he loved; for reasons that are none too clear--perhaps simply because of his antiSemitism--Dickens disliked the Old Testament, and tried repeatedly to separate it from the New.   Commenting on some religious discourses which Frank Stone had sent him, he said they contained one "fatal mistake": "Half the misery and hypocrisy of the Christian world arises (as I take it) from a stubborn determination to refuse the New Testament as a sufficient guide in itself, and to force the Old Testament into alliance with it--whereof comes all manner of camel-swallowing and of gnat straining."   The idea seems to have been that the Old Testament may involve the Christian in strenuous exploration of useless questions, so that simple Christian values are obscured; six years later, writing of the state of the Church of England, he complained of "the Master of the New Testament put out of sight, and the rage and fury almost always turning on the letter of obscure parts of the Old Testament, which itself has been the subject of accommodation, adaptation, varying interpretations without end. . . ."   The Old Testament, moreover, at least when taken literally, was discredited by the maturing of the human intellect, including the advances of modern science: commenting on a contemporary study he said that

> The position of the writers of "Essays and Reviews" is, that certain parts of the Old Testament have done their intended function in the education of the world *as it was*; but that mankind, like the individual man, is designed by the Almighty to have an infancy and a maturity, and that as it advances, the machinery of its education must advance too.   For example: inasmuch as ever since there was a sun and there was vapour, there *must have* been a rainbow under certain conditions, so surely it would be better now to recognise that indisputable fact.   Similarly, Joshua might command the sun to stand still, under the impression that it moved round the earth; but he could not possibly have inverted the relations

of the earth and the sun, whatever his impressions were. Again, it is contended that the science of geology is quite as much a revelation to man, as books of an immense age and of (at the best) doubtful origin, and that your consideration of the latter must reasonably be influenced by the former. As I understand the importance of timely suggestions such as these, it is, that the Church should not gradually shock and lose the more thoughtful and logical of human minds; but should be so gently and considerately yielding as to retain them, and, through them, hundreds of thousands. This seems to me, as I understand the temper and tendency of the time, whether for good or evil, to be a very wise and necessary position. And as I understand the danger, it is not chargeable on those who take this ground, but on those who in reply call names and argue nothing. What these bishops and such-like say about revelation, in assuming it to be finished and done with, I can't in the least understand. Nothing is discovered without God's intention and assistance, and I suppose every new knowledge of His works that is conceded to man to be distinctly a revelation by which men are to guide themselves. Lastly, in the mere matter of religious doctrine and dogmas, these men (Protestants--protesters--successors of the men who protested against human judgment being set aside) talk and write as if they were all settled by the direct act of Heaven; not as if they had been, as we know they were, a matter of temporary accomodation and adjustment among disputing mortals as fallible as you or I.

The Old Testament is old, of doubtful origin, and intended for man's "infancy." The New Testament, presumably, is new, of divine origin, and written for the mature reader. Dickens' argument that uncritical fundamentalism would alienate thinking people is surely valid, but one wishes that the writer who spent his life proclaiming that literature directed toward children was the salvation of us all would not argue that modern man has outgrown the Old Testament. Furthermore, it is not at all clear how this idea applies to the Old and not to the New Testament: Dickens could as well have argued that mankind in its maturity also finds it difficult to believe in walking on water and the restoration of life to corpses upon command. But most of the modern world will no doubt approve of Dickens' call for open-mindedness, and of his argument that the pursuit of truth is not finished (though many would add that this applies to the New Testament, as well as the Old). But for Dickens it is clearly the New Testament which is the solid rock upon which his own religion must be built. When his son Henry went off to college in 1868, he wrote him, "I most strongly and affectionately impress upon you the priceless value of the New Testament and the study of that book as the one unfailing guide in life." Angus Wilson reads *Dombey and Son* as "a parable extolling the New Testament over the old."[6]

There is not much critical commentary on eighteenth-century writing, including, sad to say, the novelists. The first of these (or for some the ur-), Defoe, is mentioned along with Richardson for his "wonderful genius for the minutest details in a narrative. . . ." One of the things that fascinated Dickens about *Robinson Crusoe* was that it interested him without affecting him--that it got by on "truth," unsupported by feeling. It was, he said, a

> wonderful testimony to the homely force of truth, that one of the most popular books on earth has nothing in it to make anyone laugh or cry. . . . In particular, I took Friday's death as one of the least tender and (in the true sense) least sentimental things ever written. It is a book I read very much; and the wonder of its prodigious effect on me and everyone, and the admiration thereof, grows on me the more I observe this curious fact.

Robinson Crusoe is included in a list of things Dickens said he had never outgrown (which also included Cervantes, Le

Sage, and Sterne). Of *The Political History of the Devil* he
wrote, "What a capital thing it is. I bought it . . . yesterday
morning, and have been quite absorbed in it ever since."
Commenting on a narrative by Lady De Lancy (sister of Basil
Hall) of her experiences with her husband at Waterloo, which
impressed him tremendously, he said, "It is a striking proof
of the power of that most extraordinary man Defoe, that I
seem to recognize in every line of the narrative, something
of him."[7]   All other allusions to eighteenth-century prose
fiction are incidental.   Richardson receives still less attention
than Defoe, and far less praise.   "Richardson is no great
favorite of mine," Dickens wrote to the Reverend Edward
Taggart, "and never seems to me to take his top-boots off,
whatever he does."   Dickens did admire Richardson's handling
of detail, as noted, but made no other appreciative comment.
In "A passage [sic] in the Life of Mr. Watkins Tottle," he
described the title character as having "a clean-cravatish
formality of manner, and kitchen-pokerness of carriage,
which Sir Charles Grandison himself might have envied," and
added that "He looked something like a vignette to one of
Richardson's novels. . . ."[8]   So much for Richardson;
psychological probing was not for Dickens (though those who
like Richardson's psychology may also occasionally object to
an excess of topboots).
      The novels of Fielding and Smollett were far closer to
Dickens' idea of what good fiction should be, yet there is
some uncertainty about his assessment of Fielding.   After
reading the least of his major works, *A Journey from This
World to the Next*, Dickens called him "one of the greatest
English writers. . . ."   When he listed his favorite novels, he
almost always included Fielding, and he quoted at least once
from his commentary on the nature of the novel.   Yet he
spoke of Smollett in more favorable terms: "'Humphrey
Clinker' is certainly Smollett's best.   I am rather divided
between "Peregrine Pickle' and 'Roderick Random,' both
extraordinarily good in their way, which is a way without
tenderness. . . ."   Frederick Locker-Lampson said that
"Dickens admired Smollett; he considered *Humphry Clinker* a
highly humorous story, and very originally told. . . ."   And
according to J. T. Fields, Dickens preferred Smollett to

Fielding, and thought *Peregrine Pickle* a better novel than
Tom Jones. George Russell put it more strongly: "Dickens
was not a great admirer of Fielding. 'Tom Jones is always in
tears and rouses my contempt,' he said, 'and excepting
Blifil, there is not an original character in the book.'"[9]
(Could Tom Jones possibly be in tears more frequently than
Florence Dombey? But of course she is a female, which may
make it all right.)

Goldsmith's plays elicit more comment than his novel,
though there is no doubt that Dickens loved *The Vicar of
Wakefield*--"that most delightful of all stories"--which he
said had "perhaps done more good in the world, and
instructed more kinds of people in virtue, than any other
fiction ever written."[10] Dickens took from Goldsmith's *The
Citizen of the World* the pen-name he used for his sketches
in the *Evening Chronicle,* "Tibbs"; his better-known pen-
name, Boz, originated in *The Vicar of Wakefield.*

Among other eighteenth-century writers who received
attention was James Boswell, whom Dickens did not like,
perhaps not so much because of his writing nor even his
character as because of his role in exposing the life of a
writer, which was naturally an anathema to the man who
burned all his letters lest posterity invade his privacy. In a
glowing commendation of Forster's *Life of Goldsmith*, he took
exception to two small matters: what he considered excessive
italicizing, and the statement that every great man should
have a Boswell recording his looks and words and deeds.

> I question very much whether it would have been a
> good thing for every great man to have had his
> Boswell, inasmuch as I think that two Boswells, or
> three at most, would have made great men
> extraordinarily false, and would have set them on
> always playing a part, and would have made
> distinguished people about them, for ever restless
> and distrustful. I can imagine a succession of
> Boswells bringing about a tremendous state of
> falsehood in society, and playing the very devil
> with confidence and friendship.

Further disparagement is made later in the same letter, which we quote below in our look at commentary on Forster, but George Russell said that Dickens thought Boswell's biography of Johnson the best in the English language, and placed even Forster's *Life of Goldsmith* second to it. Dickens did like the writing of Addison and Steele, but preferred the humorous pieces to the sober: "I don't agree with you," he wrote to Forster, who had just published a book on Richard Steele, "about the serious papers in The Spectator which I think (whether they be Steele's or Addison's) are generally as indifferent as the humour of The Spectator is delightful." The only other writer of the eighteenth century to whom I find critical reference is Richard Savage; Dickens wrote, "I do *not* think . . . that Savage *was* a man of genius, or that anything of his writing would have attracted much notice but for the bastard's reference to his mother."[11]

Comments on nineteenth-century writers are, of course, far more plentiful, but those on important figures must be sifted out from the copious commentary on insignificant writers, and when the task is finished the residue is again disappointingly small. Among major American writers, Dickens rendered critical opinion on Irving, Hawthorne, Dana, Stowe, and Bret Harte. He wrote to Washington Irving that "there is no living writer, and there are very few among the dead, whose approbation I should feel so proud to earn. And with everything you have written, upon my shelves, and in my thoughts, and in my heart of hearts, I may honestly and truly say so." The letter proves Dickens' familiarity with Irving's works by mentioning several figures from *The Sketchbook* and other works. But he did not understand Hawthorne's *The Scarlet Letter*:

> It falls off sadly after that fine opening scene. The psychological part of the story is very much overdone, and not truly done I think. Their suddenness of meeting and agreeing to go away together after all those years, is very poor. Mr. Chillingworth, ditto. The child out of nature altogether. And Mr. Dimmesdale certainly never could have begotten her.

But he said he liked Hawthorne's "earlier books," by which he meant of course his collections of short stories, especially *Mosses from an Old Manse*; it would be hard to think that a writer so committed to searching out the secrets of the human heart would not like Hawthorne. His only comment on Richard Henry Dana was to call his *Two Years Before the Mast* "about the best sea book in the English tongue."[12] In the essays of Emerson he found "among much that is dreary and fanciful . . . much more that is true and manly, honest and bold." He had a great deal more to say about Harriet Beecher Stowe, partly because while he admired some things about *Uncle Tom's Cabin* he thought her much over-rated, and disliked finding so much attention paid to so modest a talent. In 1850 the emphasis was on approval: her novel was an "admirable book" in which "the main features" of North American slavery "are painted in the freshest colours." He criticized the "overstrained conclusion and violent extremes," but finished by claiming the novel to be "A noble work; full of high power, lofty humanity; the gentlest, sweetest, and yet boldest, writing. Harriet Beecher Stowe . . . will take her place among the best writers of fiction. . . ." It was not long before he changed his mind about Stowe's fictional talent: he told an interviewer that "he thought it decidedly a story of much power, but scarcely a work of art: he thought too, he said, that Mrs. Stowe had made rather too much of her subject--had overdone in the philanthropic direction. Uncle Tom evidently struck him as an impossible piece of ebony perfection, as a monster of excellence. . . ." Dickens liked black people, he said, "but then I have no prejudices against white people." At a Mansion House Banquet at which he and Stowe represented literature, he referred to her graciously as "the author of a noble book with a noble purpose,"[13] a comment which rather confines itself to content--which may well have been what attracted Dickens to the novel in the first place. The year before, he had written to the Duke of Devonshire to say, "I don't know whether Uncle Tom is a little too celestial, or whether I am a little in the opposite direction; but, 'bating such things, it is an uncommonly fine book, and full of the the highest power."

But by 1854 in a reference to another work by Stowe, *Sunny Memories of Foreign Lands* (1854), all complimentary adjectives have disappeared: Stowe's "Moony Memories are very silly I am afraid. Some of the people remembered most moonily are terrible humbugs--moral, deadly incarnations of Cant and Quackery." When Stowe published "The true story of Lady Byron's Life," in the *Atlantic Monthly* (9/69), on a subject that had to be distasteful to Dickens, he wrote to James T. Fields (editor of the *Atlantic*), "Wish Mrs. Stowe was in the pillory," and commented to another correspondent a few days later that "It seems to me that to knock Mrs. Beecher Stowe on the head, and confiscate everything about it in a great international bonfire . . . would be the only pleasant way of putting an end to the business."[14]

The final American commented upon is Bret Harte. Dickens, shortly before his death, sent Forster

> two *Overland Monthlies* containing two sketches by a young American writer far away in California, "The Luck of Roaring Camp," and "The Outcasts of Poker Flat," in which he had found such subtle strokes of character as he had not anywhere else in late years discovered; the manner resembling himself, but the matter fresh to a degree that had surprised him; the painting in all respects masterly; and the wild rude thing painted, a wonderful reality. I have rarely known him more honestly moved."[15]

Dickens commented upon few continental writers of his time. He did not pass judgment on Gogol, but did recommend his "Tarass Boulla" to Bulwer as having the "conditions" Bulwer would need for changing the location of his play *The Captives* from Greece to Russia. To George Cattermole he wrote slightingly of Italian and German novelists, saying they were "convenient as being easily taken up and laid down again. . . ." But Manzoni's *I Promessi Sposi* drew praise: "a most charming book, and eminently remarkable for its excellent sense, and determination not to give in to conventional lies." And as everyone knows, he loved Hans Christian Andersen--at least until he became a troublesome house guest--and unfailingly praised his stories. In 1847 he wrote Marguerite Power that he would come up from his vacation spot at Broadstairs "to dine at your house and meet the Dane, whose Books I honour. . . ."[16] Earlier that year he had said of Andersen that "His spirit shines through him in all he does." The next year, writing to Andersen of his *A Christmas Greeting to my English Friends*, he said,

> Your book made my Christmas fireside, happier. We were all charmed with it. The little boy, and the old man, and the pewter soldier, are my particular favorites. I read that story over and over again, with the most unspeakable delight.
> . . . Whatever you do, don't leave off writing, for we cannot afford to lose any of your thoughts. They are too purely and simply beautiful to be kept in your own head.

Another story published that year, *The Two Baronesses*, brought equal though briefer praise: "Charming Baronesses they were; and I took them to my bosom with all honor, love, and gallantry." And almost ten years later, his opinion of Andersen was unchanged: "I have read to be or not to be and think it a very fine book--full of good purpose, admirably wrought out--a book in every way worthy of its great author."[17]
     The only other continental writers of fiction who received critical comment are Sand, Hugo, and Lamartine. Sand was given short shrift: Forster said that Dickens "was not familiar with her writings, and had no very special liking for such as he knew." Dickens thought Hugo the greatest of contemporary French writers--"a genius," whom he held "in the profoundest admiration." And he wrote to an unknown correspondent to express "l'admiration vers M. de Lamartine, cet homme illustre qui a ennobli a la fois la literature imaginative et l'histoire politique et social du siecle qu'il adorne." Angus Wilson suggests, though, that both writers appealed to him as much on political as on aesthetic

grounds.[18]

Commentary upon nineteenth-century English writers abounds in Dickens' letters and speeches, of course, but once again, how disappointing it is to find nothing about such novelists as the Brontës, and precious little about Thackeray, Eliot, Gaskell (beyond his editorial comments), or Trollope. He said nothing at all about Jane Austen, but Locker-Lampson records that "He did not unduly appreciate Miss Jane Austen's novels. . . ." We know that he loved his predecessor Scott, of course: in 1839 he wrote of "'Kenilworth', which I have just been reading with greater delight than ever. . . ." He called Scott's story of the Earl of Leicester murdering his wife "one of his best romances." He indirectly praised his productivity (a talent he always admired in writers): in a disagreement with the publisher Bentley over work to be done for him, Dickens argued that what he was committed to "would have been beyond Scott himself."[19] "I think Walter Scott is the first of all the novelists," he told Percy Fitzgerald, adding that he liked *The Bride of Lammermore* best, though he found "some weak places in it." Perhaps among the weaknesses was that which he mentioned to George Russell, to whom he spoke of Scott as "too constantly interrupting the thread of his narrative"; but he finished his thought with, "but after all, who is there like him?" In 1850 he wrote that Scott was

> Foremost and unapproachable in the bright world of fiction, gifted with a vivacity and range of invention scarcely ever equalled, and never (but in the case of Shakespeare) exceeded; endowed, as never fabled enchanter was, with spells to conjure up the past, and to give to days and men of old the spirit and freshness of yesterday; to strip religion of her gloom, Virtue of her austerity, and present them both in such attractive forms that you could not choose but love them. . . .[20]

Most of the commentary on Thackeray, in addition to that already cited, is brief and scattered. In 1843 Thackeray wrote in a private note that "Boz has written me a letter of

compliments" on his *Irish Sketch Book* of that year.   Dickens
thought *Vanity Fair* "an absolute masterpiece"; in 1858 he
toasted the novel and Thackeray, who was in the chair of a
meeting of the Royal General Theatrical Fund:

> . . . How full of wit [his books] are, how full of
> wisdom they are, how full of outspoken meaning--
> and yet, though out-speaking, how devoid of fear,
> and how devoid of favour. . . .   [Men of the
> theater may] have studied the mighty deep secrets
> of the human heart in many theatres of many
> kinds, great and small, but I am sure that none of
> them can have studied those mysterious workings
> in any theatre . . . to greater advantage, to
> greater profit, and to greater contentment than in
> the airy books of *Vanity Fair*. . . .   [He is a]
> skillful showman, who has . . . delighted us . . .
> [with] his potent art. . . .

Dickens seems to have liked Thackeray's short pieces as well
as his novels: he called one such "his very best contribution
to *Punch*, describing the grown-up cares of a poor family of
young children."   Some of Thackeray's early satirical pieces
were too sharp for him; he thought it possible that "in the
reckless vivacity of his youth, his satirical pen had even
gone astray or done amiss. . . ."   But Dickens approved of
"his   refined   knowledge   of   character,   of   his   subtle
acquaintance with the weaknesses of human nature, of his
delightful   playfulness   as   an   essayist,   of   his   quaint   and
touching ballads, his mastery over the English language," and
paid tribute to the "brilliant qualities" exhibited in his work
as editor for the *Cornhill Magazine*.   Dickens thought his
last, unfinished, work (*Denis Duval*, published in *Cornhill
Magazine*, 1864) to be "much the best of all his works."[21]
Gladys Storey says that Kate Perugini, Dickens' daughter,
told her of an incident at Gad's Hill, "when a visitor
commenced to eulogize the works of her father at the
expense of Thackeray (then dead); whereupon Dickens
immediately observed:
      'The author of *Vanity Fair* was a very great genius.'"

"We shall not see another Thackeray this century," he told another visitor."[22]

Dickens said he was "a great admirer of George Eliot"; certainly he was among the first to recognize her genius. He called Forster's attention to the publication of those tales in *Blackwood's Magazine* which were soon to be collected as *Scenes from Clerical Life*: "Do read them. They are the best things I have seen since I began my course." He wrote to Joseph Langford, asking him to "convey the note of thanks (enclosed) to the author of Scenes of Clerical Life, whose two stories I can never say enough of, I think them so truly admirable. But if those two volumes, or part of them, were not written by a woman, then should I begin to believe that I am a woman myself." To Eliot herself he wrote,

> I have been so strongly affected by the first two tales in the book you have had the kindness to send me through Messers. Blackwood, that I hope you will excuse my writing to you to express my admiration of their extraordinary merit. The exquisite truth and delicacy, both of the humour and the pathos of these stories, I have never seen the like of; and they have influenced me in a manner that I should find it very difficult to describe to you, if I had the impertinence to try.

He repeated his guess about her sex, basing it on "womanly touches" in the stories. If he was wrong, he said, "I believe that no man ever before had the art of making himself, mentally, so like a woman, since the world began."[23]

In 1859 he wrote to Eliot to repeat his admiration of the collected stories--"strong feelings of admiration . . . so noble a writer . . . such genius"--and gave still greater praise to *Adam Bede:*

> Adam Bede has taken its place among the actual experiences and endurances of my life. Every high quality that was in the former book, is in that, with a World of Power added thereunto. The conception of Hetty's character is so

extraordinary [sic] subtle and true, that I laid the
book down fifty times, to shut my eyes and think
about it. I know nothing so skilful, determined
and uncompromising. The whole country life that
the story is set in, is so real, so droll and genuine
and yet so select and polished by art, that I
cannot praise it enough to you.

And that part of the book which follows
Hetty's trial (and which I have observed to be not
as widely understood as the rest) afflicted me far
more than any other, and exalted my sympathy
with the writer to its utmost height. You must
not suppose I am writing this to *you*. I have been
saying it over and over again, here and elsewhere.

He finished by inviting Eliot to write for *All the Year
Round*, which she never did. It is interesting that Dickens
admired Hetty, who as unrepentent sexual sinner was not his
kind of fictional female (though in his own life he worked
with Miss Coutts to help many similarly "fallen" women). But
his admiration for Eliot's presentation of that which was
"genuine" yet "polished by art" is characteristic: in painting,
in drama, and in literature, that for him was the artist's
task. Four months later, he tried again to secure her genius
for *All the Year Round*: "Of my personal feeling and wish in
the matter, and of the extent to which I have it at heart as
an artist, to have such an artist working with me, I have no
right to say more. . . ."[24]

As we have seen, Dickens did manage to enlist the
services of Elizabeth Gaskell for his journal. Though their
differences over *North and South* led him to disparage that
novel in part, he had nothing but praise for the rest of her
work, beginning with *Mary Barton*; Dickens said he felt
"unaffected and great admiration of your book. . . ." Forster
affirms that Dickens "had a high admiration" of the "powers"
of Gaskell; Dickens wrote to him of a story of hers that
appeared in *Household Words* in 1853, "Don't you think Mrs.
Gaskell charming? With one ill-considered thing that looks
like a want of natural perception, I think it masterly."[25]

Most of Dickens' comments on the work of Wilkie

Collins are made on stories submitted to his journals, but he did offer opinions on Collins' plays and novels as well. The first I have found was on his *Basil: A Story of Modern Life* (1852), which Dickens liked, but also criticized: "I think the probabilities here and there require a little more respect than you are disposed to shew them. . ."; he wished that Collins had not included a "Prefatory Letter" which explained and defended the novel. "But the story contains admirable writing, and many clear evidences of a very delicate discrimination of character." Perhaps the two worked so smoothly together on a few literary ventures because, in addition to being close friends, they exchanged constructive criticism. Dickens by no means acted upon all of Collins' suggestions, but he did accept some--for example, one concerning "Tom Tiddler's Ground": "I agree entirely with you as to the necessity of writing up the compact concerning the people who come in at the gate. I have not the least doubt that it is hurried and huddled up as I have written it, and that much more can be made of it. Much more, therefore (please God), *shall* be made of it when we get to work." The admiration with which Dickens spoke of much of Collins' work indicates that he thought in most cases it needed little alteration. He said of *Hide and Seek*,

> I think it far away the cleverest novel I have ever seen written by a new hand. It is in some respects masterly. Valentine Blyth is as original and as well done, as anything can be. The scene where he shows his pictures is full of an admirable humor. Old Mat is admirably done. In short I call it a very remarkable book, and have been very much surprised by its great merit.[26]

One thing that seems to have impressed Dickens about Collins was his capacity for growth: with but little exception, each thing he did struck Dickens as better than its predecessor. He wrote to him of *The Woman in White* that

> It is a very great advance on all your former writing, and most especially in respect of

tenderness.   In character it is excellent.   Mr.
Fairlie is as good as the lawyer, and the lawyer is
as good as he.   Mr. Vesey and Miss Holcombe, in
their different ways, equally meritorious.   Sir
Percival is also most skillfully shown, though I
doubt (you see what small points I come to)
whether any man ever showed uneasiness by hand
or foot without being forced by nature to show it
in his face, too.   The story is very interesting and
the writing of it admirable.

The following year, he wrote Collins that the novel was
"your best book," an opinion he was to revise only as he
began to read *No Name*.

> I have read the story as far as you have
> written it, with strong interest and great
> admiration. . . .
> I find in the book every quality that made
> the success of the *Woman in White*, without the
> least sign of holding on to that success or being
> taken in tow by it. . . .

Eight months later, with the second volume read, the opinion
remained the same:

> I have gone through the Second Volume at a
> sitting, and I find it *wonderfully fine*.   It goes on
> with an ever-rising power and force in it that fills
> me with admiration.   It is as far before and
> beyond *The Woman in White* as that was beyond
> the wretched common level of fiction-writing.
> There are some touches in the Captain which no
> one but a born (and cultivated) writer could get
> near--could draw within hail of.   And the
> originality of Mrs. Wragge, without compromise of
> her probability, involves a really great
> achievement.   But they are all admirable; Mr. Noel
> Vanstone and the housekeeper, both in their way
> as meritorious as the rest; Magdalen wrought out

with truth, energy, sentiment, and passion, of the very first water.

The third volume of *No Name* continued to elicit praise: "Among the many excellent things in the proof, I noticed, as particularly admirable, the manner in which the amount of Mrs. Lecount's legacy is got at, and the bearing and discourse of the Scotch fly-driver." And finally, ". . . All that I thought and said of it when you finished the second volume, I think and repeat of it now you have finished the third." Some months before *The Moonstone* began its run in *All the Year Round* in January of 1868, Dickens gave it only slightly qualified praise in a letter to Wills:

> Of course it is a series of 'narratives,' and of course such and so many modes of action are open to such and such people; but it is a very curious story--wild, and yet domestic--with excellent characters in it, great mystery, and nothing belonging to disguised women or the like. It is prepared with extraordinary care, and has every chance of being a hit. It is in many respects much better than anything he has done.

Here again are the Dickensian standards: a dislike of the obvious pattern, a liking of wildness against a background of the ordinary, and of meticulous work. But by the following year, Dickens had lost much of his enthusiasm for *The Moonstone*: "I quite agree with you about the 'Moonstone,'" he wrote Wills. "The construction is wearisome beyond endurance, and there is a vein of obstinate conceit in it that makes enemies of readers."[27] It is difficult to be certain of what Dickens has in mind here, but he seems to be reacting negatively to the labored working out of the mystery of the story, and to the sense of the writer's rather smugly holding his readers in suspense.

Dickens admired Collins' capacity to arouse emotion, to create pathos, humor, and the pleasant and easy mood. But he objected to Collins' tendency to excess, to his lapses into cliché, and to the failure of his work to create that moving picture which Dickens held as the essence of good storytelling. Dickens' reaction to *The Moonstone* follows what we may see as a pattern of his criticism of friends: initial enthusiastic response, followed by a more dispassionate critical judgment.

Two words are repeated in much of the commentary on Collins: *admirable*, and *merit*. It seems likely that Collins earned these words because he continued, in Dickens' eyes, to improve, and because he did so by dint of constant application, which appealed to Dickens as much as anything else an artist could do. Dickens told Wills that Collins' "quality of taking pains, united to natural quickness, will always get him on." Pains-taking and quickness were among the higher virtues always for Dickens. *Sister Rose*, published in *Household Words* in 1855, was "An excellent story, charmingly written, and shewing everywhere an amount of pains and study in respect of the art of doing such things that I see mighty seldom." Dickens concluded his long letter of praise of *No Name* by saying,

> . . . I was certain from the *Basil* days that you were the writer who would come ahead of all the Field--being the only one who combined invention and power, both humourous and pathetic, with that invincible determination to work, and that profound conviction that nothing of worth is to be done without work, of which triflers and feigners have no conception.[28]

It was a theme he was to repeat to others about Collins.

Aside from the comments made on Bulwer's contribution to Dickens' journal, only one other non-dramatic work is given specific (though hardly helpful) criticism: Bulwer's "'Lost Tales of Miletus' is a most noble book! He is an extraordinary fellow, and fills me with admiration and wonder." One other book is mentioned, but not assessed: from Broadstairs Dickens wrote Bulwer that "I have brought Harold [a Bulwer novel] down here, and am going away now . . . to lie down on the sand with him." All other references to Bulwer are general compliments: in a speech

Dickens said that his "works of fiction . . . were known and appreciated by all the world"; in another he paid tribute to his "brilliant fancy."[29]

Commentary upon other writers whom Dickens knew are infrequent. His two brief opinions on Talfourd suggest that he was not overly enthusiastic about his work: of Talfourd's emotional dedication to his wife of his *Recollections of a First Visit to the Alps* he said, "I *do* think it is rather Adam-and-Evey." The only other reference avoids judgment by the old method--despite Dickens' disclaimer--of thanking an author for his book before reading it: "Hearty thanks for the Memorials of Lamb, . . . which I am now going to read luxuriously. . . ." Dickens thanked Frederick Marryat for "your famous book; over which I have been chuckling and grinning, and clenching my fists, and becoming warlike. . . ." Harrison Ainsworth, who by 1846 had somewhat fallen out of Dickens' favor, was referred to only as "the unintelligible novelist. . . ."[30] Dickens seems to have liked the work of George Henry Lewes: he wrote to him in 1847 that "I am reading Ranthorpe with great interest and pleasure"--though one is inclined to wonder whether that vague phrase was not at times used to fill a blank in which nothing more positive could be written, just as "very interesting" is used today. Later, though, Dickens expressed specific praise of, as well as some reservations about, *Ranthorpe:* "It has pleased me *very much indeed*; and I would I saw more of such sense and philosophy in that kind of Literature. . . . It occurred to me here and there, in the perusal, that the characters were, sometimes, not sufficiently distinct from each other, and that instead of your being metaphysical for them, they are a little too metaphysical for themselves." But Dickens' final comment on Lewes, concerning *Rose, Blanche, and Violet*-- which Jane Carlyle thought "execrable" and which Lewes himself later condemned--was purely commendatory: " . . . It has affected me extremely, and manifests, I think, very great power. It has left the strongest impression on me. The whole history of Chamberlayne and his wife, is admirably done. I had noted a great many other striking things as I went along, but this swallowed them all up. . . ."[31]

Dickens wrote fairly frequently of the work of his

friend Douglas Jerrold. Of "books" which Jerrold sent him in
1843 he said, "I have read them with perfect delight . . ."
and "I am greatly pleased with your opening paper in the
Illuminated. It is very wise, and capital; written with the
finest end of that iron pen of yours; witty, much needed, and
full of truth." The following year he wrote Jerrold, "I can't
tell you how often I read, Brown, Jones, and Robinson. . . .
It is full of melancholy and pain to me, but its truth and
wisdom are prodigious." The editors of the Pilgrim Edition
Letters suggest that "CD's response testifies more to his
concern with the subject of education than the quality of the
story." When Jerrold slightly revised his *Story of a Feather*,
first serialized in *Punch* and now collected in a volume,
Dickens wrote, "I am quite delighted to find that you have
touched the latter part again, and touched it wtih such a
delicate and tender hand. It is a wise and beautiful book."[32]
Some months later he wrote of the story that he found
"Gauntwolf's sickness and the career of that snuffbox,
masterly." Of Jerrold's *Chronicles of Clovernook, with Some
Accounts of the Hermit of Bellyfulle*, Dickens said that the
hermit "took my fancy mightily when I first saw him in the
Illuminated, and I have stowed him away in the left-hand
breast pocket of my travelling coat, that we may hold
pleasant converse together on the Rhine." Douglas Jerrold
was "a clever author," and "an author of great power. . . ."[33]
    Fields say that Dickens mentioned as among his favorite
books to talk about while walking the following:

> the writings of Cobbett, De Quincy, the *Lectures
> on Moral Philosophy* by Sydney Smith, and
> Carlyle's *French Revolution*. Of this latter
> Dickens said it was the book of all others which
> he read perpetually and of which he never tired--
> the book which always appeared more imaginative
> in proportion to the fresh imagination he brought
> to it, a book for inexhaustibleness to be placed
> before every other book.

The only other major author mentioned is Charles Reade;
Dickens was called upon to render an opinion of his *Griffith*

Gaunt in connection with a trial for libel. "I have read it with the strongest interest and admiration," he wrote. "I regard it as the work of a highly accomplished writer and a good man; a writer with a brilliant fancy and a graceful and tender imagination. I could name no other living writer who could, in my opinion, write such a story nearly so well." He also said of the poet Thomas Hood that "I have been reading poor Hood's *Tylney Hall* [a novel]: the most extraordinary jumble of impossible extravagance, and especial cleverness, that I ever saw!" And he wrote to a friend of Hood that, probably in his *Comic Annual for 1839*, he was "rather poor," though, because Hood was then ill, he would not say so in print; in his review in the *Examiner*, he called the work "pleasant and inoffensive."[34]

Dickens' general allusions to John Poole as writer probably refer to his dramatic pieces, but may also include the incidental prose which he wrote: Poole, he said while including him in the benefit originally designed only for Hunt, had written "comic pieces of great merit . . . productions of great celebrity and merit. . . . And in a piece Dickens wrote to make up a deficiency in the money garnered by the benefit, Mrs. Gamp calls Poole a man "as has made a many people merry in his time. . . ."[35]

Perhaps one other writer deserves mention here, though she is not known as a novelist. At her death Jane Carlyle had been working on a novel. "How often I thought of the unfinished novel," Dickens wrote to Forster. "No one now to finish it. None of the writing women come near her at all." It would be a shocking statement if we thought Dickens was really suggesting that Eliot, Gaskell, and the Brontës could not measure up to Jane Carlyle, but we have seen enough of his superlatives to understand him: while he thought of one author, he often considered him or her to be the best, only to render a contrary opinion when he concentrated upon another author. When he made the above statement, he doubtless had no thought of the two women he so clearly admired, but was thinking of the female authors of the romances and domestic novels he disliked--the romances, by such women as Mrs. Gore, Lady Blessington, and Lady Charlotte Bury, which he called "mawkish tales of fashionable life before which crowds fall down as if they were gilded calves," and the domestic novels, treated with such severity by Wilkie Collins in "Doctor Dulcamara, M. P."[36]

Dickens commented briefly on certain non-fictional prose writers of his time, though as always only upon those for whom some special connection such as friendship or editorship gave occasion. The first of these, naturally, was his close friend, John Forster. Forster wrote several biographies, and Dickens liked them all. Reading through *The Life and Times of Oliver Goldsmith*, he sent Forster weekly notes of commendation: "I think the Goldsmith very great indeed--exceedingly large . . ." and "Upon my soul, I think the Goldsmith *admirable*." And finally a long assessment:

> As a picture of the time, I really think it impossible to give it too much praise. It seems to me to be the very essence of all about the time that I have ever seen in biography or fiction, presented in most wise and human lights, and in a thousand new and just aspects. I have never liked Johnson half so well. Nobody's contempt for Boswell ought to be capable of increase, but I have never seen him in my mind's eye half so plainly. The introduction of him is quite a masterpiece--I should point to that, if I didn't know the author, as being done by somebody with a remarkably vivid conception of what he narrated and a most admirable and fanciful power of communicating it to another. All about Reynolds, is charming; and the first account of the Literary Club, and of [Topham] Beauclerc, as excellent a piece of description as ever I read in my life. But to read the book, is to be in the time. It lives again in as fresh and lively a manner, as if it were presented on an impossibly good stage by the very best actor that ever lived, or by the real actors come out of their graves on purpose.
>
> And as to Goldsmith himself, and *his* life, and the tracing of it out in his own writings, and the

manful and dignified assertion of him without any
sobs, whines, or convulsion of any sort, it is
throughout a noble achievement, of which, apart
from any private and personal affection for you, I
think (and really believe) I should feel proud as
one who had no indifferent perception of these
books of his--to the best of my remembrance--
when little more than a child.   I was a little
afraid in the beginning, when he committed those
very discouraging imprudences [sic] that you were
going to champion him somewhat indiscriminately;
but I very soon got over that fear, and found
reason in every page to admire the sense,
calmness, and moderation, with which you make
the love and admiration of the reader, cluster
about him: grow with his growth, and strengthen
with his strength--and weakness too, which is
better still.

Dickens then offered two objections, one to the value of
having a Boswell, and another to the over-use of italics; then
he raised a question, characteristic of his insistence upon
accurary of detail:

In that picture at the close of the third book
(a most beautiful one) of Goldsmith sitting looking
out of the window at the Temple Trees, you speak
of the "grey-eyed" rooks.   Are you sure they are
grey-eyed?   The Raven's eye is a deep lustrous
black; and so, I suspect, is the rook's except when
the light shines full into it.

After these demurs, he closed his letter with compliments:

I have reserved for a closing word--though I
don't mean to be eloquent about it: being far too
much in earnest--the admirable manner in which
the case of the Literary Man is stated throughout
this book.   It is splendid.   I don't believe that any
book was ever written, or anything ever done or

said, half so conducive to the dignity and honor of literature. . . . Lastly, I never will hear the biography compared with Boswell's except under vigorous protest. For I do say it is mere folly to put into opposite scales, a book, however amusing and curious, written by an unconscious coxcomb like that, and one which surveys and grandly understands the character. . . .[37]

Here again we have the Dickens who could read and be overwhelmed by the work of a friend, only in later reaction to render a more considered judgment (see his comment on Boswell's biography of Johnson, above). Dickens' comment on biography well done as a kind of superb drama is also characteristic, as is his constant attention to minute detail, including the color of a bird's eyes, and his great admiration of Forster's asserting the dignity of the literary man.

In 1855, Dickens offered Forster comment on his biography of Richard Steele:

I cannot express to you how very much delighted I am with the "Steele." I think it incomparably the best of the series. The pleasanter handling of the subject may commend it more to one's liking, but that again requires a delicate handling, which you have given to it in the most charming manner. It is surely not possible to approach a man with a finer sympathy, and the assertion of the claims of literature throughout is of the noblest and most gallant kind. . . . The paper is masterly. . . .

Five years later, Dickens expressed admiration for Forster's *Impeachment of the Five Members*, calling it his "most excellent, interesting, and remarkable book. . . ." Dickens defended it against the charge of being one-sided--apparently some readers felt it was pro-rebel.

In the whole narrative I saw nothing anywhere to which I demurred. I admired it all,

went with it all, and was proud of my friend's
having written it all. I felt it to be all square
and sound and right, and to be of enormous
importance in these times.

    . . . I thought the marginal references
overdone. Here and there, they had a comical
look to me for that reason, and reminded me of
shows and plays where every thing is in the bill.[38]

Dickens wrote a review of Forster's "admirable
biography" of Walter Savage Landor. Forster was, he said, a
"masterly writer. . . ." His *Life of Goldsmith* had been "a
generous and yet conscientious picture of a period," and the
present biography "a not less generous and yet conscientious
picture of one life. . . . It is essentially a sad book, and
herein lies proof of its truth and worth. The life of almost
any great man possessing gifts, would be a sad book to
himself; and this book enables us not only to see its
subject, but to be its subject, if we will." Dickens suggested
that Landor was not yet as much admired as he some day
would be, and added that, "This point admitted or doubted,"
the value of Forster's biography "remains the same." Later,
he wrote that

Nothing in the book is more remarkable than his
examination of each of Landor's successive pieces
of writing, his delicate discernment of their
beauties, and his strong desire to impart his own
perceptions in this wise to the great audience that
is yet to come. It rarely befalls an author to have
such a commentator: to become that subject of so
much artistic skill and knowledge, combined with
such infinite and loving pains. Alike as a piece of
Biography, and as a commentary upon the beauties
of a great writer, the book is a massive book. . .
. Sometimes . . . the balance held by Mr. Forster
has seemed for a moment to turn a little heavily
against the infirmities of temperament of a grand
old friend . . . but we have not once been able to
gainsay the justice of the scales.[39]

Though Dickens himself rarely wrote analysis of literature for its own sake, here and in a few other places he approves of such writing by others. But when it came to biographical comment, one gets the feeling that fine judgment is less important to Dickens than friendship, and that he wished that Forster had adhered to Dickens' own rule and held his tongue a bit more (though as reviewer, Dickens obviously feels the necessity of *using* his own tongue). Here again as well is Dickens' love of the combination of talent and pains-taking.

Dickens' comments on other non-fictional writers are brief. He said that Lamb's *Popular Fallacies* consisted of "most happy glances. . . ." He thought that the *Memoirs, Journal and Correspondence* of Thomas Moore, edited by Lord John Russell, was "extraordinarily good as a little gossiping piece of his time; I think the best Diary since Pepys." He praised Macaulay's "brilliant history," but objected to his contemptuous remarks about "clerks and milliners." And in 1842 he wrote to Mrs. Trollope of her book on America that "there is no writer who has so well and accurately (I need not add so entertainingly) described it [American society], in many of its aspects, as you have done. . . ." He wrote to W. H. Prescott that his *History of the Conquest of Mexico* was a "noble book. . . . I am half way through it already, and am *full of delight and pleasure*--dreaming of it, talking of it, and thinking of it." The book quickly won a high reputation, and is established as an important historical work. Dickens wrote to Felton about the book, "with which I was perfectly charmed. I think his descriptions, Masterly; his style, brilliant; his purpose, manly and gallant always. The introductory account of Aztec civilization impressed me. . . . From beginning to end, the whole History is enchanting and full of Genius."[40]

It may be well to pick from Dickens' comment on minor figures a few names which will be familiar to Dickensians and to students of the century. Dickens wrote of a lecture by Albert Smith, "Mont Blanc," that "It is extremely well and unaffectedly done." He said of *Young England's Library*, to which Smith had contributed, that it "entertained me very much indeed. It is full of a pleasant humor and capital observation." To Charles Knight, of his *William Shakespeare, a Biography*, Dickens wrote, "I . . . read it with great pleasure as a charming piece of honest enthusiasm and perseverence . . ."--rather faint praise for what is perhaps the first truly important biography of the Bard. Dickens also commented on the second of Knight's "Weekly Volumes" of *Mind Amongst the Spindles: a Selection from the Lowell Offering (1844)*: "I think the subject excellently chosen, the introduction exactly what it should be, the allusion to the International Copyright question most honourable and manly, and the whole scheme full of the highest interest."[41]

Though Dickens apparently did not admire the contributions of Lady Blessington to romantic fiction, he did compliment her on some of her work--perhaps indicating that not only would he hold his tongue for a friend, but even file it to some extent. He wrote to her of her *Memoirs of a Femme de Chambre* (1846) that "I have been greatly entertained by the Femme de Chambre . . . [which is] sometimes, like a female Gil Blas." (Hard to think that Dickens would truly have enjoyed a female Gil Blas.) He told her that her illustrated annuals, *Book of Beauty* and *Keepsake*, "have given me--through your graceful but strong-handed share in them--. . . great pleasure." And to her friend Count D'Orsay he wrote of her *Marmaduke Herbert, or the Fatal Error* (1847), "Le livre de Milady est un gran success. Il-y-a beaucoup de choses dans ce livre, tout-a-fait extraordinaire." Perhaps he meant the compliment, but it is tempting to think he may have found it easier to lay it on in French than in his native tongue. Dickens commented too on some of the work of his young acquaintance Marguerite Power, niece of Lady Blessington. Of a book which she had translated from the French and sent to him he commented, "I read [it] . . . with the greatest pleasure. It is a charming story gracefully told, and very gracefully and worthily translated. I have not been better pleased with a book for a long time." He tried to get the publisher Chapman (Hall was now dead) to publish it.[42]

As may be expected, Dickens wrote again and again to offer advice, consolation and, when required, rebuke to his

humble apprentice, John Overs.   Coaching him in 1840, he
wrote about an Overs paper on Wat Tyler, "I think it is a
good magazine piece--I am speaking, mind, as if I knew
nothing of the author, or the circumstances under which it
was written--and *quite equal* to the general run of such
things."   He objected to "making Wat such a thorough paced
villain," on grounds of sympathy, but added, "Apart from this,
I have been greatly pleased with the performance, and I
speak most seriously when I say that in the way of
improvement, you have *done wonders*."   The last comment
indicates that Dickens had carefully overseen at least one
earlier version of the paper, as seems also to have been true
of another, finally titled "Norris and Anne Boleyn"; Dickens
said that "The Improvement is *immense* . . ." and added that
"The new introduction is--except the latter part--the best of
the whole.   When you do anything fresh, throttle your
jesters, remoselessly."   He said of Overs that "he really
writes, in the intervals of his daily labour, *very well*"; he
told Macready, in recommending something Overs was to send
him, that Overs "has written"--and he wrote "poetry" but
struck it out in favor of--"pretty ballads and good little
prose sketches. . . ."[43]   But when Overs sent him a draft of
a proposed letter to Macready, protesting what he considered
to be ill usage, Dickens took him down sharply: "I strongly
disapprove of it"; it was "inconsiderate" in being too long,
and Overs seemed "to vaunt your independence too much"; a
paragraph criticizing Macready's changes in the theater was
"presumptuous and impertinent"; on the whole, "your letter is
in execrable taste. . . ."   But Dickens by no means abandoned
Overs after this; in 1843 several letters show him trying his
best to get writing work for Overs--the last as a reporter on
the *Sun Newspaper*--and inviting Overs to send him MS.   In
1844 he was still offering advice, though not about writing.[44]
In that same year, he wrote the Introduction to Overs'
Evenings of a Working Man.
    Among other names of some interest, Dickens mentioned
John Lockhart, biographer of Scott: "There is a terrible paper
on Theodore Hook, in the last Quarterly--admirably written--
as I think, from its internal evidence, by Lockhart.   I have
not seen anything for a long time so very moving.   It fills

me with grief and sorrow." He wrote to S. Laman Blanchard to praise a "leader" he had written for the *Courier*: "I . . . was greatly amused with the 'leader.' It seemed to me exceedingly happy, terse, pointed, smart, and quite an off [hand] leader in short." (Dickens' brackets.) Of *A New Spirit of the Age* (1844), by R. H. Horne, he wrote, "Horne's book is syncretic. Shadows of Martinuzzi, Gregory the Seventh, and Co. darken its pages, and make the leaves hideous." But writing to Horne of his "didactic fantasy," first called "A Romance of Science" and later titled *The Poor Artist* (1849), Dickens expressed approval: "I am delighted with the story. I think it quite novel in the idea, and admirably executed. A bookseller *might* suggest that the introduction and the conclusion are scarcely so thoroughly allied to the main notion as they might be. . . ." Dickens sent Horne detailed advice on the closing section.[45]

Dickens liked the work of Sydney Smith, as one would imagine. To his wife, in thanks for the gift of his *Sermons* (1846), he said, "The wisdom, truth and beauty, of it . . . perfectly enchanted me." And when Mrs. Smith caused her husband's *Elementary Sketches of Moral Philosophy*, a series of lectures which was, said Dickens, "delivered six years before I was born," to be published in 1849, Dickens said, "I think you have exercised a sound discretion in not permitting such a book to perish. . . . Everywhere it bears the mark of his hand and heart; and the earnest purity of its intention is no less manifest in every page." They were, he said, "beautiful lectures. . . ." In 1855 he wrote to a friend that "Sydney Smith's daughter has privately printed a life of her father with selections from his letters, which has great merit. . . . I have strongly urged her to publish it. . . ."[46]

Peter Cunningham, with whom Dickens had correspondence concerning benefit performances of his amateur dramatic productions (Cunningham was secretary of the Shakespeare Society), was cited by Dickens for his *A Handbook for London, Past and Present* (1849); Dickens congratulated him "on the admirable manner in which you have executed a task of very great difficulty. . . ."

I have gone over several parts of both

> volumes which I know to be difficult ground, and I
> cannot tell you how well I think they are done.
> The poetical illustrations give a charm to the
> whole which sets up the old theatres again, and
> fills them with the old company, and delights the
> fancy; while the district authority is stated with a
> precision and conciseness, worthy of all imitation.
> In both respects you have taken such
> extraordinary pains and read so much, that . . . I
> should rather have believed you had been Seventy
> years, then seven, over your work.

In a speech at the Commercial Travellers' School's annual
dinner, Dickens spoke of Cunningham's 'able edition of
Goldsmith's *Traveller* [and] his admirable *Handbook*."[47]

Dickens wrote to the Reverend James White, of his four
"Letters to the Rev. Charles Fustian, an Anglo-Catholic,"

> I have a hundred times at least wanted to say
> to you how good I thought those papers in
> "Blackwood"--how excellent their purpose, and how
> delicately and charmingly worked out. Their subtle
> and delightful humour, and their grasp of the
> whole question, were something more pleasant to
> me than I can possibly express.

The content of the "Letters" would have appealed to Dickens:
they satirized the introduction of "Foreign mummeries and
superstitions"--i.e., Roman Catholic ritual--into Anglican
service. Dickens also took an interest in the work of
Edmund Yates, as Forster tells us. "If you will read *Kissing
the Rod*," he wrote to Forster, "a book I have read today,
you will not find it hard to take an interest in the author of
such a book." Forster uses this quotation to support his
contention that Dickens had no greater interest "than to help
young novelists to popularity." No doubt Dickens helped
Yates; in 1866 we find him passing judgment on one of his
books [*Flaneur*?] by which he had been "profoundly
affected." "It has touched me deeply," he wrote, "and moved
me to many tears. Hold fast, I adjure you, to the deeper

emotional faculty that you unquestionably possess, and do justice to the tendernesss that is most beautifully and pathetically brought out in the last of these three volumes."[48]

Dickens took interest, also, in the writings of nonprofessional friends such as Miss Coutts, whose pamphlet on education he called "very good indeed. Very plain, very easily remembered, very direct to the purpose." He approved of Mary Boyle's "little Christmas book. Very gracefully and charmingly done. The right feeling, the right touch; a very neat hand, and a very true heart." As can be seen, a certain style was adopted for comments to such writers: brief phrasing, a few complimentary adjectives, and a good deal of *very*. A slightly different tone is adopted for writers of a somewhat more serious stamp, like Sir Arthur Helps: "I have been reading your book with great pleasure. It is full of matter to set one thinking, most charmingly suggested."[49] Only a little less vague, but rather more formal.

Among others Dickens commented on is his friend Charles Kent: "I have been charmed with your book," he wrote him in 1865. He thanked Fitzgerald for his "charming book on Charles Lamb," telling of "with what interest and pleasure I read it . . ." and called it "a graceful sympathetic book." (Both of these books, it might be noted, were dedicated to Dickens.) Dickens told Fitzgerald he was "a fellow-labourer whose writings I highly esteem." Dickens also liked another book on Lamb, this one by the poet B. W. Procter:

> I have read your biography of Charles Lamb with inexpressible pleasure and interest. I do not think it possible to tell a pathetic story with a more unaffected and manly tenderness. And as to the force and vigor of the style, if I did not know you I should have made sure that there was a printer's error in the opening of your introduction, and that the word "seventy" occupied the place of "forty.". . . .
>
> It is not an ordinary triumph to do such justice to the memory of such a man. And I

venture to add that the fresh spirit with which you have done it impresses me with being perfectly wonderful.[50]

Dickens had one occasion to compliment his son Charles on a paper sumitted to *All the Year Round*. "Your paper is remarkably good," he wrote him from New York. "There is not the least doubt that you can write constantly for A.Y.R. I am very pleased with it." He was not at all pleased with the papers of Chauncy Hare Townshend, which were loaded upon him for editing at Townshend's death; to Cerjat he wrote that "To publish them without alteration [as Townshend had directed] is absolutely impossible, for they are . . . fragments . . . and produce a most incoherent and tautological result. . . . I would certainly publish nothing about them, if I had a discretion in the matter. Having none, I suppose a book must be made."[51]   And so a portion of the scant year and a half that Dickens had left was devoted to this unrewarding task for a friend.

As we have seen, far more detailed opinions than these were sent to those who submitted their work to Dickens for comment.   Henry F. Chorley, who wrote for Dickens, got a long judgment of his romance:

I think Roccabella a very remarkable book indeed. Apart--quite apart--from my interest in you, I am certain that if I had taken it up under any ordinarily favourable circumstances as a book of which I knew nothing whatever, I should not-- could not--have relinquished it until I had read it through.   I had turned but a few pages, and come to the shadow on the bright sofa at the foot of the bed, when I knew myself to be in the hands of an artist. . . .   Your story seems to me remarkably ingenious.   I had not the least idea of the purport of the sealed paper until you chose to enlighten me; and then I felt it to be quite natural, quite easy, thoroughly in keeping with the character and presentation of the Liverpool man. The position of the Bell family in the story has a

special air of nature and truth; is quite new to me,
and is so dextrously and delicately done that I
find the deaf daughter no less real and distinct
than the clergyman's wife. . . .   Your characters
have really surprised me.   From the lawyer to the
Princess, I swear to them as true; and in your
fathoming of Rosamund altogether, there is a
profound wise knowledge that I admire and
respect. . . .[52]

Here are several of the Dickens tenets of prose fiction: the
use of foreshadowing symbol, gradual unfolding of plot, and
consistency and reality of character.

Dickens commented briefly on one work by his friend,
(Charles William) Shirley Brooks, the editor of *Punch*.   "I
have read your little book concerning our friend the
Autogryph, with very great pleasure," he wrote to him,
probably of his series of traveling letters in 1853 for the
Morning Chronicle, from Russia, Syria, and Egypt.   "I have
not travelled in more agreeable company this many a long
day.   It is full of good writing, good observation, good
humour, and good sense."   The only other name of some
interest is Henry Austin, Dickens' brother-in-law, to whom
Dickens wrote concerning his "Thoughts on the Abuses of the
Present System of Competition in Architecture": "The
Pamphlet is extremely well got up, and looks capital."[53]

I have found comments on sixty-nine other writers, all
of virtually no reputation.   But what an irony it is that this
man, described as having merely an animal intelligence,
should have expressed so many opinions about so many
writers, most of which--even if jotted down in a short
letter--are sound and pertinent judgments, revealing a
consistent and solid aesthetic which our remaining chapters
will further explore.

4

Literary Practise: Unicorns and Griffins

Dickens' great dislike of shop talk, and especially of talk about his own work, prevented him from making that kind of complete pronouncement on his art which we have from some other novelists. Still, in his editorial comments, his advice to would-be writers, and his casual references to prose fiction, he said enough to show that he understood his art thoroughly. He had a definite method of writing, minor details of which changed slightly during his lifetime, but the main facets of which he strictly followed. He gave attention to all aspects of writing, including such elementary concerns as punctuation, spelling, and grammar. Hardwork and careful revision were a *sine qua non*. He wrote about organization, including the potential of interpolation; in particular, he gave careful attention to the problems of serialization. He liked fiction in which the author submerged himself. And he made strong comments on style; he was especially critical of slang, vulgarisms, professional language, pretentiousness, and his old enemy, cant.

Dickens' first principle for literature, whether written, read, or discussed, was serious application. "I cannot honestly encourage you," he wrote a correspondent in 1850, "to believe that there is any short cut or smooth road to the honors and perils of print." In contrast to the usual representation of him as slavishly desiring to please his audience, he demanded the same seriousness of the reader, too: in *American Notes* he wrote of Philadephia that ". . . There is, in the fair city, an assumption of taste and criticism, savoring rather of those genteel discussions . . . in connection with Shakspeare [sic] and the Musical Glasses, of which we read in the *Vicar of Wakefield*." No such toying could be tolerated in connection with literature, the vehicle of truth: in 1857 he wrote of "that perpetual struggle after an expression of the Truth, which is at once the pleasure and the pain in the loves of us workers of the arts. . . ."[1]

Considered a rapid and careless writer in his own time (and uncomfortably close to ours), Dickens was accorded better judgment when examination of his manuscripts proved that, as Richard Stang says, "emphasis on careful composition, method, technique and form became a dominant concern in his theory of the novel. . . ." It was not only a concern in the novel: the letters themselves, though they numbered in the thousands and were often hastily written, impress one with their careful correctness; only occasionally is a writing slip allowed to pass. As for their content, as they discussed his own work, edited the work of others, and offered advice to those who came to him for help, Dickens' letters sounded incessantly the same note: good writing is the result of hard work, of meticulous attention to every detail of form. Abstract considerations of the relation of form to meaning were not often his concern, but that form should express meaning as clearly and concisely and effectively as possible was a maxim he urged upon everyone he advised.[2]

Dickens was touchingly patient with humble amateurs who sought his advice, but he could be angrily impatient with poor writing. He railed against the "intensely weary and commonplace" writing submitted to his journals. "Everybody could write such things I imagine," he said, "but how anybody can contentedly sit down to do it is inscrutable. . . . People don't plunge into churches and play the organ without knowing the notes or having a ghost of an ear. Yet fifty people a day will rush into manuscript. . . ." American students of the '70's, brought up to consider unfettered expression to be the ideal, would not have liked Charles Dickens as a teacher. He wrote a good description of their kind of writer, in the person of the "Voluntary Correspondent" who sent unsolicited manuscripts to *Household Words*:

He has a general idea that literature is the easiest amusement in the world. He figures a successful author as a radient [sic] personage whose whole time is devoted to idleness and pastime--who keeps a prolific mind in a sort of corn-sieve, and lightly shakes a bushel of it out sometimes, in an odd half hour after breakfast. It would amaze his incredulity beyond all measure, to be told that such elements as patience, study, punctuality, determination, self-denial, training of mind and body, hours of application and seclusion to produce what he reads in seconds, enter into such a career. He has not more conception of the necessity of entire devotion to it, than he has of an eternity from the beginning. Correction and re-correction in the blotted manuscript, consideration, new observation, the patient massing of many reflections, experiences and imaginings for one minute purpose, and the patient separation from the heap of all the fragments that will unite to serve it--these would be Unicorns or Griffins to him--fables altogether. Hence, he can often afford to dispense with the low rudiments of orthography; and of the principles of composition it is obvious that he need know nothing.[3]

No rudiment was too humble to escape Dickens' attention: he insisted upon the elements of grammar, upon spelling, upon punctuation, in everything that came near him. When the first issue of his first periodical, the *Daily News*, came out, he was horrified by the number of typographical errors, and, posing as a reader, wrote a letter of humorous reproof, and an editorial reply:

Sir,
    Will you excuse my calling your attention to a variety of typographical errors in you first number? Several letters are standing on their heads, and several others seem to have gone out of town; while others, like people who are drawn for the militia, appear by deputy, and are sometimes very oddly represented. I have an interest in the subject, as I intend to be,
                    If you will allow me,
                        Your Constant Reader

***   We   can   assure   our   good-humoured correspondent that we are quite conscious of the errors he does us the favour to point out so leniently. The very many inaccuracies and omissions in our first impression are attributable to the disadvantageous circumstances attending the production of a first number. They will not occur, we trust, in any other.[4]

Attention to inaccuracies and omissions continued throughout his editorial career, as did his aversion to certain conventions of printing and punctuation. He complained to Wills of an article "where the Italics (of which, take care that not one is left), and the marks of elision where the vowels are omitted, are irritating and vulgar. . . ." He explained his dislike of italics in a letter to Angela Burdett Coutts; he had not, he said, put certain words into italics on the placards hung in the rooms of Urania Cottage (the home he helped her maintain for wayward women) because "I doubt whether it would not direct attention rather to bits and scraps of the explanation than to the whole of it; and secondly, because Italics are always considered objectionable in printed text, with a view to clearness and general plainness." In another context he wrote that he could not

help objecting to that practice (begun I think or greatly enlarged, by Hunt) of italicizing lines and words and whole paragraphs in extract, without some very special reason indeed. It does appear to be a kind of assertion of the editor over the reader--almost over the author himself--which grates upon me. The author might almost as well do it himself, to my thinking, as a disagreeable thing; and it is such a strange contrast to the modest, quiet, tranquil beauty of the Deserted Village for instance, that I would almost as soon hear the town crier speak the lines. The practice always reminds me of a man seeing a beautiful view, and not thinking how beautiful it is, half so much as what he shall say about it.[5]

(Note the quotation from Shakespeare.)

He suggested that Bulwer drop the practice of using an initial plus dash for the name of a town in his story, and supply a fictitious name instead: "I suppose a blank or a dash rather fends a good many people off--because it always has the effect on me." On more than one occasion he brought Wills up for inattention to "pointing": "Again I observe one or two of the articles in a very slovenly state, both as to the Queen's English and pointing."[6] Of another, "There are 6 &C.'s in the compass of one column of the Chinese Francis Moore." [sic] Apparently he was no less careful in going over his own work: Kathleen Tillotson tells us that the revision of *Oliver Twist* for its publication in monthly parts "included the introduction of a new and individual system of punctuation which . . . is related to oral delivery. . . ."[7]

Spelling received similar attention. ". . . Nobody can write properly without spelling well," he advised a correspondent. Using in haste the spelling "Shakspeare," he paused to ask Forster to "put an e before the s; I like it much better . . ."--possibly because Forster used that spelling in the *Examiner*. In response to a query by Angela Burdett Coutts he wrote,

> I spell Harbor without the letter u, because the modern spelling of such words as "Harbor, arbor, parlor," etc [sic] (modern within the last quarter of a century) discards that vowel, as belonging in that connexion to another sound--such as hour and sour. But, if it will be the slightest satisfaction to you, I will take that vowel up again, and fight for it as long as I live. U and I shall be inseparable, and nothing shall every part us[8]

--an example of Dickens' love of modest flirting with his female correspondents; perhaps no one else would have found a way of injecting romance into orthography.

Grammar was another constant concern. Dickens gently

scolded no less famous an author than Wilkie Collins on one occasion for an error which still drives English teachers mad. About his novel *No Name*, Dickens said that "There is one slight slip, occurring more than once, which you have not corrected. Magdalen 'laid down,' and I think someone else 'laid down'. It is clear that she must either lay herself down, or lie down. To lay is verb active, and to lie down is a verb neuter, consequently she lay down, or laid herself down." When a woman asked him to help place some translations she had made, he as usual declined, but did correct some of her verb tenses. He asked Fitzgerald, in contributions to *Household Words*, to "Please keep, on abrupt transitions into the present tense, *your critical eye*."[9] "Talented," he wrote R. H. Horne, "cannot be a word, I think, because you cannot make a participle in English out of a substantive." (Talented had occasionally been so used since the seventeenth century, but in Dickens' time the practice had become more common, and was considered objectionable by many.) He pointed out to Wills that the word "both" in a poem by Robert Lytton "is used as applied to several things." And on occasion he came down on excessive use of slang: he advised Wills, of an unidentified article, "It wants . . . the omission of a familiar slang phrase here and there," and voted against "Under a Cloud" as title for what Wilkie Collins finally called *No Name* because "it has a semi-slang acceptation that is dead against it and makes it small." He wrote to Henry Morely, who helped with editing when Wills was ill, that he was "almost demented by the intolerably confused change of mood, time, and person, into which the writers fall. . . ."[10]

Perhaps no editor ever worked harder to root out basic illiteracies. We have glanced at but a sampling of the extent to which he, as Stone says, made changes in "punctuation, allusions, phrasings, and figures of speech." He worked no less hard at his own writing, though at a much higher level than eliminating fundamental errors. Circumstances of his private life demonstrate the same concern for detail. "Dickens was very particular concerning the terms of speech used by his children," Gladys Storey tells us. "He disliked the expression 'awfully nice' or 'awfully pretty'; it simply

could not and must not be used." True, he wrote to John
Overs "I . . . correct but very little, and that invariably as I
write." But a young Dickens speaks these words; later
comments indicate a different kind of writing. Dickens
rarely posed as writer, but one is tempted to believe he
struck something of an attitude for the humble Overs in his
statement. The second half of it, as we shall shortly see,
may have been true, but the first half was true, if at all,
only for the very early writer; we will see evidence of
careful revision as early as *Oliver Twist*. Forster tells us
that when Dickens was writing portions of *David Copperfield*
taken from his abortive autobiography, there was "no
blotting, as when writing fiction. . . ." And the study of
his manuscripts by Butt and Tillotson proves that in his
fiction he blotted often: after agreeing that he wrote rapidly
in early novels, they say:

> But at the height of his powers, he found more
> difficulty in satisfying himself, and from *Dombey &
> Son* onwards his manuscripts are characterized by
> frequent erasures and interlineations. . . . His
> habit was to correct as he wrote, sentence by
> sentence. . . . He rarely needed to make any later
> alteration.[11]

Thus the statement to Overs may be valid, yet it gives the
wrong impression: Dickens did not write without correction.
If he did not throw away a thousand pages of one novel, as
D. H. Lawrence claimed to do, yet, according to Gladys
Storey, "Sometimes . . . his waste-paper basket would be
filled with discarded manuscript," which gives a somewhat
different picture even from the "sentence by sentence"
statement of Butt and Tillotson: sometimes, it would seem,
Dickens corrected pages by pages. (Evidence of alteration is
found in the letters as well as the manuscripts.) He changed
the name of a character in *The Chimes* from Jessie to Lillian
because "It is prettier in sound, and suits my music better."
In 1849 he thanked the Reverend George Frederick Hill for
sending him corrections of Yarmouth venacular used in the
early numbers of *David Copperfield*; he corrected some of

these in an *errata* list for these numbers, and used the corrected spellings in later numbers.[12]

Even Dickens' public letters and other nonfictional writing were carefully revised. In an appeal for funds for Italian refugees of the war for Italian independence, he changed "almost as new in Rome as Rome is old" to "new in Rome," and "let us remember" to "it must not be forgotten." Derek Hudson tells us that, of *A Child's History of England*, ". . . there is autograph manuscript, heavily corrected, in the Victorian and Albert Museum for [several] chapters. . . ." When George Dolby said "It is well known with what care and elaboration Mr. Dickens prepared his books," he was probably thinking not only of writing, but of such incidents as that in which Dickens consulted with his publishers on the timing of the printing of *David Copperfield*, "so that it should not commence at a dead time of the year." As I have shown elsewhere, his attention to the details of reproducing illustrations in his novels was equally exhaustive.[13]

Many other friends bore witness to Dickens' careful revision of manuscript. A friend wrote that "A famous artist, who once painted his portrait while he was in the act of writing one of the most popular of his stories, relates that he was astonished at the trouble Dickens seemed to take over his work, at the number of forms in which he would write down a thought before he hit out the one which seemed to his fastidious fancy the best, and at the comparative smallness of manuscript each day's sitting seemed to have produced." It is generally agreed that he wrote rapidly in his early years, and that his pace slowed only later in his career, but as early as *The Old Curiosity Shop* he wrote to Forster that composing a number (two chapters) "takes a long time doing, I can tell you." Kathleen Tillotson noted the "detailed revision" of an even earlier novel, *Oliver Twist*; she and John Butt also speak of "the care which he took in revising" his sketches when they were collected in book form, at about the same time: he "made extensive cuts, rewrote whole paragraphs, and made innumerable minute changes both of substance and style; . . . he continued to revise in successive editions . . ." though they add that much of this was "'political and topical' revision," rather than literary improvement.[14]

From the time of *Dombey and Son* on, still something less than half way through his career, Dickens' letters mention hard work with increasing frequency. Of that novel he wrote to Forster, "I take enormous pains with it." Of the next, *David Copperfield*, he said "I have been tremendously at work these two days, eight hours at a stretch yesterday, and six hours and a half today, with the Ham and Steerforth chapter, which has completely knocked me over--utterly defeated me." Perhaps partly in reaction to the popular idea that he scribbled, he now let David enunciate his principle within his fiction:

> Whatever I have tried to do in life, I have tried with all my heart to do well. What I have devoted myself to, I have devoted myself to completely. Never to put one hand to anything in which I could throw my whole self, and never to affect depreciation of my work whatever it was, I find now to have been my golden rule.

Forster found the passage so characteristic of the author as well as the fictional character that he put it in his biography, in which he himself later commented that Dickens "did not think lightly of his work; and the work that occupied him at the time was for the time paramount with him."[15] Working on his next novel, *Bleak House*, Dickens lamented his inability to "grind sparks out of this dull blade," and of *Little Dorrit* he said, "It would not be easy to increase the pains I take with her." Upon finishing *Great Expectations* he said that "the work has been pretty close," and that he was exhausted. By the time of his last full novel, *Our Mutual Friend*, he was saying "I have grown hard to satisfy, and write very slowly. . . ."[16] The slowness seems to have been caused by some problems with invention--either too much or too little. At one point Dickens told Forster that he had been "wanting in invention," but elsewhere he suggested that the reverse was true: "I work slowly and with great care, and never give way to my invention recklessly, but constantly restrain it. . . ."

Perhaps what he meant by the first statement was that he had been wanting in satisfying invention, for he also told Forster, while working on *Our Mutual Friend*, that "I have so much bad fiction, that will be thought of when I don't want to think of it, that I am forced to take more care than I ever took." His publisher Frederick Chapman attested to "the very careful sketching and plotting that he put into his later books," and said that he did much rewriting both at the manuscript and proof stages. Whatever he may have thought earlier, by the end of his career Dickens himself knew that invention alone was not enough; about six months before his death he told the annual meeting of the Birmingham and Midland Institute at Birmingham that "My own invention or imagination, such as it is, I can most truthfully assure you, would never have served me as it has, but for the habit of commonplace, humble, patient, daily, toily, drudging attention."[17]

Two years before his death, Dickens encouraged his son Henry in his work by telling him,

> I should never have made my success in life if I
> had been shy of taking pains, or if I had not
> bestowed upon the least thing I have ever
> undertaken exactly the same attention and care
> that I have bestowed upon the greatest. . . . Look
> at such of my manuscripts as are in the library at
> Gad's, and think of the patient hours devoted year
> after year to single lines.

The claim has been given scholarly sanction only in our time, but several of Dickens' contemporaries were well aware that it was true. Charles Kent said that in the manuscripts "the countless alterations, erasures, interpolations, transpositions, interlineations, shew plainly enough the minute and conscientious thought devoted to the perfecting, so far as might be in any way possible, of the work of composition." Frederick Chapman said that Dickens "was exacting with himself in his MSS., changing this part and interleaving that part, so that often it was almost indecipherable. Also he made extensive alterations to his proofs up to the moment that, as a book, they went out into the world."[18]

Dickens did not often complain openly about the popular misconception of his craftsmanship, but he did not like the notion that his or any good literature could be written without painstaking effort. At a banquet in his honor in Liverpool he said that his "literary brethren" knew (and so by implication others might not know) "how true it is, of all art, that what seems the easiest done is oftentimes the most difficult to do, and that the smallest truth may come of the greatest pains. . . ." He wrote a letter to Peter Cunningham objecting to a piece he thought Cunningham had written in the *Illustrated London News* claiming that *Hard Times* was inspired by Dickens' going to see the strike at Preston; such a statement, he said, "encourages the public to believe in the impossibility that books are produced in that very sudden and cavalier manner. . . ." He must have been delighted with an Irish child who, when Dickens asked him if he could write, replied, "Not yet. Things comes by deegrays."[19]

He had no patience with writers who excused their faults on the grounds of haste. To one such, a would-be poet named R. S. Horrell, he wrote,

> In answer to some of the objections I ventured to suggest to you, you plead the absence of needful revision and correction. Now, I must say you are foolish and wrong in this. The question you wish me to decide, has reference, not only to what you think but to your power of expressing what you think. How can I judge of that, upon your mere assurance that you have the power of writing regular verse, but have not taken the trouble to exert it? For aught I know, a great many men may *think* poetry--I dare say they do--but the matter between us, is, whether you can write it or no.

> Do not suppose that the entertaining a distaste for such extremely light labour as reading and revising your own writings, is a part of the true poetical temperament. Whatever Genius does, it does well; and the man who is constantly

beginning things and never finishing them is no
true Genius, take my word for it.   I do not
remember to have ever had, within the last four or
five years, any composition sent to me by a young
man (and I have had a great number) who did not
give me to understand that it was the worst he
had ever written, and that he had much better
ones at home.

The other side of the coin was the writer who made
mistakes, but learned from them: Dickens said of George
Augustus Sala that "he looks sharply at the alterations [made
by Dickens] in his articles, and takes the hint next time."[20]
     Writing was not a mere matter of application, but
Dickens believed that it was not the product of mere
inspiration, either.   Henry said that his father "had no faith
in the waiting-for-inspiration theory, nor did he fall into the
opposite error of forcing himself willy-nilly to turn out so
much manuscript every day. . . .   It was his business to sit
at his desk during just those particular hours in the day, my
father used to say, and, whether the day turned out well or
ill, there he sat accordingly."   At times the day could turn
out ill because of mood: "I have been rather slack in point of
work;" he wrote in 1842, "not being in the vein."   Certain
vexations could also get him out of the vein: when his
publisher William Hall made an incautious remark about a slip
in sales, he said "I am so irritated . . . that a wrong kind of
fire is burning in my head, and I don't think I _can_ write.
Nevertheless, I am trying."   Asked if inspiration always came
during the morning he invariably spent at work, he replied,
"No--sometimes I have to coax it; sometimes I do little else
than draw figures or make dots on the paper, and plan and
dream til perhaps my time is nearly up.   But I always sit
here, for that certain time. . . ."   When his time was up, he
added, he left for his daily tramp, "hardly waiting to
complete a sentence."   It seemed necessary for him to close
off his imagination when he came back into the "real" world:
James T. Fields said that he had taught himself to shut his
characters away when he shut his study door, "and only meet
them again when he came back to resume his task."[21]

It was always difficult for him to begin a novel; an acquaintance said that "Sometimes he would scarcely eat or sleep when beginning a new book." The effort affected his personality: near the end of 1842 he told Miss Coutts that he was

> in the agonies of plotting and contriving a new book; in which stage of the tremendous process, I am accustomed to walk up and down the house, smiting my forehead dejectedly; and to be so horribly cross and surly, that the boldest fly at my approach.
>   . . . Unless I were to shut myself up, obstinately and selfishly in my own room for a great many days without writing a word, I don't think I should ever make a beginning.

Once he has written the first number, he said, "I go on with great nonchalance,"[22] which an observer confirmed: " . . . when the pages covered with writing began to pile up, I knew that pretty soon he would ease off considerably." No doubt this was because he did the hardest work before he began to write: he would develop and organize everything in his mind before putting anything on paper. "I never commit thought to paper until I am obligated to write," he said, "being better able to keep them in regular order, on different shelves of my brain, ready ticketed and labelled, to be brought out when I want them." His son Charley reported that

> . . . Very often, I have known a day to be barren of copy, but to have been a very good day, notwithstanding. Often . . . I have seen that he had scarcely written a line, and have heard him report at lunch time that he had a bad morning, but have known from the expressive working of his face and from a certain intent look that I learnt to know well, that he had been, almost unconsciously, diligently thinking all round his subject; and that the next day's work would result

in the comparatively easy production of a goodly number of those wonderful sheets full of blue lines, and erasures, and "baloonings out," and interlineations, and all kinds of traps for compositors, which you may see at South Kensington.

Frederick Chapman described it thus: " . . . After getting hold of a central idea he revolved it in his mind until he had fully thought it out.   Then he made what I may call a programme of the story and its characters, drawing up each character in skeleton form.   Upon this skeleton he set to work and gave it the literary blood, sinew and vitality of a *David Copperfield* or an *Oliver Twist*."   The same principle seems to have applied to other kinds of composition: George Dolby said that when Dickens put together a speech

. . . his habit was to take a long walk . . . during which he would decide on the various heads to be dealt with.   These being arranged in their proper order, he would in his "mind's eye", liken the whole subject to the tire of a cart wheel--he being the hub.   From the hub to the tire he would run as many spokes as there were subjects to be treated; and during the progress of the speech he would deal with each spoke separately, elaborating them as he went round the wheel; and when all the spokes had dropped out one by one . . . he would know that he had accomplished his task, and that his speech was at the end.[23]

At times Dickens did write notes and outlines, but however he planned, he planned carefully.   His description of the steps of composition, in a piece in *Household Words*, is worth repeating in this connection: "Consideration, new observation, the patient massing of many reflections, experiences and imaginings fo one minute purpose, and the patient separation from the heap of all the fragments that will unite to serve it. . . ."   One thinks, observes, experiences, and imagines; then one takes from each, paring away--as Henry James also advised--all that is not essential, and forming the pure matter into a whole.   As he developed as an artist, Dickens gave increasing attention to the latter steps, and expressed regret for failure to do so in earlier works: in his preface to the Cheap Edition of *Pickwick Papers*, he said that he could "perhaps wish now that these chapters were strung together on a stronger thread of general interest."   As early as the writing of *Master Humphrey's Clock* he was concerned with its episodic nature, and wrote his publishers that he was "trying . . . to connect the stories more immediately with the clock, and to give the work a less discursive appearance."   In his Preface to *The Old Curiosity Shop* he admitted that he was "made uneasy by the desultory character of the work."   Organization formed a part of his advice to several writers: he told John Overs that a story of his was not as good as a preceding one, "except in the one respect of being very compact and close, and in that essential quality a great improvement."   He wrote to Richard H. Horne of his *The Poor Artist* that he was

> *delighted* with the story. I think it quite novel in the idea, and admirably executed. A bookseller *might* suggest that the introduction and the conclusion are scarcely so thoroughly allied to the main notion as they might be, but we will leave the animal in question to find it out if he can

--a rare instance of Dickens' leaving any work, his or anyone else's, unimproved when improvable.   As editor, too, he insisted upon well-organized fiction: he wrote to Forster in June of 1856 that he had a story "to hack and hew into some form for Household Words this morning, which has taken me four hours of close attention.   And I am perfectly addled by its horrible want of continuity. . . ."[24]
    But he was also intrigued by the possible advantages of breaking continuity.   In *Little Dorrit* he tried the eighteenth-century device of digression; he wrote to Forster of what was to become Miss Wade's chapter,

> I don't see the practicability of making the History

of a Self-Tormenter, with which I took great pains, a written narrative. But I do see the possibility of making it a chapter by itself. . . . I have no doubt that a great point of Fielding's reason for the introduced story, and Smollett's, also, was, that it is sometimes really impossible to present, in a full book, the idea it contains (which yet it may be on all accounts desirable to present), without supposing the reader to be possessed of almost as much romantic allowance as would put him on a level with the writer. In Miss Wade I have had an idea, which I thought a new one, of making the introduced story so fit into surroundings impossible of separation from the main story, as to make the blood of the book circulate through both.

The interpolated and purely digressive tales of *Pickwick Papers* were replaced by a story both separate from yet integrated with the rest of the novel: as Sterne had put it, Dickens would digress in order to progress. But Dickens was always aware of the danger of the method, and on occasion rejected it: " a story within a story," he said to Collins through Wills concerning a project for his journal, ". . . is complicated and difficult for our peculiar purposes."[25]

Possibly because of *Arabian Nights*, he liked the framework structure, trying it out early and not successfully in *Master Humphrey's Clock*, and employing it again in several of the Christmas numbers. "He had a taste for these schemes or frameworks for many tales," Chesterton said. "He liked to have story within story, like room within room of some labyrinthine but comfortable castle."[26]

Chapter division was always carefully considered, as Butt and Tillotson have shown in their study. Writing of his trip to Lowell in *American Notes*, he said, "I assign a separate chapter to this visit . . . because I remember it as a thing by itself, and am desirous that my reader should do the same." He was expert in the division of fiction for the purpose of serialization. As early as *Nicholas Nickleby* he complained of the enormous difficulty of writing his novels in numbers: "It is very difficult indeed to wind up so many people in parts, and make each part tell by itself. . . ." As editor of *All the Year Round*, he rejected a story submitted by Mrs. Brookfield partly because it could not be divided into monthly parts:

> the scheme of the chapters, the manner of introducing the people, the progress of the interest, the places in which the principal places [sic] fall, are all hopelessly against it. It would seem as though the story were never coming, and hardly ever moving. There must be a special design to overcome that specially trying mode of publication, and I cannot better express the difficulty and labour of it than by asking you to run over any two weekly numbers of 'A Tale of Two Cities,' or 'Great Expectations,' or Bulwer's story, or Wilkie Collins's, or Reade's, or "At the Bar," and notice how patiently and expressly the thing has to be planned for presentation in these fragments, and yet for afterward fusing together an as uninterrupted whole.

Later in the same letter he offered more advice:

> As a mere piece of mechanical workmanship, I think all your chapters should be shorter; that is to say, that they should be subdivided. Also, when you change from narrative to dialogue, or *vice versa*, you should make the transition more carefully. Also, taking the pains to sit down and recall the principal landmarks in your story, you should then make them far more elaborate and conspicuous than the rest.[27]

Though Dickens used *Great Expectations* as an example of well-executed division for a novel to be published in numbers, he had expressed concern while writing that novel that such division might injure it:

It is a pity that the third portion cannot be read
all at once, because its purpose would be much
more apparent; and the pity is the greater, because
the general turn and tone of the working out and
winding up, will be away from all such things as
they conventionally go.   But what must be, must
be. As to the planning out from week to week,
nobody can imagine what the difficulty is, without
trying.   But, as in all cases, when it is overcome
the pleasure is proportionate.

As far back as *Nicholas Nickleby* he had faced the fact that
the requirements of weekly or monthly numbers would clash
with the needs of the entire work: "I am afraid that I must
spoil a number now and then, for the sake of the book.   It's
a hard case, but I ought to be hard as iron to my own
inclinations and do so."   It is instructive that the earlier
regret is for the loss incurred by the number, while the later
is for the impairment to the whole.   In the novel following
Nicholas Nickleby, *The Old Curiosity Shop*, he was still
complaining about the damage which lack of space forced
upon him by numbers did to the parts of the novel: writing
to Forster, perhaps of Chapters 11 and 12, in which Kit
invites Nell and her grandfather to stay in the Nubbles
cottage, he said, "I was obliged to cramp most dreadfully
what I thought a pretty idea in the last chapter.   I hadn't
room to turn."[28]   Butt and Tillotson show us that by the
time of *David Copperfield* he was doing this fairly often, but
by now his only mention of it in his letters is that he was
"eschewing all sorts of things that present themselves to my
fancy--coming in such crowds!"   He deleted with care, but
each time he did so something was lost.   Forster speaks of
the loss to the preceding work, *Dombey and Son*:

These cuttings, absolutely necessary as they were,
were not without much disadvantage; and in the
course of them he had to sacrifice a passage
foreshadowing his final intention as to Dombey.   It
would have shown, thus early, something of the
struggle with itself that such pride must always go

through. . . .[29]

A major criticism of *Dombey and Son* has been that its protagonist changes abruptly at the end, without sufficient preparation.

Dickens expressed pride in his ability to make his novels dense: " . . . In every one of my books published in twenty numbers there is about three times the amount of matter comprised in an ordinary Novel." When he wrote a relatively short novel like *A Tale of Two Cities*, he appears to have suffered: "Nothing but the interest of the subject, and the pleasure of striving with the difficulty of the form of treatment--nothing in the way of mere money, I mean-- could else repay the time and trouble of the incessant condensation." The shorter *Hard Times* was also painful, both for its brevity and its weekly publication: ". . . the compression and close condensation necessary for that disjointed form of publication gave me perpetual trouble."[30] On the other side of the coin, Dickens was not above "padding" a number when necessary: on occasion a number had too much space, instead of too little. Writing to Forster of the second number of *Nicholas Nickleby*, he said that he had "yet five slips to finish, and don't know what to put in them, for I have reached the point I meant to leave off with." Forster says he can remember two other such occasions; I have discovered only one. Of the sixth number of *Dombey and Son* Dickens said, "I am horrified to find that the first chapter makes *at least* two pages less than I had supposed. . . ."[31] At times, the practical exigencies of space, too much or too little, obliged the meticulous craftsman to compromise.

But though serial publication sometimes cramped or elongated his genius, all other matters of form, Forster tells us, would appear to have given way to his imagination: this, his biographer says, was "his method in all his writings." Forster quotes Dickens' sketch for *The Chimes*, and adds:

> His idea is in it so thoroughly, that, by comparison with the tale as printed, we see the strength of its mastery over his first design. Thus always,

whether his tale was to be written in one or in twenty numbers, his fancy controlled him. He never, in any of his books, accomplished what he had wholly preconceived, often as he attempted it. Few men of genius ever did.

Dickens himself did not speak of the overpowering of his original plan by his fancy, though he did once complain of the failure of his writing to present what his imagination had conceived. In a letter to Forster Dickens said he had put into *The Old Curiosity Shop* a "description of the road we travelled between Birmingham and Wolverhampton; but I had conceived it so well in my mind that the execution doesn't please me quite as well as I expected."[32]

Dickens often advised writers to tighten their material. In a letter to Mary Boyle about her paper, "My Mahogany Friend," he said he was "endeavoring to bring it closer, and to lighten it, and to give it that sort of compactness which a habit of composition, and of disciplining one's thoughts like a regiment, and of studying the art of putting each soldier into his right place, may have gradually taught me to think necessary." "Compactness" is a word many readers will not associate with Charles Dickens: students in my classes are fond of asking me if he was paid by the word. But one of his principles of craftsmanship was economy: as we have seen, as editor he probably did nothing so often as shorten the works of his writers: Harry Stone says that "Major rewriting and drastic cutting were the two most crucial kinds of revision that Dickens performed." One of his first objections in the increasingly unhappy relationship with Bentley, while he was editing *Bentley's Miscellany*, was that translations sent him for inclusion were too long. He complained of a piece for *All the Year Round*, entitled "Through Lambeth to Vauxhall," that "It is fully as long again as it ought to be. However estimable these clergymen are, it is quite out of the question for us to go on spinning out dry catalogues of what they do. . . ."[33]

He wrote to Emily Jolly, of her "The Wife's Story," "I observe some parts of the story which would be strengthened, even in their psychological interest, by condensation here and there. If you will leave that to me, I will perform the task as conscientiously and carefully as if it were my own." Of a piece entitled "The Metropolitan Protectives," written by himself and Wills, he said, "I have cut down the number of cases, to save tediousness. Two drunken men, for example, could scarcely have been done with."[34]

He subjected his own work to the same careful process. He wrote Wilkie Collins about *The Frozen Deep* (which he virtually co-wrote with Collins), "I should like to shew you some cuts I have made in the second act (subject to authorial sanction, of course). They are mostly verbal, and all bring the Play closer together." Of his account of Niagara in *American Notes* he wrote Forster "I have made the description very brief (as it should be) . . . ." Writing of the riot scenes in *Barnaby Rudge*, Dickens said,

> . . . In the description of such scenes, a broad, bold, hurried effect must be produced, or the reader instead of being forced and driven along by imaginary crowds will find himself dawdling very comfortably through the town, and greatly wondering what may be the matter. In this kind of work the object is,--not to tell everything, but to select the striking points and beat them into the page with a sledge-hammer. . . . My object has been to convey an idea of multitudes, violence, and fury; and even to lose my own dramatic personae in the throng, or only see them dimly, through the fire and smoke.

Speaking of *The Haunted Man*, he wrote that

> The process of my mind in the construction of such a picture as the opening one of twilight, is one of incessant process of *rejection*. I bring it down to that, by working at it very slowly, and with infinite pains--rejecting things, day after day, as they come into my thoughts, and whipping the cream of them.

He complained that R. H. Horne, who was sending him a series of articles from Australia entitled *A Digger's Diary*, had written "eighty-four columns--and the man not aboard ship at the London Docks until within the three last." Dickens would be under the necessity of "cutting it to shreds. . . ."[35]

To those who sought his opinion of their work, Dickens also often advised concision. Typical is his advice to W. B. Archer that in an unidentified story he "would condense--greatly condense--the opening scene with the priest, so that the reader might come to the story. I would materially shorten the commencement of the story itself. . . ."[36] But of course condensation never meant (except under the tremendous pressure of serialization) the eliminating of essential material. Dickens had a great respect for detail. Part of his admiration for Defoe, and about the only thing he admired in Richardson, was the "wonderful genius" of each for "the minutest details in a narrative," and he urged the use of detail upon writers who neglected it. Speaking of a scene in a story which had failed to impress him, he told its writer to

> Suppose yourself telling that affecting incident in a letter to a friend. Wouldn't you describe how you went through the life and stir of the streets and roads to the sick-room? Wouldn't you say what kind of a room it was, what kind of day it was, whether it was sunlight, starlight, or moonlight? Wouldn't you have a strong impression on your mind of how you were received, when you first met the look of the dying man, what strange contrasts were about you and struck you? I don't want you, in a novel, to present *yourself* to tell such things, but I want the things to be there.

Such detail, he continued, was not "a meretricious adornment, but positively necessary to good work and good art. . . ."[37]

STYLE: A BOLD AGILE GRACE

Garrett Stewart sums up what one can learn about Dickens' style from his novels:

> Dickens' faith in language was a faith in style, in its ability to confer form, to make fancy expressive. It was an evangelistical faith, and there are characters in every novel who bear it witness, just as there are villains of imagination who warn us against its shams and blasphemies.
>
> The Dickensian style can at any moment turn away from the world, and with a bold agile grace remake it.[38]

Dickens' comments confirm his belief in "expressive fancy." He often urged imagination as essential to the journals he edited: looking over the back numbers of *Household Words*, he told Wills that "Wherever they fail, it is in wanting elegance of fancy. They lapse too much into a dreary, arithmetical . . . dustyness that is powerfully depressing." He called particular pieces "colorless, shapeless," "heavy," and "pale literary boiled veal."[39]

He believed that style (as well as content) was innate to the writer. Asked how he had developed his style, he replied, "The style of expression and manner of thought . . . come naturally to me, and are (as it were) a part of myself." But this did not mean that style was mere reflex, or instinctive act: he was well aware of the qualities of his own style, as his recognition of his tendency to fall into blank verse shows. He asked Forster to help him guard against the habit, but defended it when one Charles Watson criticized it:

> I am perfectly aware that there are several passages in my books which, with very little alteration--sometimes with none at all--will fall into blank verse, if divided off into Lines. It is not an affectation in me, nor have I the least desire to write them in that metre; but I run into it, involuntarily and unconsciously, when I am very

much in earnest. I even do so, in speaking.

I am not prepared to say that this may not be a defect in prose composition; but I attach less importance to it than I do to earnestness. And considering that it is a very melodious and agreeable march of words, usually; and may be perfectly plain and free; I cannot agree with you that it is likely to be considered by discreet readers as turgid or bombastic, unless the sentiments expressed in it, be of that character. Then indeed it matters very little how they are attired, as they cannot fail to be disagreeable in any garb.

Upon the whole I am inclined to think that if I had altered the passages which give you offense, you would not have liked my books so well as you are kind enough to say you do . . . .[40]

He paid close attention to language in everything he read. In one article he criticized an address to the Queen by a group of mayors as "a species of literary hunting-field, in which every substantive is a terrified stag, run down by a pack of yelping tautological adjectives." He liked to raise questions of word choice, and of interpretation of words, with his friends, no doubt far more frequently in conversation than in correspondence. Not all such discussions were fortuitous ones: he suggested to Forster that "to take arms against a sea of troubles" might have "been originally written 'make arms,' which is the action of swimming. It would get rid of a horrible grievance in the figure, and make it plain and apt." This is ingenious, but painfully wide of the mark, for the "grievance" is the point of the passage: the knowing commitment to the senselessness of wielding a sword against waves. Forster merely replied that "swimming through your troubles would not be 'opposing' them."[41]

Frequently he urged plain and direct style upon those who sent him writing of any kind for advice. When Fanny Kelly consulted him about a letter with which she hoped to solicit engagements for her readings of Shakespeare, he

wrote, "I should like your letter . . . better, if it were more
direct. I don't think going, like the old riddle, 'round and
round the house without ever touching the house,' is a good
course. . . ." As we have seen, he disliked tricks of
printing, such as the italicizing of certain words in a
passage, or the use of underlined space: unsolicited
contributions from the typical female poet, he said, invariably
bore the title "To a Child" or "To _____":

> We don't know who _____ is, but we wish he
> would lead her to the altar. In prose, she
> addresses the Gentle Reader constantly, and
> sprinkles with French words. She is invariably
> persuaded that blanks heighten the interest, and
> convey an air of reality. She generally begins, "It
> was on a summer evening in the year eighteen
> hundred and (blank), near the pretty little town of
> (blank), where the (blank) river murmurs its
> rippling way among the rushes, that a youth of
> handsome mein and fine figure, who might have
> numbered two-and-twenty summers, and whose
> expressive countenance was cast in the pure Greek
> mould."[42] [sic]

He was also aware that word-devices could be harmful,
and admitted to one such lapse in his own writing:
responding to cordial criticism by the Earl of Carlyle of *The
Haunted Man*, he defended several points, but added, "William
Swidger's catchword, I give up. The temptation to
intemperance in that wise, in a little book, where it is very
difficult to make the individuality of the characters, is
great." He was cautious about special use of language, such
as slang or professional jargon; of "Licensed to Juggle" he
asked Wills to "Look to the slang of it, and don't let 'ya'
stand for 'you'." In another case he objected to "that"
being used in place of "who," which he called "a great
vulgarity," and said that "vowed him revenge" was "extremely
bad." And he declared that he would not burden his readers
with professional lingo in any form. When he was obliged to
send Wilkie Collins a business letter couched in semi-legal

language, he appended a second letter in which he prayed, "May the Spirit of English Style be merciful to me!"[43]

Pretentious language was, indeed, the first foe in his literary field, attacked more often both in his novels and his direct comments on style than any other evil. Garrett Stewart again expresses it perfectly for the novels: "Bombast, circumlocution, and evasive delicacies of expression--the whole smothering atmosphere of euphemism and magniloquence Dickens is out to get. His own comic style, with its humorous circuities and overdone expressions, is a frontal assault on the very concept of style as sensibility in its most priggish advocacy." Did Dickens' love of "that which is overdone" in plays teach him what fun and what critical impact could be gained from overdoing it in his own prose? Certainly he inveighed again and again against pretentious language, arty diction, and the cliché. In one piece, for example, he cited the clichés of the English Bore in the areas of travel, politics, places, illness, gossip, and argument. Elsewhere he mocked the hackneyed English of political campaigns and of Parliament: "Why must an honorable gentleman always 'come down' to this house? Why can't he sometimes 'come up'--like a horse--or 'come in' like a man? . . . Why is he always 'free to confess'? It is well known that Britons never will be slaves; then why can't he say what he has to say, without this superfluous assertion of his freedom?"[44]

But the greatest offense of all was cant. He wrote to Douglas Jerrold:

> Supposing fifty families were to emigrate into the wilds of North America--yours, mine, and forty-eight others--picked for their concurrence of opinion on all important subjects and for their resolution to found a colony of common-sense, how soon would that devil, Cant, present itself among them in one shape or other? The day they landed, do you say, or the day after?

And in a letter to a Mr. David Dickson, who had protested against a passage in *Pickwick Papers*, he wrote,

. . . Sacred things are degraded, vulgarized,
and rendered absurd when persons who are utterly
incompetent to teach the commonest things take
upon themselves to expound such mysteries. . . .
In making mere cant phrases of divine words,
these persons miss the spirit in which they had
their origin.
. . . That every man who seeks heaven must
be born again, in good thoughts of his Maker, I
sincerely believe.   That it is expedient for every
hound to say so in a certain snuffling form of
words, to which he attaches no good meaning [sic]
I do not believe.

In *The Chimes*, he wrote Jerrold, he had "tried to strike a
blow upon that part of the brass countenance of wicked
Cant, when such a compliment is sorely needed. . . ."   A
blow is often the image he used to express his intention
against the cliché: describing the getting of Tavistock House
ready, he ended with, "Then Stone presents himself, with a
most exasperatingly mysterious visage, and says that a rat
has appeared in the kitchen, and it's his opinion (Stone's,
not the rat's) that the drain wants 'compo-ing;' for the use
of which explicit language I could fell him without remorse."
He often made fun of patriotic clichés: "I, a free-born
Briton, who never, never will--or rather, who never, never,
would, if I could help it. . . ."   And he made fun of the trite
phrases of his own profession.   At the beginning of *Pictures
from Italy* he assured his reader that his story would not
begin "where two travellers might have been observed slowly
making their way over that picturesque and broken ground by
which the first chapter of a Middle-Aged novel is usually
attained. . . ."   And in an article he made a point by saying
that "as standard novelists expressly inform us--'all was a
blank!'"   One reason for liking American transcendentalism,
he said, lay in its "hearty disgust of Cant, and an aptitude to
detect her in all the million varieties of her everlasting
wardrobe."[45]

OUTSIDE INFLUENCE: INNUMERABLE SUGGESTIONS

After all these homilies on craft, the attention to the slightest detail in his own writing and the work of others, the strictness concerning punctuation, the striving for organization, the effort to exclude all but the essential, it comes as a surprise to find Dickens leaving not only minor details of his novels to another hand, but also altering his own decisions about points of plot and character at the behest of someone who never wrote a novel. How could such a meticulous workman have trusted anyone, even such as close friend and admired colleague as John Forster, to exercise control over parts of his fiction?

Dickens did exactly this. Working on *The Old Curiosity Shop*, he took a vacation at Broadstairs, and left final correction of its numbers to Forster; the editors of Pilgrim Edition *Letters* tell us that Forster made cuts, altered style, and added "heavily to Charles Dickens's very sketchy punctuation." Butt and Tillotson say that as early as 1837, four years before this, Forster had "been accustomed to lend a hand. . . ." Edgar Johnson is more precise: "From the fifteenth number of *Pickwick* on there was no work of Dickens's that [Forster] did not see in manuscript or in proofs, making innumerable suggestions . . ."; Forster himself claims to have been the first to suggest that Little Nell should die. Whether he was or not, certainly he exerted considerable influence on Nell's story, as is seen in the number of letters to him from the author, asking him to make changes, granting permission to alter without prior approval, seeking his opinions. ". . . If there be anything here you object to," one such letter suggests, "knock it out ruthlessly."[46] Anything: Dickens never gave the best of his illustrators such leeway with their own drawings.

Carte blanche extended to the next novel, *Barnaby Rudge*: "Deal with it as you like." By *Martin Chuzzlewit* blanket permission to change is not mentioned, but advice is sought, and acted upon: "I . . . substituted for the action you didn't like some words expressive of the hurry of the scene." In the Christmas story for 1844, *The Chimes*, when Forster objected to one of the characters, a "Young England

Gentleman," Dickens dutifully substituted another character, and granted Forster permission to "File away at Filer, as you please." By *Dombey and Son*, he was still seeking counsel:

> It is a great question with me, now, whether I had not better take this last chapter bodily out, and make it the last chapter of the second number; writing some other new one to close the first number. I think it would be impossible to take out six pages without great pangs. Do you think such a proceeding as I suggest would weaken number one very much? . . . I shall be anxious to hear your opinion.

Again in this novel, Forster was given permission to make changes on his own: obliged to make cuts in Chapters 1 to 3 to make room for Chapter 4, Dickens wrote, "In case more cutting is wanted, I must ask you to try your hand. I shall agree to whatever you propose." And two weeks later: "I shall gladly acquiesce in whatever more changes or omissions you propose." About two months later Dickens again asked for more advice, this time about making "number three a kind of half-way house between Paul's infancy, and his being eight or nine years old?"[47] By now we are almost half-way through Dickens' novels, and Forster still has final say on certain matters.

In the same month, Dickens sent Forster the last part of that year's Christmas story, *The Battle of Life*, agreeing to make changes apparently already suggested, asking for further suggestions, and calling for an opinion about the final paragraph, which hints at the eventual marriage of Marion and Michael Warden and also contains a personal reference to the author; Forster apparently approved of it as it was, for it was allowed to stand. At the end of the month, another letter discussed Forster's opinion "that the marriage of Grace and Alfred [was] . . . rather unsatisfactory . . ." and proposed changes for Forster to consider; the letter also stated that Dickens saw no purpose in continuing the story until he heard from Forster. Five days later, Dickens suggested "another good place for introducing a few

lines of dialogue. . . ."   Three days passed, and Dickens was
dealing with a series of questions raised by Foster about
preparing "the way for the last paragraph of the tale . . .";
Dickens also explained certain additions he proposed to make.
A week later, he returned to Forster proofs of *The Battle of
Life*, with "amendments": "If there should still be anything
wanting, in your opinion, pray suggest it to me in Paris.   I
am bent on having it right, if I can."   About a week later,
another letter: "I am glad you like the alterations.   I feel
that they make it complete, and that it would have been
incomplete without your suggestions."   In the same month,
concerning the third number of *Dombey and Son*, he added,
"I have taken out about two pages and a half, and the rest I
must ask you to take out with the assurance that you will
satisfy me in whatever you do."[48]   A towering assurance,
surely.

Returning to *Dombey and Son* near the end of the
following year, Dickens in his letters again allowed Forster
to influence important aspects of the novel.   Discussing
Edith, he said "I have no question that what you suggest will
be an improvement."   Forster says the subject was "a nice
point in the management of her character and destiny"--
probably in connection with her apparent intent to commit
adultery.   The next month, Dickens was asking advice about
the same problem: "What do you think of a kind of inverted
Maid's Tragedy, and a tremendous scene of her undeceiving
Carker, and giving him to know that she never meant that?"
And when the novel was finished, Forster was asked to
correct the inadvertent omission of Florence's dog in the
usual final mention of characters:

> I suddenly remember that I have forgot
> Diogenes.   Will you put him in the last little
> chapter?   After the word "favorite" in reference to
> Miss Tox, you can add, "except with Diogenes, who
> is growing old and wilful."   Or, on the last page
> of all, after "and with them two children, boy and
> girl" (I quote from memory) you might say, "and an
> old dog is generally in their company," or to that
> effect. Just what you think best.[49]

Forster chose the second suggestion.

By the end of this year, 1848, with *The Haunted Man* in hand, Forster was still making final corrections; Dickens wrote to his publisher Bradbury that "My corrections had better be made, and then the fresh proof go to Mr. Forster for the usual corrections." In 1849 the subject was *David Copperfield*, and again Forster affected a detail of character. He urged that Dickens' original idea of the cause of Mr. Dick's illusion was "a little too farcical for that . . . touching delineation of character," and Dickens agreed: "Your suggestion is perfectly wise and sound. I have acted on it."[50] In regard to suggestions accepted, Forster was still batting a thousand.

Nor was fiction the only ballpark: evidence concerning Forster's influence on Dickens' editorial work is less clear, but it seems certain that in at least some instances final judgment about articles in *Household Words* was left to him. When Dickens and his sub-editor Wills differed about some matter, Dickens wrote that they should leave the decision to Forster: "We will abide by his black or white ball." Wills, on the other hand, was *not* given final powers, at least not to change articles which Dickens had already approved; when the sub-editor tried some unauthorized alterations in a piece by Alexander Mackay ["The Devil's Acre," HW 6/22/50], Dickens at once brought him up: " . . . In future don't touch my articles without first consulting me." Mrs. Gaskell, we remember, also didn't allow her work to be revised; when Forster got involved in a decision concerning her, he was removed from the discussion by Dickens: in the resolving of some sort of disagreement over *North and South*, Dickens instructed Wills that "As to Forster, put him entirely out of the question and leave the settlement of any such dispute to me. . . ." One guesses that Dickens may well have either been removing the irascible Forster from a worsening situation, or protecting him from Mrs. Gaskell's ire because of something he had said; surely he was not denying him a voice because he objected to his judgment. Forster's fiery nature makes the second guess the better one; apparently not even in his work with Dickens on the novels did Forster

always keep his temper. On one occasion he complained to
their mutual friend Macready that, as Macready recorded it
in his diary, "Dickens was so intensely fixed on his own
opinions and in his admiration of his own works (who could
have believed it?) that he, Forster, was useless to him as a
counsel. . . ." It would all end, Forster darkly predicted, in
"incurable evil."[51] This was in 1845, and was perhaps owing
to some imagined slight of the moment, for Forster continued
for many years to serve as a kind of *amicus libri*. Indeed,
given the extent to which he had by that time influenced
Dickens' novels, Forster's comment is at the least
disingenuous.

Why did a writer who paid such attention to the least
detail of his work subject it so frequently to the shaping
hand of another? Would a painter ask what colors he should
use, or lend his brush to an artist of another genre and ask
him to add whatever he pleased? The analogy is probably
not tight, and Dickens is certainly not the only novelist who
has submitted his writing to critical correction, but one must
wonder whether any other great writer has done so as often
and as easily as Dickens did with Forster. The situation
strikes one as different from other famous cases of literary
influence. Thomas Wolfe put his pages in the hands of an
editor and let him have his way, but Wolfe is nowhere near
the heights of Dickens, and has no reputation as a meticulous
craftsman. No one has attempted a full explanation of this
unusual working relationship--perhaps because there is no
explanation, though there are partial ones, surely. Obviously
Dickens liked Forster, respected his judgment tremendously,
trusted him. Dickens worked hard most of his life, and like
artists who paint huge murals, perhaps could not have done
all he did without help. Habit may help to explain the
relationship: begun in his first novel, while he was feeling
his way, perhaps the use of an informal editor simply became
a part of his creative process.

Forster himself comments on Dickens' willingness to
take advice, but offers little to explain why; after recording
some of the letters we have quoted, he added,

But see how easily this fine writer takes every

suggestion, how little of self-sufficiency there is, with what a consciousness of the tendency of his humour to exuberance he surrenders what is needful to restrain it, and of what small account to him is any special piece of work in his care and his considerateness for the general design.

At the same time that he compliments Dickens for this creative lack of self-sufficiency, he raises the question of whether it helped or hurt: citing Ben Jonson's statement about the need at times to curb "Shakespeare's phantasy," he adds, "Whether he, as well as the writer of later time, might not with more advantage have been left alone, is the only question."[52]   One is inclined to agree, but to wish that Dickens' closest friend through much of his life might have attempted something more of an answer.   Is it possible that raising the question was a kind of answer--that Forster either regretted or had doubts about his influence on Dickens' novels?   Given his imperious Podsnappian nature, it seems unlikely, but he does ask the question, one in which later Dickensians have shown relatively little interest.

All that can be done in our little space is to examine the slight evidence in the letters.   Certainly there is some indication that Dickens at times felt unsure of himself, that he sought help in areas where he doubted his own judgment. Writing to Forster in 1841, he said, "Don't fail to erase anything that seems to you too strong.   It is difficult for me to judge what tells too much, and what does not."   It was difficult for him, too, to judge his own style at times: he asked Forster, "If in going over the proofs you find the tendency to blank verse (I *cannot* help it, when I am very much in earnest) too strong, knock out a word's brains here and there."[53]   But we may note in reviewing the letters that much (though by no means all) of the work done by Forster was not aesthetic, but practical: it was owing not to Dickens' need to improve his art but to the necessity of shaping his fiction to a certain method of publication.   With the postboy at the door, as Angus Wilson has put it, Dickens wrote enough to fill the anticipated number; when he wrote too much, Forster was there to cut the number down to size in proof, especially when Dickens was not in London, and could not do so himself. While Forster certainly exercised considerable influence over Dickens in the writing of his novels, that influence was limited to relatively few aesthetic decisions.

Still, Dickens' willingness to take advice is worthy of more attention than criticism has yet given it. Despite Forster's petulant remark to Macready, Dickens seems to have been ready to subject both his art and his editorship to the scrutiny and possible revision of others. On at least one occasion he took the advice of another friend, Bulwer, and changed the ending of *Great Expectations*. The manager of his public readings, George Dolby, says that Dickens was willing to take advice about them, too: "He was always open to conviction, and did not disdain to defer to the judgment of another in whom he had faith, even though his own mind had been made up on any particular point. . . ."[54] This hardly sounds like the Dickens of iron will we read about in the biographies, but perhaps the Dickens who wrote was a different man from the Dickens who ruled his family, dealt arbitrarily with his publishers, and took the advice of no one in personal matters. Surely the deference he sometimes paid to the opinion of others was not evidence of occasional indifference to his craft; perhaps it was the final proof that, as he said to Forster, he was "bent on having it right, if I can," even if that meant subjecting his massive talent to the opinions of others.

5

The Idea of Literature: Hug the Theory

LITERARY INFLUENCE: QUEST OF THE ROMANTIC

It is in the study of Dickens' literary theory that his reluctance to commit his thought to paper, at least in any single extended treatise, is most frustrating. Enough has already been cited to erase any doubts of his being a conscious and conscientious student of language, who thought about what he was doing and would, when called upon, give voice to his convictions concerning the nature of literature, but it is not easy to build a coherent picture of his thought from the scattered fragments of off-hand comment we have. For example, one may attempt to understand a man's ideas about his art by seeking evidence of the influence of others upon him, but though Dickens' literary masters may be tracked in his fiction, their prints are almost untraceable in the occasional patches of his critical snow. He read Fielding's comments on the novel, as an allusion to them attests, but there is no word about such ideas as, for example, Fielding's theory of the novel as a comic epic in prose. Of theoretical discussions of his own time, he must have been familiar with the writings of such friends as Lewes and Hutton; surely he talked with them and other friends like Forster and Wilkie Collins and Bulwer about their literary ideas. But in his infrequent comments on literature there are few allusions to them, no recognition of intellectual debt, little citing of aesthetic influences. The only clear source of Dickens' sense of the nature and purpose of literature is-- and even here it must be perceived not so much through overt statement as by implication--the Romantic Movement. As Angus Wilson said, Dickens was "the heir of the Wordworthian romantic tradition. . . ." Monroe Engel in an essay on Dickens said the same for Dickens' age: "It will not do to posit any real separation between the Romantics and the Victorians."[1]

The evidence for Wilson's statement from sources other than the novels is slight, though there is enough to support his further assertion that "like most Victorian Romantics Dickens fed upon and renounced" his Romantic predecessors. He did not love all the English Romantic poets, nor adhere to all their convictions; still, he was greatly influenced by Romantic thought, which is found often in his comments on literature; a number of his statements echo Wordsworth. As Harry Stone points out, loving the *Arabian Nights* ("a familiar genre of Romantic writing, an almost archetypal way of rejecting the ordered strictness of neoclassicism,") as much as he did, it was probable that he should adhere to much in Romantic theory. There is little to indicate that he studied Romanticism in anything like scholarly fashion, on the other hand, and some suggestion that he was ignorant of much of it: if he was aware of Coleridge's distinction between the primary and secondary imagination, for example, he never alluded to it, and made no such distinction himself. And he did not accept all of the Romantic tenets of which he did speak. Along with his age, he was troubled by what he perceived to be a moral laxity in Romantic writers: in "Received, a Blank Child," he said that "parents of depraved and abandoned character" were "unconsciously emulative of Jean Jacques Rousseau,"[2] which suggests that he considered the moral standards of the Frenchman as flawed as he thought those of Byron and Shelley to be. He also despised the noble savage: despite his typically Romantic assault upon many of the institutions of society, he preferred civilization to nature, and mocked the idea that natural man was better than the product of culture: "The noble savage is a wearisome imposter wherever he is, and has five hundred thousand volumes of indifferent rhyme and no reason, to answer for." "I have not the least belief in the noble savage," he wrote elsewhere.

> I consider him a prodigious nuisance, and an enormous superstition. His calling rum fire-water, and me a pale face, wholly fail to reconcile me to him. I don't care what he calls me. I call him a

savage, and I call a savage a something highly
desirable to be civilized off the face of the earth.
I think a mere gent (which I take to be the lowest
form of civilization) better than a howling,
whistling, clucking, stamping, jumping, tearing
savage . . .--cruel, false, thievish, murderous; . . .
a conceited, tiresome, bloodthirsty, monotonous
humbug.

"My position is," he added, "that if we have anything to
learn from the Noble Savage, it is what to avoid. His
virtues are a fable; his happiness is a delusion; his nobility,
nonsense." Of all the characters in his fiction, Angus Wilson
believes, only Jo of *Bleak House* (and possibly Hugh of
Barnaby Rudge) is "Dickens' one concession to the idea of
the noble savage"--because of his "natural decency."[3]
    On the other hand, Dickens did not share the opinion
of that unusual Romantic, Blake, that nature was a fallen
state, and destructive to man. In "A Child's Dream of a
Star," he imagined two children who

used to say to one another, sometimes, Supposing
all the children upon earth were to die, would the
flowers, and the water, and the sky be sorry?
They believed they would be sorry. For, said they,
the buds are the children of the flowers, and the
little playful streams that gambol down the hill-
side are the children of the water; and the
smallest bright specks playing at hide and seek in
the sky all night, might surely be the children of
the stars; and they would all be grieved to see
their playmates, the children of men, no more.

Sorry as this is as art (it is painfully close to the tone of a
"Robins" passage which he fiercely resented in Edward
Stirling's dramatization of *Oliver Twist*), it expresses the
pathetic fallacy, finds nature sympathetic to man, and
perhaps even suggests an ability in the child to see nature as
Wordsworth's adult, grown into his earth-prison, cannot (see
"Ode: Intimations of Immortality"). Much as he loved the

city, Dickens sometimes spoke of nature with affection: he wrote to an admirer "in the backwoods of America" to say, "Believe me that your expressions of affectionate remembrance and approval, sounding from the green forests on the banks of the Mississippi, sink deeper into my heart and gratify it more than all the honorary distinctions that all the courts in Europe could confer." One of the qualities he praised in the *Lowell Offering* was that "A strong feeling for the beauties of nature . . . breathes through its pages like wholesome village air. . . ." On the American frontier, on the other hand, Dickens found little loveliness or romantic delight in nature, as passages in *American Notes*[4] and the chapters about the Mississippi in *Martin Chuzzlewit* reveal. As Humphrey House says, in both his travel books Dickens "paid little attention to nature for its own sake." But Kate Perugini said that her father had "an intense enjoyment of outdoor life, and a sincere and passionate love of nature." He was a great lover of art, but he loved nature more, she said. Perhaps so, but he certainly kept the two mistresses from meeting: one was his vocation, the other merely his vacation. Forster says that "the love of nature was as much a passion with him in his intervals of leisure, as the craving for crowds and streets when he was busy with the creatures of his fancy. . . ." The separation of imagination from nature is interesting because, like the Romantics, he seems to have found spirituality in nature: he wrote that he "would far rather that my children acquired their first principles of religion from a contemplation of nature and all the goodness and beneficence of the Great Being Who created it" than under a "strict construction ever to open a Bible or Prayer Book, or enter a place of Worship." It is not unusual for him to support a point by saying that it "is a lesson taught us in the great book of nature."[5] Yet this great source of spirituality would appear, quite unlike the Romantics, to have played no part in awakening his imagination.

Unlike the Romantic, too, he did not seek escape from his time and place through travels of the imagination. He read about other parts of the world, but rather for interest than for flight. Instead of idealizing the past, he denigrated it throughout his novels, and wrote a prologue to a tragedy arguing that the present could provide tragic material quite as well as any earlier age. "If ever I destroy myself," he wrote Douglas Jerrold, "it will be in the bitterness of hearing those infernal and damnably good old times extolled." He felt he could not convey in words the quality of Venice as he saw it in the present, but he had no such hesitation about describing what some of it had been like in the past:

> . . . Oh God! the cells below the water, underneath the Bridge of sighs; the nook where the monk came at midnight to confess the political offender; the bench where he was strangled; the deadly little vault in which they tied him in a sack, and the stealthy crouching little door through which they hurried him into a boat, and bore him away to sink him where no fisherman dare cast his net--all shown by torches that blink and wink, as if they were ashamed to look upon the gloomy theatre of sad horrors; past and gone as they are, these things stir a man's blood, like a great wrong or passion of the instant. And with these in their minds, and with a museum there, having a chamber full of such frightful instruments of torture as the devil in a brain fever could scarcely invent, there are hundreds of parrots, who will declaim to you in speech and print, by the hour together, on the degeneracy of the times in which a railroad is building across the water at Venice; instead of going down on their knees, the drivellers, and thanking Heaven that they live in a time when iron makes roads, instead of prison bars and engines for driving screws into the skulls of innocent men.

He wrote of his intention to put into *The Chimes* a character "who recognizes no virtue in anything but the good old times, and talks of them, parrot-like, whatever the matter is." Mrs. Skewton is such a character in *Dombey and Son*. "Good God," he cried elsewhere, "the greatest mystery in all the earth, to me, is how or why the world was tolerated by

its Creator through the good old times, and wasn't dashed to
fragments."[6]   A part of this distaste for the past seems to
have been political: Dickens associated it with the Tory
enemy.   In a squib in the *Examiner* he offered a song "To be
said or sung at all Conservative Dinners," the refrain of
which was,

> In the fine old English Tory time;
> Soon may they come again.

In *American Notes* he referred to "those good old customs of
the good old times" in which England's criminal code made
her "one of the most bloody-minded and barbarous countries
on the earth."   His study at Gad's Hill had a series of false
book-backs, one set of which was entitled "The Wisdom of
Our Ancestors," and contained the headings, "I. Ignorance. II.
Superstition. III. The Block. IV. The Stake.   V. The Rack.
VI. Dirt. VII. Disease."[7]

Once, Dickens wrote something in favor of the past.   In
a little song a boy asks his father what "honour" is, and the
father replies,

> It is a name,--a name, my child,--
>   It lived in other days,
> When men were rude, their passions wild,
>   Their sport, thick battle-frays.
>
> When in armour bright, the warrior bold,
>   Knelt to his lady's eyes:
> Beneath the abbey-pavement old
>   That warrior's dust now lies.
>
> The iron hearts of that old day
>   Have moulder'd in the grave;
> And chivalry has pass'd away,
>   With knights so true and brave;
>
> The honour, which to them was life,
>   Throbs in no bosom now;
> It only gilds the gambler's strife,

Or decks the worthless vow.[8]

It is difficult to believe, in view of all else that he wrote, that such a sentiment was more than a passing mood for Dickens.

Dickens' personal past, we ought to note, was quite another matter. Humphrey House's assertion that he "was apt to ruminate upon the departed glories" is supported by many passages like the following, quoted by Forster: "The old days--the old days! Shall I ever, I wonder, get the frame of mind back as it used to be then? Something of it perhaps-- but never quite as it used to be." In another mood, he wrote to Mrs. Richard Watson that ". . . We must not think of old times as sad times, or regard them as anything but the fathers and mothers of the present." And he was capable of mocking those who dwelt on the past: in his facetious "Threatening Letter to Thomas Hood, from an Ancient Gentleman," his crusty speaker says, "Ah! governments were governments, and judges were judges, in my day, Mr. Hood. There was no nonsense then." But nostalgia was the more common condition; when he was contacted by the mature Maria Beadnell, whom he had loved as a young man, he wrote that "it is impossible to be spoken to out of the old times without a softened emotion."[9]

Little that Dickens said overtly connects him closely with the Romantic, in particular the Wordsworthian, idea of making the commonplace world beautiful by our way-- especially the imaginative way of the child--of seeing it, but it is implicit in much of his writing. He said that "In Bleak House I have purposely dwelt upon the romantic side of familiar things." Walter Phillips said that to show "the quest of the romantic in the commonplace" was "the first distinction of the Dickensian group," consisting of Dickens, Collins, and Reade. To my knowledge, Harry Stone is the only scholar who has noticed the importance of "A Christmas Tree" in this regard. In this article Dickens uses a Christmas tree as a pattern of his childhood, tracing his early years on branches of the tree, each reminding him of experiences, toys, favorite books, plays, *et cetera*. The imaginative light which shines on the tree, bathing the

Arabian Nights and other childhood possessions, is right out of Wordsworth's "Intimations of Immortality": "Oh, now all common things become uncommon to me," and "Yes, on every object . . . I see the fairy light!" In an article Dickens wrote that "Childhood is usually so beautiful and engaging that . . . there is a mournful shadow of the common lot, in the notion of its changing and fading into anything else," which is close to a paraphrase of stanzas of the same poem. Dickens himself believed deeply, as Forster tells us, in his own childhood vision:

> It seems almost too much to assert of a child, say at nine or ten years old, that his observation of everything was as close and good, or that he had as much intuitive understanding of the character and weaknesses of the grown-up people around him, as when the same keen and wonderful faculty had made him famous among men. But my experience of him led me to put implicit faith in the assertion he unvaryingly himself made, that he had never seen any cause to correct or change what in his boyhood was his own secret impression of anybody, when he had, as a grown man, the opportunity of testing in later years.

It is not at all too much to assert if one calls the child "best philosopher," as Wordsworth did. Several other comments by Dickens reflect a Wordworthian turn of mind, for example Dickens' thinking of his childhood as the parent of his adulthood: he remembers "when I was this exceedingly uncomfortable and disreputable father of my present self."[10] There is no evidence, to my knowledge, that Dickens read Wordworth's (or any other Romantic's) poetical theory, but several allusions indicate that he read his (and their) poetry.

Dickens' strongest and most obvious tie to Romanticism is to be found in his advocacy of the primacy of emotion in literature, a subject to which it will be necessary to pay more attention in a later place. His love of drama was in good part owing to his conviction that it was the most

effective purveyor of feeling; art, music, and literature, he
thought, could do no better than adopt its affective methods.
We will see Dickens speaking of literature as a rational
amusement, and devoting his own fiction to the improvement
of man's economic and social lot.   But high above all such
laudable objectives was the need of literature to touch the
human heart, and make it beat in human sympathy.   If
Florence of *Dombey and Son* weeps more often even than the
notorious hero of Mackensie's *The Man of Feeling*, Dickens
makes no apology: it is good to weep, whether one is a
character in or a reader of a book.   The people of his
century loved to cry over their books, certain that there are
worse things to cry about, and less helpful things than tears.

Despite his love of sentiment, Dickens was aware of the
problems of excess; he agreed with Wilkie Collins' picture of
a young female reading Charlotte Mary Yonge's *The Heir of
Redclyffe*: "She reads for five minutes, and goes up-stairs to
fetch a dry pocket handkerchief; comes down again, and
reads for another five minutes; goes up-stairs again, and
fetches another dry pocket handkerchief."   Sentiment, he
knew, could be affected, and the stimulation of such
affectation inhibited true feeling.   At the home for reclaimed
prostitutes, the practice was "to discourage shows of
sentiment" which might prompt the girls to feign what they
thought their superiors wanted them to feel.   But he shared
the belief of his age that true tears are one of literature's
best pleasures and benefits, tears that are related to yet
mercifully separated from the sorrow of life, and as he
created his stories he experienced the emotions he tried to
make his reader feel: speaking of *The Haunted Man*, he said,
"I finished last night, having been crying my eyes out over
it--not painfully but pleasantly as I hope the readers will--
these last three days."[11]

Whenever he found that a man or woman could feel, he
responded with enthusiasm.   Speaking of Miss Coutts' porter,
who had told him "with extraordinary emotion and
excitement" of a railway accident, he said, "I esteem him
much more than I did, finding a capacity of emotion in him
for which I was wholly unprepared."   Feeling could even
make tolerable the thought of death, the end of all feeling;

death itself could be valuable for its "softening influences" upon the living. At an Edinburgh banquet in his honor, he said that he had written the death of Little Nell to "substitute a garland of fresh flowers for the sculptured horrors which disgrace the tomb." He wanted to "fill the young mind with better thoughts of death, or soften the grief of older hearts, . . . afford pleasure or consolation to old or young in time of trial. . . ." As important as making death acceptable was making life endurable. The printed description of *The Household Narrative*, a monthly supplement to *Household Words*, promised, in treating "facts and realities," to "soften what is hard in them, to exalt what is held in little consideration, and to show the latent hope there is in what may seem unpromising. . . ."[12] "As long as I can make you laugh or cry," he told an audience at the Birmingham Polytechnic Institute, "I will." Believing as he did that feeling was the surest road to truth, Dickens was mystified by the fact that some of his favorite books were devoid of it. *Robinson Crusoe* had nothing in it to make anyone laugh or cry and Smollett's *Roderick Random* and *Peregrine Pickle* were "both extraordinarily good in their way, which is a way without tenderness. . . ."[13] That a story could hold the attention without the dramatic necessity of legitimate emotion aroused in the reader by careful art was hard for him to believe.

Indeed, though Dickens often used the word *natural* simply to mean *real*, *believable*, he also used it frequently to identify human emotion as the norm. As Humphrey House says, "The word 'natural' often slips into Dickens' sentences," as in one in which he said that a slight adjustment to the opening of *No Thoroughfare* had made "the opening . . . far more natural. . . ." Dickens usually opposed anything that struck him as unnatural: "To confine exaggeration within limits," Forster said, "was an art he laboriously studied." He was as aware as Twain that reality could be far less "natural," in this sense, than fiction could afford to be, but when it came to feeling he still found it hard to accept the difference: whatever reality might insist, he found it unnatural not to feel. Of Lady De Lancy's narrative of her experiences at Waterloo, he wrote to a friend to ask "Have you ever thought within yourself of that part where having suffered so much by the news of [her husband's] death, she will not believe he is alive?   I should have supposed that unnatural if I had seen it in Fiction."[14]   Almost always his criticism of an "unnatural feeling" is directed at an artist's failure to make his or her character sufficiently sensitive. For him as for his master Scott, romance and reality were not necessary antithetical: in *Waverley* (Ch. 72) Scott argued that "the most romantic parts of this narrative are precisely those which have a formulation in fact."

Turning from Romanticism to other elements of Dickens' literary theory, we find a considerable body of thought.   If it does not cover every concept pondered in such a modern work as Wellek and Warren's *Theory of Literature*, it nevertheless represents a respectable and revealing awareness of the nature and needs of prose fiction in certain areas. Prominent among these is the relationship between reader and writer, in which Dickens demonstrates his own personal desire for the widest and largest possible audience for himself, as well as his general principle that most art should be made available to most people.   He is aware that not all levels can be reached by all that art has to say, but he is convinced that his own fiction, at least, can so be made that it will offer something to any mind that focuses upon it.   If his great affection for his extensive audience cannot be called an aesthetic principle, perhaps his pressing desire to feel a personal relation with his readers, an almost physical contact--as he puts it, to write a book in company--can.   He took his relation with his reader as a trust, which he understood as a commitment not to injure or offend (though he always asserted his and every author's right to define *hurt* and *offense*), and to entertain and give pleasure, and to teach.   He had a hatred of moral preaching, and was not so much interested in improving the manners or even morals of his readers as he was in heightening their capacity to feel human emotion, and, above all, to use their imagination. The great object of literature for him was to improve both society and the individual.

Dickens felt the imagination to be the supreme human quality, of first importance because it led more powerfully than any other to the deepening and broadening of human nature at its best. He sought to strengthen the imagination of others by utilizing his own, by creating in his fiction a world better (in being more meaningful, not nicer) than this one yet never divorced from it: fiction consisted of the imagination playing over and casting a Wordsworthian light upon reality, clothing it in an illumination which both revealed and improved. One great method of achieving this was, as we have seen, to return the reader to the childlike state, for as in Wordsworth the child was the best philosopher, capable of seeing and accepting the potential for good in existence. If we must lose childhood yet we may, again as in Wordsworth, keep it alive in the memory, a power by which our lives may be sustained and improved. Though Dickens was aware of the limitations of the imagination, he thought it capable, if it did not tear free from reality, of finding Truth--perhaps even of replacing reality with that greater Truth.

Yet he never ignored reality, or sought to pretend to some ideality as alternative to it. His concept of reality was not the modern complexity but, simply conceived, he found it essential to art, and found it an enemy only when others conceived of it as totally divorced from imagination, founded entirely on cold, hard fact. Fiction, he believed, should give the effect of reality--indeed, must be based upon it--but must never be enslaved by it. Dickens began his own writing by careful, almost photo-like observation, but always subjected what he saw to the power of the imagination to elevate interest, add meaning, and offer hope.

Dickens was also fascinated with the act of creating character, especially, once again, as he contemplated the relation between fictional and actual humanity. The line between the two was for him thin indeed, at times almost nonexistent: the creations of his own stories and those of others had for him as powerful a force of conviction, of emotional involvement, as any in the real world. He was no more certain than any other individual about how the artist created his characters, but he knew that, as with the rest of a story, one began with one's experience of real people, then let the imagination focus upon the reality until it was transmuted into something new.   He saw the method as essentially dramatic: characters should not be psychoanalysed but should reveal themselves, with as little help from their creator and narrator as possible, through their actions and particularly through their speech.   The truth of human nature was best conveyed when dramatic color and vividness helped to compose the picture.   Essential too was distinctness: characters should be touched with individuality, and though types could offer truths of general human nature, they raised the danger of stereotype, which he found destructive.   To be believable, characters should, surprisingly in the writer of such novels as *Nicholas Nickleby* and *The Old Curiosity Shop*, be mixtures of good and bad qualities.   Dickens shows an interest in first-person narration, using a character to tell his tale, but is also cautious about the dangers of such technique.

Finally, the commentary made by Dickens conveys most powerfully his great desire not merely to communicate but to commune with his readers; some things he says suggest his powerful awareness of the deep chasm that lies between human minds, and his determination to cross the space so effectively that his audience will both understand and feel what he meant when he created his fanciful realities.   Art, he says, is what makes life bearable, both as he writes and, he fervently desires, as his great audience reads.

WRITING IN COMPANY

The primary purpose of literature, then, was to make the reader feel.   With this principle we enter the area of Dickens' greatest literary concern, that which he wrote and spoke about more often and with greater vigor than any other: the responsibility of art toward its audience.   The topic may hardly seem worth consideration, for, as Laurence W. Mazzeno has said, "the idea that Dickens wrote with an eye constantly turned toward his readers is a critical commonplace," but the commonplace has been so often understood simply as obsequiousness and desire to cull the customer's coin that attention must be paid, for the issue is considerably more complex.   To begin with, Dickens did not accept the Romantic stress of self-expression and corresponding de-emphasis of communication with the reader; he would have rejected Rousseau's famous authorial declaration that he knew his reader didn't need to know what he was saying, but he needed to tell him. Dickens would have disagreed even more with an unnamed modern novelist, interviewed by Anatole Broyard, who said that he "used to write for people," but gave up:

> What can you hope for from people? Think of how parochial, how limited, how small people are. Writing for them is like shouting into the wrong end of a megaphone. Now I go to the source. I hurdle right over their heads and address myself to the world.

Dickens never wrote to so amorphous a thing as the world, which may be one reason why almost everyone in it has read him, though for many years it was also a reason why many thought him an inferior novelist, afflicted by "an undignified and nervous dependence on the goodwill of his public," as one critic wrote in 1964. "We have come in our time to equate a writer's desire for audience with his desire for money and make them both vulgar," a wiser critic, Monroe Engel, said. "But for Dickens, a writer seemed to have no function without an audience. . . ."[15]

To put it another way, Dickens' audience *was* the world--not the impersonal aggregate of Broyard's novelist but the world of people, few of whom he thought of as small, and all of whom he believed he could reach; he aimed not over their heads but into them. Much in the history of the printing of his novels and the planning of his journals indicates how sincerely he tried to address as large an audience as possible--and not only for profit. *The Household Narrative* was to be offered "at a price that will render it accessible to the humblest purchaser of books. . . ." And his own books were made accessible to the same purchaser. "His first novel, *Pickwick Papers*," Butt and Tillotson say, "shows him attempting to reach a larger number of readers [than could the expensive three-volume novels, which prevailed at half a guinea per volume] by cutting the price to suit their pockets"--that is, by issuing the novels in monthly parts, at less than one-third of the price of a novel. Butt and Tilotson also believe that Dickens felt monthly publication kept him closer to his reader:

> Through serial publication an author could recover something of the intimate relationship between story-teller and audience . . .; for an author like Dickens, who was peculiarly susceptible to the influence of his readers, this intimate relationship outweighs the disadvantages of the [monthly] system.[16]

The comments in Dickens' letters and speeches all show that he felt it his first and most important duty as an artist to communicate with every possible reader--the humble as well as the high, the simple as well as the intelligent. No doubt all writers for whom profit is a motive have a similar ambition, but though Dickens was by no means indifferent to money, also important to him was the deep affection he felt for his great audience. Master Humphrey hoped of his readers that there might "spring up between them and me feelings of homely affection and regard," but his creator, Angus Wilson suggests, went even further: "it would hardly be too much to say that Dickens's relations with his readers were the high point of his life--what Mrs. Tillotson has called 'the most interesting love-affair of his life.'" Certainly it was no distant relationship for Dickens. "A Preliminary Word" in the first issue of *Household Words* declared that "We aspire to live in the affections and to be numbered among the Household thoughts, of our readers."[17] "Go where I will," he said elsewhere, "in out of the way places and odd corners of the country, I always find something of personal affection in people whom I have never seen, mixed up with my public reputation. This is the best part of it, and it makes me very happy." His readers were, indeed, ubiquitous; Forster tells the story of a man crossing the Sierra Nevada and coming across a crude hermit whose only companions were copies of *Nicholas Nickleby* and

Pickwick Papers. In the Preface to *David Copperfield*, he spoke of "the reader whom I love," and elsewhere talked of the play as an experience which was "like writing a book in company; a satisfaction of a most singular kind, which has no exact parallel in my life; a something that I suppose to belong to the life of a laborer in art alone. . . ."[18] "Although he disliked being lionized in private society," K. J. Fielding said, "he was obviously attracted by appearing before the public he created." The attraction was not in being admired--"He was never merely content with homage and applause"--but in experiencing affectionate personal contact with those to and for whom he wrote. If it was not quite, as Angus Wilson puts it, "a sort of orgy of warm personal communication with his great mass of readers," no doubt at times it came close. Drama itself lost its power, he believed, when it rejected any part of its audience: he attributed its decline in his time in part to "that fine spirit of humour which . . . jeered at every simple recreation within the reach of the common people. . . ."[19]

In his first public reading for money he said,

> I long held the opinion . . . that in these times whatever brings a public man and his public face to face, on terms of mutual confidence and respect, is a good thing. . . . I have had a pretty large experience of the interest my hearers are so generous as to take in these occasions, and of the delight they give to me, as a tried means of strengthening those relations--I may almost say of personal friendship--which it is my great privilege and pride, as it is my great responsibility, to hold with a multitude of persons who will never hear my voice nor see my face.

Speaking of international copyright, the issue which caused such a furor during his visit to the United States, Dickens said, "I would rather have the affectionate regard of my fellow men, than I would have heaps and mines of gold." At the same meeting (the 1842 banquet honoring him in Boston), he spoke of the many readers who had written to him after the death of Little Nell, and added, "and my correspondent has always addressed me, not as a writer of books for sale, resident some four or five thousand miles away, but as a friend to whom he might freely impart the joys and sorrows of his own fireside. . . . I do assure you that no circumstance of my life has given me one-hundredth part of the gratification I have derived from this source." ". . . To commune with you, in any form," he wrote to the readers of *Master Humphrey's Clock*, "is to me a labour of love. . . ." The word *commune* is worth noting: Dickens sought more than a communicating relation with his readers. It was painful for him to read the death of Paul, his friend and manager George Dolby said, because of his "intuitive identification of himself with his audience. . . ."[20]

Perhaps it was because of this closeness that Dickens was so widely known--more widely, probably, than any writer who preceded him. According to Charles Kent, "Everyone, even to the illiterate wayfarers in the public streets, had, to a certain extent, long since come to know what manner of man Charles Dickens was by means of his widely-scattered photographs." No doubt the new art-form helped, but it was the sense that Dickens was *their* writer that caused the pictures to be widely distributed among the populace. I have found but three incidents in which an ignorance of Dickens is recorded, two of which are supplied by George Dolby. While he was arranging one of Dickens' reading tours, Dolby asked the local agent at Aberdeen about the potential for success of a Dickens reading there, and got the following answer: "Weel, Misther Doalby, I'm no prepared t' state positively what yewr receats 'll be, *for ye see, amangst ma ain freends there are vairy few wha ha' iver haird o' Chairles Dickens*." And Dolby says that the Mayor of New Haven, Connecticut (the seat of Yale University), while chairing a committee formed to resolve problems concerning tickets for a Dickens reading, declared that "until then he had never heard of Mr. Charles Dickens in his life"--perhaps as clear an example of the gap between town and gown in that city as we could possibly be given. The third instance comes from Dickens' sub-editor, Wills. At the bottom of a letter in which Dickens had instructed him to send some

notices to a paper, Wills added the word "Fame!" and the
information that, when Dickens' servant John had delivered
them to the *Morning Advertiser* and declined to pay for their
inclusion on the grounds that newspapers did not charge
Charles Dickens for announcements, the clerk had replied,
"Charles Dickens?--Charles Dickens? *What house does he
keep?*" A story revealing the other side of the coin is told
by William Howard Russell.   Dickens was invited to a
shooting party, but his note declining the invitation did not
reach the hostess until the party was about to begin.   At
once she called to her cook, "Martin, don't roast the
ortolans; Mr. Dickens isn't coming."   Thackeray, who was
present, "never felt so small," according to Russell.   "There's
a test of popularity for you!   No ortolans for Pendennis," he
quotes Thackeray as saying.[21]

After poring through the thousands of attestations of
admiration and affection recorded in Dickens' time, one is
tempted to believe that only the three above-mentioned
people were ignorant of him, and that all the rest of
mankind preserved their ortolans only for him: they not only
knew of him, but felt that they *knew* him, as we know those
who are close to us.   Intimacy with his characters made them
feel intimate with *him*: to love, laugh, and suffer with
Pickwicks and Olivers was equivalent to doing the same with
their creator.   Dickens sensed this.   At a banquet in his
honor at Edinburgh, he said that he felt

> as if the deaths of the fictitious creatures, in
> which you have been kind enough to expose an
> interest, had endeared us to each other as real
> afflictions deepen friendship in actual life; I feel
> as if they had been real persons, whose fortunes
> we had pursued together in inseparable connexion,
> and that I had never known them apart from you.

The "as if" is comparable to his expression of pleasure when
listeners reacted to his readings--"as if they saw" and heard
the realities before them, he said.   At the banquet in Boston,
he told his audience that "At every act of kindness on your
part, I say to myself, 'That's for Oliver; I should not wonder

if that were meant for Smike; I have no doubt that is intended for Nell'. . . ."[22] His readers were not just readers of his fiction; they were people with whom he had mutual friends.   Until he hit upon the idea of dramatic readings, this was as close as he could come to writing a book in company.

Dickens often declared how seriously he took the relationship with his readers.   "We have considered what an ambition it is to be admitted into many homes with affection and confidence," he said in "A Preliminary Word"; ". . . We know the great responsibility of such a privilege. . . ."   "As to my art," he said, "I have as great a delight in it as the most enthusiastic of my readers; and the sense of my trust and responsibility in that wise, is always upon me when I take pen in hand.   If I were soured, I should still try to sweeten the lives and fancies of others. . . ."   The first obligation of every writer is to his art, but Dickens believed that the first obligation of his art was to the reader.   He saw nothing wrong with providing things the ordinary reader would like: in his proposal for what was to become *Master Humphrey's Clock*, he expressed concern that the work should be "popular," should begin with "some pleasant fiction," should "introduce fresh characters constantly," be "amusing," treat "the various foibles of the day," be careful to "vary the form" and "diversify the contents," present "fun, raillery, and interest," include "satirical papers," and "give fresh novelty & interest."   In his preface to the second volume of the work, Dickens quoted approvingly from of Fielding's Introduction to *Tom Jones*:

> An author ought to consider himself, not as the gentleman who gives a private or eleemosynary treat, but rather as one who keeps a public ordinary, to which all persons are welcome for their money.   Men who pay for what they eat, will insist on gratifying their palates, however nice and whimsical these may prove, and if everything is not agreeable to their taste, will challenge a right to censure, to abuse, and to damn their dinner without control.

On several occasions, Dickens used the same metaphor; as editor, he applied the same principle: Harry Stone says that the articles in *Household Words* "are remarkable for their diversity, clarity, and appeal."[23]

The sense of responsibility to his reader can be seen in passage after passage in Dickens' letters. As he faced the possibility that he would have to give up his Christmas book for 1847 in order to finish *Dombey and Son*, he expressed reluctance to "lose the money. And still more so to leave any gap at Christmas firesides which I ought to fill." So seriously did Dickens take his obligation to his readers that, as John Butt and Kathleen Tillotson have pointed out, he would supply his printer additional lines if he found that he had not sent enough to fill out the monthly numbers of his journals to a full thirty-two pages: "he disliked giving his readers short measure. The text of a number must usually end well down on the thirty-second page." To the end of his life Dickens adhered to this practice; in 1867 he sent directions to Wills: "In making up *A.Y.R.* try to bring the matter close down to the foot of the last page of the No."[24]

Upon occasion Dickens even extended this principle to his novels: Butt and Tillotson tell us that, in the eighteenth number of *David Copperfield*, "Proofs showed that the number would end high on the thirty-second page. Honest dealing with the reader demanded that he should get full measure for his shilling, and the page must therefore be completed."[25] When college freshmen scribble something to fill up their themes to the length required by the instructor, he strikes out the worthless addition with red ink, and writes "Deadwood!" in the margin. Dickens was not a college student, and his fill was doubtless worth reading, but it is questionable whether any other great novelist would have risked the integrity of any corner of his work by adding something not required by his artistry, simply to save his reader from purchasing a partially-blank page; no stronger evidence could be offered that the sense of obligation to his reader stood at the very top of Dickens' artistic credo.

The reader who came to Dickens' public ordinary could expect to be entertained. Writing much as Sleary would speak in *Hard Times*, Dickens said that "the people . . . *will* be amused somewhere. It is of no use to blink that fact, or to pretend to the contrary. We had far better apply ourselves to improving the character of their amusement." Here of course he has the lower classes in mind--no one has ever felt called upon to insist on the right of the upper classes to be amused--but clearly it was a principle he held for all readers. As Edgar Johnson puts it, "Dickens knew that . . . his readers . . . could not be argued or battered into liking what they did not like. Though he was not afraid to assert views to which they might be opposed, he worked assiduously to provide a kind of writing that they would enjoy. Good fortune had given him the command of their laughter and tears, and he never despised the gift."[26]

Responding to the actor and dramatist (Richard) Nelson Lee, who had sent him "the manuscript of [his] life," Dickens afforded the work some of his best aesthetic compliments-- "modesty," "manliness," "natural," "agreeable,"--but advised against attempting publication because readers would not find in it "that variety and oddity of adventure which people attracted by the nature of the subject, would expect to find there"; he stressed the need to distinguish between writing which may be of interest to a small circle, and that which will appeal to the "public." Though the collected letters of Henry Coleman, an American who had come to Europe to write reports about agriculture, seem to be (as glimpsed in the fragments quoted by Dickens in his comments on them) not badly written, and certainly are in their descriptions of nineteenth-century life of interest to a twentieth-century reader, Dickens argued that they were too redundant and narrow in scope to merit publication:

What Mr. Coleman may choose to write, in this private aspect of himself, to his friends, is a very different thing from what he is justified in calling upon the public to read. A man may play at horses with his children, in his own parlour, and give nobody offense; but if he should hire the Opera House in London, or the Théâtre Français in Paris, for the exhibition of that performance at so much a head, he would challenge criticism. . . .[27]

As editor, Dickens distinguished between what interested him and his colleagues and what would interest their readers. Of a piece submitted to him he wrote,

> Starting a paper in India [the title of the article] is very droll--to us. But it is full of references that the public don't understand, and don't in the least care for. Bourgeois, braver, minion, and nonpareil, long primer, turn-ups, dummy advertisements and reprints, back form, imposing stone, and locking up, are all quite out of their way and a sort of slang that they have no interest in.

When Angela Burdett Coutts suggested that hieroglyphics would make a good subject for an article in *Household Words*, he thanked her, but said "the difficulty in treating it for so large an audience is to find anyone well acquainted with it, who has the power of sufficiently popularizing it." Repeatedly he sought to strengthen the appeal of stories sent him by increasing the potential for eliciting emotion. He wrote that he thought William Moy Thomas's "Miss Furbey" "very good indeed. Close, original, vigorous, and graphic. It strikes me that I see better things in it than he has done yet." But then he added

> An alteration occurs to me--easily made-- which I think would greatly improve it, in respect of interest and quiet pathos, and a close sentiment of pleasure to the reader. It should be delicately expressed that the man (admirably described) who comes a-courting Miss Furbey might have always had a miniature of him, hanging up, or in a pet drawer and sometimes brought out, taken when he was a young man; and that when the narrator begins to observe him and his visits, she should still see in the grey hair and the worn face something of that portrait.[28]

The corollary to pleasing readers was to protect them from unnecessary unpleasantness. Dickens was convinced that certain kinds of subject matter were potentially harmful not only to the reader but to the story in which they might appear, and again and again he counseled, in his roles as editor and as adviser to would-be writers, that such materials either be handled with great care or entirely excluded. Writing to Walter Thornbury about a contribution to *All the Year Round*, he said, "We must not have too many murders. They not only become distasteful to periodical readers, but will seriously damage your book." And he rejected another piece by the same author about a criminal as "not wholesome for a large audience . . ."--though he admitted that proper treatment, distinguishing such a story from "mere Newgate Calendar," could make it admissible. In his own piece, "Gin Shops," he said that "We have sketched this subject very slightly, not only because our limits compel us to do so, but because, if it were pursued further, it would be painful and repulsive." And in the very next piece, "The Pawnbroker's Shop," he promised "nothing to disgust even the most fastidious reader."[29] In his review of a spiritual book, he recounted the experience of a pregnant woman who feels the fetus move within her, and then apologized for including "this nauseous matter. . . ." Writing about Landor's unhappy marriage, he felt called upon to say that "We verge on delicate ground. . . ." Once, though one hopes humorously, he used the word "waistcoat" and added "if I may be allowed the expression. . . ."[30]

Obviously, several forces are at work in Dickens as he makes these statements. There is the editor's concern that the customer not be offended; there is the writer's dislike of mere sensationalism. But the note most often struck is that the reader should not find himself engaged in what might be distasteful.

It is well to remember that in his avoidance of offensive material Dickens was not alone: Richard Stang tells us that "As an editor, Thackeray was extremely cautious about offending his public, and even Trollope and Elizabeth Barrett Browning had manuscripts refused for indecency." George Eliot, we may recall, declined to read the coarse

Balzac. But perhaps in no other Victorian author--perhaps in no author of any time--does one sense the same degree of brooding care for the reader that must be felt by anyone who peruses Dickens' correspondence. When a reader accused him of writing something that might damage the morals of his reader he replied, "Nothing, sir, could give me so great pain as to know that any word of mine had for one moment diverted a human soul from the path of rectitude."[31]

As editor Dickens assiduously avoided not only the distasteful but also the potentially painful. When he read "Gilbert Massinger," a story which Holme Lee (Harriet Parr) had submitted to *Household Words*, he was overcome by its pathos and pleased with its art. Wills suggested that it was too long and should be cut, but Dickens disagreed, though he did concede that its length made it unsuitable for his journal. But an equally important reason for rejecting it was

> the nature of the idea on which it turns. So many happy people are, by no fault of their own, linked to a similar terrible possibility--or even probability--that I am afraid it might cause prodigious unhappiness if we could address it to our large audience. I shrink from the responsibility of awakening so much slumbering fear and despair.[32]

Of an article submitted by Wilkie Collins, he wrote "I doubt the subject of hereditary insanity--not with an eye to the feelings of the public in general, but with a consideration for those numerous families in which there is such a taint." An ending, particularly, should if at all possible affirm the positive in life, the goodness in humanity. To a query from Collins about *A House to Let*, the Christmas Number for 1858, concerning the materials of the house, he replied,

> I am not clear about following up the old Materials, and making them doomed and destructive. I think it would end the thing with unseasonable grimness. If I could build them into a good school, or infirmary, or child's hospital, or

> something of that sort, it might be a more
> pleasant end, and a working round of the thing to
> something brighter.

One notes the qualifying reference to season: the great
Christmas writer could not darken December.   Dickens did
not insist that all endings be joyous, as the reader of *The
Old Curiosity Shop* and *Great Expectations* (to say nothing of
his short fiction) will attest, but he saw no reason to sadden
his reader unless he had to: of a story submitted for *All the
Year Round* he said, "If I had written it, I should have made
the woman love the man at last."   And he changed another
in *Household Words* ("Evil is Wrought," by Coventry Patmore)
because "It left off with a disagreeable impression as to the
feeling between the sisters."[33]

However, subjects not personally painful could, even if
they were offensive, be used, provided they were necessary,
and properly treated: of Dickens' own use of prostitution in
his novels he said, "It is difficult to approach in pages that
are intended for readers of all classes and all ages of life;
but I have not the least misgiving about being able to bring
people gently to its consideration."   In addition to the
"gently," one notes the reference to classes and ages:
Dickens distinguished between levels of readers in judging
what might be written.   After his early writing for
newspapers, which might in his time be safely considered as
read only by men, he never wrote again for any smaller
audience than all classes and all ages, but if he had, he
might have exposed his readers to still bolder subjects, and
with less gentleness.   The convention of the Gentle Reader,
in fact, was one he despised: he urged an anonymous
contributor "forever and a day, to dismiss the Gentle Reader
as a monster of the Great Mad Period, who has no kind of
business on the face of the literary earth. . . ."   Gentle or
not, though, when it came to the carnal he believed readers
of all classes should be protected: Dickens never dealt with
sex without employing the most conscientious delicacy, and
he urged others to do the same.   To John Overs he suggested
that nothing should be written that could not be spoken in
any company:

> Beware of writing things for the eyes of
> everybody, which you would feel the smallest
> delicacy of saying anywhere. Mrs. Scutfidge may
> have stripped in public--I have no doubt she did--
> but I should be sorry to have to tell young ladies
> so in the nineteenth Century, for all that.[34]

Did Dickens anticipate an age in which young ladies could be
told about stripping in public? It is more likely that he
complimented his age upon its advance in feminine delicacy
over preceding generations.

Dickens felt strongly that readers not prepared for
certain kinds of materials would be damaged by them.
Writing about Charles Reade's *Griffith Gaunt*, charged with
being an immoral novel, he undertook to defend the work,
but admitted that, as "the Editor of a periodical of large
circulation," he would not have "passed" several passages
because "what was pure to an artist might be impurely
suggestive to inferior minds (of which there must necessarily
be many among a large mass of readers). . . ." In the same
letter, speaking of certain relationships he would not have
allowed to be treated in *All the Year Round*, he said, "I
consider those relative situations extremely coarse and
disagreeable." It was not that the reader should be
protected from *anything* coarse or disagreeable; it was that
he should be exposed only if art required it--and then,
exposed to only just so much as was necessary, and no more.
When he worked with offensive material of a nonsexual
nature, Dickens used both humor and diminished
representation to protect the reader from unnecessary excess:
writing about *Nicholas Nickleby*, he said,

> Depend upon it that the rascalities of those
> Yorkshire schoolmasters *cannot* easily be
> exaggerated, and that I have kept down the strong
> truth and thrown as much comicality over it as I
> could, rather than disgust and weary the reader
> with its fouler aspects.

He was not willing to say with Joyce that if his novel was

not fit to be read, then life was not fit to be lived: it was
the job of the artist so to represent life that it would be
neither distorted nor disgusting; if the foul and the coarse
should not be rigidly excluded from fiction (as many thinking
members of his time argued), they should at the least be
mitigated.   Though he rejected a story submitted to *All the
Year Round* on several grounds, Dickens praised its
characters because they were "remarkably well observed, and
with a rare mixture of delicacy and truthfulness."[35]

 At times it seems that he would have *nothing* presented
to an audience which might pain its members, but such is not
the case.   When, overseeing Edward Stirling's stage
presentation of *A Christmas Carol*, he saw Tiny Tim dressed
in bandages and irons, he said, "No, Stirling, no; this won't
do! remember how painful it would be to many of the
audience having crippled children." This, from the man who
killed off Little Nell and Paul Dombey over the pleas of
readers, some of whom had doubtless lost their own children,
seems surprising, until we apply the principle of necessity:
for the needs of his fiction, Nell and Paul must die, but from
stressing the suffering of Tiny Tim nothing could be gained
but theatrical effect--which as spectator Dickens often
enjoyed, but as artist usually deplored, and which by no
means he could allow to justify pain for even a few members
of the audience.   (Perhaps, too, he felt some difference
between that which the audience could take in a novel, and
that which it might endure in a visual stage presentation.)
Dickens did not banish such dangerous subjects as hereditary
madness from all art, just from his family journal: for
subjects other than sexual some kind of adjusting of the
nature of content in relation to level of reader seems to
have been acceptable.   His caution to John Overs was about
writing for the eyes of everybody; in writing directed to a
special audience, he appears to have accepted a less rigid
standard, as his comparatively relaxed language for his
newspaper sketches indicates: Butt and Tillotson note that
among the revisions of pieces going into the book form of
Sketches by Boz "was the removal of the (very occasional)
touches of indelicacy and profanity; Boz's column in the
newspaper [where the sketches first appeared] would probably

be read only by men, but a book which wished to pass
through the 'needle's eye' into 'families' must be more
circumspect."[36]
Because Dickens prided himself on being a family
author, it was at this delicate level that he wrote his novels,
but he was willing to allow a greater latitude for others:
though as editor of a family journal he would have
suppressed some passages of *Griffith Gaunt*, he did defend
the novel against charges of indecency. Even in his own
writing and journals he refused to cater completely to Mrs.
Grundy: he poked fun at those who had found something
objectionable in Wilkie Collins' "Picking Up Waifs at Sea"
(included in the Christmas Number of 1858) and in his own
"The Bloomsbury Christening" for *Sketches by Boz*. He
suggested what the special peeves of censors might do to
great literature:

> Imagine a Total abstinence edition of *Robinson
> Crusoe*, with the rum left out. Imagine a Peace
> edition, with the gunpowder left out, and the rum
> left in. Imagine a Vegetarian edition, with the
> goat's flesh left out. Imagine a Kentucky edition,
> to introduce a flogging of that tarnal old nigger
> Friday, twice a week. Imagine an Aborigines
> Protection society edition, to deny the cannibalism
> and make Robinson embrace the amiable savages
> whenever they landed. Robinson Crusoe would be
> "edited" out of his island in a hundred years, and
> the island would be swallowed up in the editorial
> ocean.

Dickens' care to protect his reader did not extend to literary
emasculation. When someone suggested that the Thugee
exhibition in the British Museum was responsible for a series
of garrotings in London, he mockingly proposed to bar *Romeo
and Juliet* and *Hamlet* to prevent poisoning, *Lear* to stop
brothers from plotting against each other, and *Paradise Lost*
to keep Satan's words out of the heads of gullible people.
He opined that "Sloggins" (a character he used to represent
the criminal by nature, as opposed to good men led into

crime) "would raise a Devil out of any Art or Grace in life; therefore hamstring all the Arts and Graces, and lock the cripples up."[37]

Dickens had little reservation about the right of the artist to decide where protection for the reader should be overridden by concern for the integrity of his work. In only one place, in "The Amusements of the People, I," did he say anything that might be understood to the contrary; in that article he seems at one point to be suggesting that the Dramatic Licenser see to it that "the pieces represented in these theatres [for the lower class] should have, at least, a good, plain, healthy purpose in them." No doubt this was owing to his strong belief that plays were an important means of elevating the masses. Elsewhere, Dickens did not always agree with the judgment of writers about the relative claims of the reader to protection and of art to integrity, but he spoke earnestly against the imposition of rigid restrictions on writing, arguing that they could hurt both the art and the reader. In "Mr. Barlow" he speaks sarcastically of a comedy he attended in which "the characters were life-like (and consequently not improving)." He surely shared the concern expressed by Wilkie Collins in an article in *Household Words* in which he decried that class of reader "which looks to the obtrusively professed intention of a book solely, and knows and cares nothing about the execution." Writing to Mrs. Samuel Hall about a magazine she proposed to begin, he said, ". . . If its high end be not too much insisted on, or held too prominently before the reader's eyes, it will do great good."[38]

Even in his family novels, he refused to restrict content beyond a certain point, a point of his own making. Writing of a character in *Dombey and Son*, he said that he "felt that Mrs. Brown was strong, but I was not at all afraid of giving as heavy a blow as I could to a piece of hot iron that lay ready at my hand." Elsewhere he wrote,

> I have . . . an invincible repugnance to that noble-eyed philosophy which loves the darkness, and winks and scowls in the light. I believe that Virtue shows quite as well in rags and patches as

she does in purple and fine linen. I believe that
she and every beautiful object in external nature,
claim some sympathy in the breast of the poorest
man who breaks his scanty loaf of daily bread. I
believe that she goes barefoot as well as shod. I
believe that she dwells rather oftener in alleys and
by-ways than she does in courts and palaces, and
that it is good, and pleasant, and profitable to
track her out, and follow her. I believe that to
lay one's hand upon some one of those rejected
ones whom the world has too long forgotten, and
too often misused, and to say to the proudest and
most thoughtless--these creatures have the same
elements and capacities of goodness as yourselves,
they are moulded in the same form, and made of
the same clay; and though ten times worse than
you, may, in having retained anything of their
original nature amidst the trials and distresses of
their condition, be really ten times better.--I
believe that to do this is to pursue a worthy and
not useless avocation.

Thus did Dickens reply to those who damned anything that
was "low" in his work; it was a prime object of literature to
seek out those very subjects which many theorists of his
time decried as debasing to art. "I have no faith," he wrote
in his preface to *Oliver Twist*, "in the delicacy which cannot
bear to look upon" the low and the real.

I have no desire to make proselytes among such
people. I . . . do not write for their amusement.
No less consulting my own taste, than the
manners of the age, I endeavored, while I painted
it in all its fallen and degraded aspect, to banish
from the lips of the lowest character I introduced,
any expression that could possibly offend. . . .
It is useless to discuss whether the conduct
and character of the girl [Nancy] seems natural or
unnatural, probable or improbable, right or wrong.
IT IS TRUE.

Both for his own standards and for those of his time, he so shaped his art as to avoid offense, but those who were offended by the truth his art conveyed would simply have to turn elsewhere.   In other passages, Dickens went further, differentiating his "own taste" from at least some of the "manners of the age" which would have restricted his art beyond the bounds he himself considered proper: "What seems to have disturbed him most deeply in the depiction of characters" in his own work, Delores Lehr believes, "was the limitation imposed by the public's insistently narrow interpretation of society." Dickens himself said,

> I have always a fine feeling of the honest state in which we have got, when some smooth gentleman says to me or to someone else when I am by, how odd it is that the hero of an English book is always uninteresting--too good--not natural & c.   I am continually hearing this of Scott from English people here who pass their lives with Balzac and Sand.   But O my smooth friend, what a shining imposter you must think yourself and what an ass you must think me, when you suppose that by putting a brazen face upon it you can blot out of my knowledge the fact that this same unnatural gentleman . . . whom you meet in these other books and in mine *must be* presented to you in that unnatural aspect by reason of your morality, and is not to have, I will not say any of the indecencies you like but not even any of of the experiences, trials, perplexities, and confusions inseparable from the making or unmaking of all men.[39]

Thackeray makes much the same comment in places in *Pendennis*.

Dickens had reason to be resentful: despite his great care to avoid unnecessary offense and to shape his fiction for the reader's improvement, he was criticized not only for the low life he had shown in *Oliver Twist*, but for failing to point a moral in *The Old Curiosity Shop*: at least one magazine found fault with him for killing off Little Nell:

> The author should always bear in mind the
> vast extent of the number of his readers, and
> think how many of these there be who are, not at
> all, or only slightly, imbued with religious
> principles. Moral, mere moral justice would have
> awarded a happier fate to the poor girl.

When an author could be condemned for allowing a character
to die, there was little hope that the reputation of his art, if
not the art itself, would not suffer. But Dickens had no
sympathy with those who insisted on finding offense, and
when, in the middle of his reading from *Martin Chuzzlewit*
about Mrs. Gamp's thinking Pecksniff was calling on her
services as midwife instead of sitter with the dead, a
schoolmistress huffily gathered her brood and left, he merely
"appeared highly amused." Well before *Bleak House* he
showed himself willing to use "strong" (by which he meant
possibly painful or even offensive) materials. When friends
feared his great popular reputation might be damaged by
frank criticisms of America in *American Notes*, he replied
that he had never

> been deterred by hopes of promotion or visions of
> greatness, from pointing out abuses. . . . And if
> my being an honest man, bring down caprice, and
> weathercock fickleness, and the falsest kind of
> insult on my head, what matters it to me. . . .
>   What is to prevent my writing? The
> certainty of not pleasing them. . . . If we yielded
> to such reasons . . . in five year's [sic] time there
> would be no such thing as Truth in the world.

We can never know how far Dickens would have carried his
commitment to truth in the face of mounting opposition;
nothing he ever did made it mount enough to test him. But
the steel of his will is well known, and he was likely, had he
been put on, to have proved most royally capable of writing
what he wanted to write in the teeth of all hostility, despite

his reputation for bowing to the wishes of his readers.   As Stang points out, several articles in his magazines lodged "a vigorous protest against the attempt to restrict the subject matter of novels to ordinary domestic relations."[40]   And while these articles were not written by Dickens, he allowed nothing into his journals of which he did not approve.

In his last completed novel, Dickens laughed at those who would ban from all intercourse anything that might bring "a blush to the cheek of the young person."   The laughter seems in direct opposition to Dickens' advice to Overs about Mrs. Scutfidge, and may suggest some degree of change in his attitude by the time of his later writing, though in *Our Mutual Friend* Podsnap's idea of what would (or ought to) make a maiden blush is certainly something much more modest than a woman stripping in public.

The balance must not be tipped too far: Dickens' objections to censorship are by a wide margin outnumbered by his declarations that the reader needs protection.   Richard Stang is right in saying that Dickens "was essentially in agreement with Bulwer about the freedom of the artist to choose his own subject matter," and that he would have sympathized with that novelist's objection to treating literature as "a kind of medicated farina to be adapted with the daintiest nicety to the digestion of the weakly and diseased. . . ."   But the fact remains that most of the things Dickens said and wrote were on the side of shielding the reader, not granting license to the writer.   If Dickens believed in bringing Truth to his reader, he did not think it necessary to smack his face with it.   Hard work in his novels to bring the world as it is to his audience without rendering that world gross or repulsive earned the encomium Forster accorded him in his "Closing Word" of criticism near the end of his biography:

> Looking back over the series of his writings, the first reflection that rises to the mind of any thoughtful person, is one of thankfulness that the most popular of writers, who had carried into the lowest scenes and conditions an amount of observation, fun, and humour not approached by

any of his contemporaries, should never have sullied that world-wide influence by a hint of impurity or a possibility of harm.[41]

Though this may not be the first reflection of the modern thoughtful reader of Dickens, the magnitude of the achievement may still be appreciated.

Altruism was not the sole motive for protecting the reader; Dickens knew that it did a writer no good to give offense (at least in his day), and that the writer who did could hardly expect to achieve his first principle of literature: to be widely read. To a contributor to his journal, Dickens wrote to inquire whether

> . . . there are some passages in the story . . . which are calculated (and very naturally so) to give offense to the very class of persons with whom you desire to stand well--whether it does not appear to be designed more for the correction of parents than the instruction of children-- whether the points about the grandmamma do not touch upon very delicate ground and one upon which there is always more or less of sore feeling in families where there is a grandmamma and whether, the teaching children (who always apply stories to their own cases) to decide so positively in her favour against their own parent is exactly judicious and very likely to create a prepossession in your own favour?

(Dickens was right in being cautious: when *Pickwick Papers* was published, Butt and Tillotson say, "two members of a circulating Book Society opposed the notion [sic] to take in the numbers [the monthly issues] because 'they considered the work vulgar.'")[42] Even here, though, the readers--the potentially sore parents and mistaught children--are given as much consideration as is the position of the writer. Dickens was never inattentive to his own welfare or to that of his writers, but his professed concern for his reader is always sincere.

The effect of all this on Dickens' art has been the subject of much speculation. Engel suggests that it may have acted as a harmful "curb," though he admits that "Sometimes the curb can be justified by the contention that what the public wants is also what art requires." Faulkner sees no harm done: "If there are flaws on his genius, . . . I don't think [they] are particularly related to the absence of permissiveness in his society. . . ." Dickens' own art is not our subject, but nothing he said suggested that he felt his self-imposed restraints to be an encumbrance, and much to indicate that he considered them an essential element of his aesthetic. Advising Charles Lever on the publication of a book, he spoke of "the Public; with whom it is no less prudent than right to keep the strictest faith." "Right" is open to interpretation, but Dickens surely was thinking not only of moral but of artistic integrity. Some things he said elsewhere suggest that he thought the two things could not or at least should not be divorced from each other. In a letter to Francis Fuller he stated his belief in "raising the character of the people and raising the character of their amusements; always supposing that no endeavor towards that end either patronizes them, or otherwise treats them as children."[43] He had faith that the common reading public, though it extended far beyond Milton's fit few, was capable of responding to superior literature, and would have loved a remark attributed to Orson Welles: "Audiences are more intelligent than the individuals who create their entertainment." ". . . Don't think that it is necessary to write down to any part of our audience," he advised in his editorial position. "I always hold that to be as great a mistake as can be made." Writing to Bulwer about a novel concerning which the latter had asked advice, Dickens said

> I counsel you most strongly *not* to append the proposed dialogue . . . and not to enter upon any explanation beyond the title-page and the motto, unless it be in some very brief preface. Decidedly I would not help the reader, if it were only for the reason that that anticipates his being in need of help. . . . Let the book explain itself.

Though he liked some things about Wilkie Collins' *The Woman in White*, he criticized its propensity to "give an audience credit for nothing, which necessarily involves the forcing of points on their attention. . . ."[44] In his "Address" in the Cheap Edition of *Pickwick Papers* (1847) he wrote, "It is not for an author to describe his own books.   If they cannot speak for themselves, he is likely to do little service by speaking for them."

(It is asserted by an anonymous authority that in Dickens' time humble people were accustomed to gather about the bust of Milton in Westminster Abbey and chant, "We've come a long way, baby.")

Is there an inconsistency in Dickens' having faith in his readers, yet feeling it necessary to protect them from so many things?   In guarding them from the scatological, for example, did he not apply to them a standard lower than that which he held for himself?   Some believe that he did. Faulkner argues that Dickens was rather freer in his own private conversation than in his writing, but the incident that he advances to support this--a conversation about male chastity which shocked the visiting Emerson--may well have been an English put-on of the naive American, not a fair representation of Dickens' usual level of permissiveness.   F. W. Dupee also believes that "in his moral sense the Dickens of the letters was more urbane, sinuous, experimental than the reader of his novels might expect him to be."   To some extent this may be true, but there is much to indicate that in his private world Dickens was just as concerned with propriety as in his public writing--that he took almost as much care to protect himself from the salacious as he did to protect his readers.   George Russell said that "in the course of a long and intimate friendship of many years, I never heard him say a word which might not have been spoken in the society of ladies."[45]

Rarely are coarse or even slightly rough words found in his letters: "damn" appears occasionally, "arthe'" (ass) once, and "bitch" but once; there is hardly any other language that could offend anyone.   References to matters pertaining to sex, such as pregnancy, are invariably couched in euphemism--all this in letters written mostly to male friends of long standing. Dickens once created a remarkable to-do by invoking a rarely-used law to have a girl arrested for speaking profanely in the street, and when he gave permission to the Higham Cricket Club to play a second time in his meadow, mentioned that he did so despite having heard "some expressions . . . which would have been better avoided . . ." when they were there before. He found nothing of value in ribaldry anywhere, and complained bitterly about the comments scribbled in guest books at Niagara:

> My wrath is kindled, past all human powers of extinction, by the disgusting entries in the books which are kept at the Guide's house; and which, made in such a spot, and preserved afterwards, are a disgrace and a degradation to our nature. If I were a despot, I would force these Hogs to live for the rest of their lives on all Fours, and to wallow in filth expressly provided for them by scavengers who should be maintained at the public expense. Their drink should be the public ditch, and their food the rankest garbage; and every morning they should each receive as many stripes as there are letters in their detestable obscenities.[46]

If literature should not be confined to narrow moral lessons on the one hand, neither should it have unrestricted license; Dickens refused to expose his readers to that which he himself found offensive.

None of this is to offer Charles Dickens as a prude. His work on behalf of prostitutes, carried on over a number of years with his philanthropist friend Angela Burdett-Coutts, is well known. He praised George Eliot's handling of Hetty Sorrel in *Adam Bede*, though that character is remarkably un-Dickensian in her lack of proper repentance for her sexual sin. To his friend Mary Nichols he wrote, "that too many women are dreadfully cruel to their sister-women who have illegitimate children is painfully true." F. W. Dupee is certainly right when he says that "The Victorian smugness, which in its very excess of feeling seems to advertise an

uneasy relation to the popular morality, is wholly alien to
Dickens." At the same time, we have seen enough to be
certain that Dickens did not write just for himself,
coincidentally as it were pleasing his audience as well. Only
once, when the sales of the early numbers of *David
Copperfield* fell well below those of the preceding novel,
Dombey and Son, did he pretend indifference to his audience;
writing to Forster, he said that he was "not sorry I cannot
bring myself to care much for what opinions people may
form. . . ." But care he did: his greatest fear as an artist
was that he might some day lose his audience, and though
loss of income was undoubtedly a part of his fear, there is
also no doubt that he deeply felt the need for approval by
his readers. Frederick Locker-Lampson said that Dickens

> told me that genuine appreciation of his works was
> as fresh and precious to him [in 1869] as it had
> been thirty years before; indeed, he was still so
> sensitive to neglect that, in a railway carriage, if
> his opposite neighbor were reading one of his
> novels, he did not dare to watch him, lest he
> should see the book thrown aside with
> indifference.

The editorial positions he accepted early in his life were
taken partly as a protection against the possibility of losing
income from his readers, but when no doubt remained that he
could keep them as long as he lived, his public readings
were, though again motivated in part by profit, also in part a
means of assuring himself of the affection and understanding
of his reading public. One of his major concerns as he
thought about giving performances for remuneration was the
possible harmful effect on his readers: he asked his published
F. M. Evans whether

> such an use of the personal (I may almost say
> affectionate) relations which subsist between me
> and the public and make my stand with them very
> peculiar, [would] at all affect my position with
> them as a writer? Would it be likely to have any

influence on my next book? If it had any
influence at all, would it be likely to be of a
weakening or a strengthening kind?[47]

He wrote in 1845 that the reason for his taking on the
editorship of the *Daily News* was "that possibility of . . .
fading popularity," though he added, "At the worst, I have
written to little purpose, if I cannot write myself *right* in
people's minds. . . ." At times one senses in his
correspondence a remarkable similarity to the Scheherezade
of his beloved *Arabian Nights*, who fended off death by
keeping her stories going in installments. Angus Wilson
seems to sense this when he says that for Dickens "The
printer's boy at the door, waiting for the next installment,
was a sort of threatening executioner."[48] Wilson is thinking
simply of the threat of not meeting a deadline, but behind
that danger lay the greater: the death of Dickens' love affair
with his readers. If Scheherezade lost her husband's interest
she lost her life; Dickens seems to have felt that his risk
was hardly less.

It was this danger of losing touch with his beloved
reader, at least as much as any practical consideration, that
made Dickens as responsive as he was to reader opinion.
Forster tells us that Dickens "was sensitive in a passionate
degree to praise and blame. . . ." Did such sensitivity induce
him to change his writing? Johnson implies that it did,
though only for the nonprofessional reader: "The verdict that
he might resent from a reviewer, he accepted from the
beating of the readers' hearts." Some passages in Dickens'
letters suggest that Humphrey House is only partly correct
when he says that "Dickens did not deliberately set out,
after a course of sales research, to find what the public
wanted. He wrote about what he wanted himself." Sales
research was not available in Dickens' day, but if it had been
it is just possible that upon occasion he might have availed
himself of it. When he was considering whether he could
allow Walter Gay of *Dombey and Son* to sink gradually into
dissipation, he consulted John Forster, who was as close to a
research department as he had, asking, "What do you think?
Do you think it may be done, without making people angry?"

The nearest thing Dickens could find to sales research advised that it might, and Walter remains the young hero of *Dombey and Son*. Angus Wilson seems closer than House to the truth when he says that Dickens "frequently made changes, sometimes major changes, to maintain his link with his readers." Wilson concedes that some such changes may have been for the purposes of his own developing art, but concludes that Dickens "must always have feared getting out of touch with his public . . ." and adds that he "sought by various means to forge new links with his public" that would protect him in case of change of public taste, change in his own creative powers, or even diminution of those powers. His son Henry said that "He was haunted at times . . . by a dread of failure, or of a sudden waning of his imaginative powers. . . ."[49]

The great scheherezadian fear may have caused the few qualifications Dickens ever made concerning his faith in the ability of the masses to appreciate good fiction. *Could* one always write true literature that all the world would read (and buy)? When the sales of *Martin Chuzzlewit* fell off, Dickens wrote to Forster of his confidence in his power to "sustain my place in the minds of thinking men," but added,

> how many readers do *not* think! How many take it
> upon trust from knaves and idiots, that one writes
> too fast, or runs a thing to death! . . . If I wrote
> for forty thousand Forsters, or for forty thousand
> people who know I write because I can't help it, I
> should have no need to leave the scene.

Though it might be a mistake to write down to readers, obviously it would be a good thing if they could at times read up to the writer. It was not the falling-off of sales alone that brought this thought to Dickens: in a speech delivered at the Manchester Aethenium, a month before the decline of sales of *Martin Chuzzlewit*, he had already said that "the more intelligent and reflective society in the mass becomes, and the more readers there are, the more distinctly writers of all kinds will be able to throw themselves upon the truthful feelings of the people, and the more honoured and the more useful literature must be." Neither his determination to write for all readers nor his belief that one should never write down to his audience led Dickens to the foolish conclusion that all of everything he wrote should be intelligible to all of his audience--if he had, one supposes, he would have written at the level of today's television situation comedy. "I strongly object," he wrote to G. H. Lewes,

> to printing anything in italics but a word here and there which requires particular emphasis, and that not often. It is framing and glazing an idea and desiring the ladies and gentleman [sic] to walk up and admire it. The truth is, that I am a very modest man, and furthermore that if readers cannot detect the point of a passage without having their attention called to it only by the writer, I would much rather they lost it and looked out for something else.[50]

Of course, Dickens was always prepared to provide a "something else" for readers who missed the deeper points of his passages: he did want all his readers to get *something*. But clearly "not writing down" was accompanied by the understanding that, if one is to write up, one must in some instances write something that will be above the heads of some readers. "Dickens never talked down to the people," G. K. Chesterton claimed. "He talked up to the people. He approached the people like a deity. . . ." But Dickens himself put it a little differently; a good writer should talk the people up to himself, as he said at a presentation made to him at a Banquet to Literature and Art at Birmingham:

> I believe no true man, with anything to tell, need have the least misgiving, either for himself or for his message, before a large number of hearers-- always supposing that he be not afflicted with the coxcombical idea of writing down to the popular intelligence, instead of writing the popular intelligence up to himself, if, perchance, he be above it; and provided always that he deliver

himself plainly of what is in him, which seems to
be no unreasonable stipulation, it being supposed
that he has some dim design of making himself
understood.

Despite the "supposed," it is clear that Dickens considered it
a tenet of art to be understood. There is evidence that he
recognized the several levels of perception he should expect
in a large audience--just as he recognized levels of
endurance of pain and toleration of indelicacy--even while
suffering no misgivings about writing for all of them. When
in 1864 the sales of *All the Year Round* fell off, Dickens
agreed that he and Wills should consider why. One possible
reason he hit upon was a contributor, George Augustus Sala.
"Of course we have to consider that Sala's is not a good
name," Dickens wrote to Wills, "and that he is accustomed
to address a lower audience." Writing to Charles Lever about
his novel *A Day's Ride*, soon to be serialized in *All the Year
Round*, Dickens said, "Do not be afraid to trust the audience
with anything that is good. Though a very large one, it is a
fine one."[51] One notes the implication that not *all* large
audiences are fine; statements such as this show that, though
he desired to be read by everybody, Dickens understood that
his readers, though far more numerous than other great
authors might hope for, would not include everyone, however
much he might wish it: there would always be someone who
had "never heard of Charles Dickens."

Listening as well as reading audiences, Dickens said,
could receive on different levels; he thought of one such that
his favorite readings, from *David Copperfield*, "may perhaps
be a thought too delicate for them. . . ." Dickens seems to
have felt that the reading required a special sensitivity; when
he first tried it in 1861, he wrote that "It seems to have a
strong interest, and an expression of a young spirit in it that
addresses people of sensitive perception curiously." He
thought his American audiences missed some things: "They do
not (I think) perceive touches of art to be art but they are
responsive to the broad results of such touches."[52] Many of
his comments note the greater or lesser capacity of an
audience to understand him; he must have realized that the

same was true of his readers.

Though the first advertisement for *Household Words* indicated that it was "Designed for the Entertainment and Instruction of all classes of readers," Dickens did not insist that all writers or all writing be for all classes; one of the baleful consequences of the lack of international copyright about which he complained was that an author "should have no choice of his audience." But his own choice was, in a sense, not to choose: he would write for all who could read him--just as he read for all. When he read *A Christmas Carol* and *The Chimes* for the benefit of the new Industrial and Literary Institute at Birmingham, he insisted that the last of the evenings be reserved, at a reduced rate, for "working men and their families";[53] Edgar Johnson says that he considered them to be "the best audience of them all." Speaking of his readings, but obviously thinking of his writing as well, he referred to "my large miscellaneous following, which is limited to no class. . . ."[54]

Not only novels, but all forms of art should be made available for people, Dickens believed, and special effort should be made to attract them to it. He admired an exhibition of art treasures at Manchester, and added

> The care for the common people, in the provision made for their comfort and refreshment, is also admirable and worthy of all commendation. But they want more amusement, and particularly (as it strikes me) *something* in motion, though it were only a twisting-fountain. The thing is too still after their lives of machinery, and art flies over their heads in consequence.

A part of his admiration for his painter-friend Daniel Maclise was owing to the breadth of audience he could reach; indeed, it was one of the best features of the age, he believed, that it could make almost all art available to almost all people; Mr. Booley, a traveler in one of his stories, says:

> It is a delightful characteristic of these times, that new and cheap means are continually being devised

for conveying the results of actual experiences to those who are unable to obtain such experiences for themselves; and to bring them within the reach of the people--emphatically of the people; for it is they at large who are addressed in these endeavors, and not exclusive audiences.[55]

The ideal, as one gleans it from the fragmentary comments on audience in Dickens' writing, is to create an art both for those who could perceive its touches and for those who could respond only to the broad effects. Perhaps because reputable artists traditionally have little to do with the humble mind, he took a special delight in reaching simple people, particularly when he felt that they had understood him as deeply as those of higher social rank. He met a delegation of carmen from Hartford, "who presented themselves in a body in their blue frocks, among a crowd of well-dressed ladies and gentlemen," and exulted, "They had all read my books, and all perfectly understood them." Writing from Liverpool, where he was giving readings, he said that "One of the pleasantest things I have experienced here this time, is the manner in which I am stopped in the streets by working men, who want to shake hands with me, and tell me they know my books. I never go out but this happens." When James Staples told Dickens that he had read *A Christmas Carol* to an audience of poor people, and that his friends had "pugh-pughed" his effort, as "casting pearls before swine," Dickens replied, "I have great faith in the poor. . . . I try to deserve their attention."[56]
Dickens felt that the key to making most writing reach the most people was, reasonably enough, to offer it to them as directly and as forthrightly as the nature of the content and the artistry would allow. In "The Amusements of the People" he speculated that the major cause of the success of low-class theaters was their greater provision for common people of seats near the stage, instead of tucking them into remote parts of the building as was done in the National Theaters. "In whatever way the common people are addressed," he said, "whether in churches, chapels, schools, lecture-rooms, or theatres, to be successfully addressed they

must be directly appealed to. No matter how good the feast they will not come to it on mere sufferance."[57]

When the writing had addressed the readers, when Dickens had pleased and carefully protected them, when he had miraculously reached all levels and made all audiences his, what did he hope to do to them? We have seen enough to be sure that he hoped to do something more than merely amuse, or hold his mirror up to nature: Forster said that equal to his desire to reveal the world in his fiction was "the hope and design to leave it better than he found it." Nothing upset him more than the assumption (which lasted among major critics as late as F. R. Leavis) that he wrote merely to entertain. "Pray do not," he wrote to a correspondent,

> . . . be induced to suppose that I ever write merely to amuse, or without an object. I wish I were as clear of every offense before Heaven, as I am of that. I may try to insinuate it into people's hearts sometimes, in preference to knocking them down and breaking their heads with it (which I have observed them apt to resent; and then they fall upon the object and do it an injury) but I always have it. Without it, my pursuit--and the steadiness, patience, seclusion, regularity, hard work and self-concentration it demands--would be utterly worthless to me. I should die at the oar, and could die a more contemptible and worthless death in no man's eyes than in my own.

He protested when critics condemned him for being something more than entertaining; responding to an article entitled "The License of Modern Novelists" in the *Edinburgh Review*, he objected to that publication's being

> angry with Mr. Dickens and other modern novelists, for not confining themselves to the mere amusement of their readers, and for testifying in their works that they seriously feel the interest of true Englishmen in the welfare and honor [sic] of

their country. To them should be left the making
of easy occasional books for idle young gentlemen
and ladies to take up and lay down on sofas,
drawing-room tables, and window-seats. . . .[58]

But again, though amusement was not to be all, neither
was it to be slighted, for Dickens shared the eighteenth
century belief that instruction must be conveyed through
entertainment. At times, indeed, he seemed to be saying that
literature which was no more than cheery was, if it had no
harm in it, sufficient: in an appeal to the Literary Fund on
behalf of the family of William Hone he said, ". . . His
contributions to the stack of cheerful blameless Literature,
are deserving of remembrance. . . ." But here his definition
of good literature was stretched slightly to include a needy
writer; of his own efforts, he always mentioned the
importance of something like instruction. His idea for
Household Words was that the materials should be "as
amusing as possible, but all distinctly and boldly going to
what in one's own view ought to be the spirit of the people
and the time." Writing to Dudley Costello he said, "The
world would not take another Pickwick from me, now; but we
can be cheerful and merry I hope, notwithstanding, and with
a little more purpose in us."[59]

The "objects" of Dickens' writing are many but perhaps
they may be gathered under two main Aristotelian headings:
the improvement of society and the improvement of the
indivdual. Each kind, of course, would contribute to the
other. Francesco Burger said that "As his creed was
practical sympathy for the entire human race, so he held
that the object of Art was to add to the comfort and
happiness of the many, rather than provide aesthetic pleasure
for the few." To the extent that it can be distinguised from
improving the nature of the individual, social betterment is
mentioned in his nonfictional writing less often than the
need to entertain and to improve the people; he had much
more to say about the benefits of literature for the
individual reader than for society. When Dickens said that
"every effort of my pen has been intended to elevate the
masses of society . . ." he surely had social reform in mind,

but as other comments make clear, he had in mind too each individual composing the mass. He did comment occasionally on the service literature could render in exposing social ills and urging reform. Speaking of the wretchedness he had seen in the dark corners of London, to which other authors had given no attention, he said, "I thought I could render some service to humanity by bringing these scenes before the minds of those who, from never having witnessed them, suppose they cannot exist. . . . I think it makes the heart better to seek out the suffering and relieve them." Included among his promises to readers of the "pleasant" and "amusing" and "fun" they would find in *Master Humphrey's Clock*, is his intention to be "satirical" and, like an Addison, Steele, or Johnson, to comment "on the various foibles of the day." It was his business, he believed, to know the world and, within the limits of what he considered decency, to show its faults: he called his novels "A Private Working School . . . wherein I am teacher and scholar too. . . ."[60]

But the improvement of the individual was still more important. He believed, as Engel says, in "the capacity of art to affect people's lives," not only in such matters as income and social status but also by fulfillment, enrichment, meaningfulness, and human decency. As Stone says, though Dickens "viewed art as a deeply social force, as a way of humanizing life," "he also felt that art satisfied psychological and aesthetic values." The idea of the article, "Shakespeare and Newgate," Stone says, is "that art can make life bearable, and that the alternative to this saving grace is violence and depravity." In the article, Dickens says that

> There are not many things of which the English nation as a people stand in greater need than sound rational amusement. As a necessary element in any popular education worthy of the name; as a wholesome incentive to the fancy, depressed by the business of life; as a rest and relief from realities that are not and never can be all-sufficient for the mind,--sound rational public amusement is very much to be desired.

The purpose of his art was to accomplish that which Forster so admired in *The Old Curiosity Shop*: to "strengthen in the heart what most needs help and encouragement, to sustain kindly and innocent impulses, to awaken everywhere the sleeping germ of good." At a banquet in his honor at Coventry he said, "I can assure you, gentlemen, that after this night the object of these labours will not less than before be to uphold the right and do good." Speaking at a banquet celebrating the laying of a foundation for the Southwerk Literary and Scientific Institution, Dickens said that the Society (and therefore, presumably, literature) "tended not only to enlarge the mind and awaken the best energies of our natures, but to improve and ameliorate the hearts of mankind." The Society, he said, "had laid a moral foundation. . . ."[61] Looking at the gallery audience in a low-class theater, he said that "It required no close observation of the attentive faces . . . to impress a stranger with a sense of its being highly desirable to lose no possible chance of effecting any mental improvement in that great audience." In comments upon modest literary efforts, Dickens sometimes fell into language rather too close to the strait-laced piety he elsewhere decried: he praised *The Lowell Offering*, a journal put out by the working women of the Massachusetts textile mill, because its tales "inculcate habits of self-denial and contentment, and teach good doctrine of enlarged benevolence." Perhaps it is this kind of statement that led Angus Wilson to characterize Dickens' insistence upon the necessity of literature as a tool for human improvement as proof of his "bourgeois morality."[62]

But the balance must always be kept in mind: instruction was not stern and rigid, but cheerful and positive. Dickens considered Byronic "gloomy greatness" distinctly inferior to cheerfulness as an improving agent. His intention in *Household Words* was, he wrote to the Reverend James White, "to be as cheery and as pleasant as we can." He spoke of himself as "an author who seeks to beguile men of their cares. . . ."[63] In part this impulse to the cheerful seems to have been simple affirmation of the goodness of life. But cheerfulness and pleasant things should be neither deceptive nor a mere cover for moral preaching. Despite his violent reaction to George Cruikshank's insidious use of children's stories to preach morality, Dickens did use fairy tales for his own satirical purposes, but he never employed them to sermonize the young: his dislike of Cruikshank's assault on children was surpassed only by his disgust with such admonitory novels as *Sandford and Merton*, from which he took the character of the preachy Mr. Barlow as spokesman for those who would ram home moral lessons upon the unsuspecting through fiction. James T. Fields said that "he had an almost supernatural hatred for Barlow, because he was so very *instructive*, and always hinting doubts with regard to the veracity of 'Sinbad the Sailor,' and had no belief whatsoever in "The Wonderful Lamp' or 'The enchanted [sic] Horse'!" Dickens was always on guard against the Barlows, always alert to the damage stories might cause when they were too narrowly instructive, injecting the sensitive reader with a cold moral at the risk of freezing the fancy. In a letter to Angela Burdett Coutts, he took exception to a series of books--each a collection of papers on such subjects as "Household Work" and "Needlework"--for which she had given prizes, and to the publication of some of which she had contributed. "I think them not natural," Dickens wrote, "--overdone--full of a conventional sort of surface morality-- disagreeably like one another--and, in short, just as affected as they claim to be unaffected." When another friend urged him to ally himself against *"street-Punch"* performances because they did not lead children to proper thoughts, he replied,

> In my opinion the Street Punch is one of those extravagant reliefs from the realities of life which would lose its hold upon the people if it were made moral and instructive. I regard it as quite harmless in its influence. . . .
>
> In countries where Punch is still a censor of the follies of the day, his influence is not beneficial. In the most popular Theatre in Naples, that is still his character every day and night; and Naples is perhaps the Wickedest City upon earth.[64]

No entertainment should load itself down with moral lessons; at a meeting of the Playground and General Recreation Society, Dickens expressed his concern lest supervision of children's games become too devoted to improvement: "I have some individual doubt whether it might not become a little too wise, and whether, taking too deliberate an aim at these young birds, it might not blow them away with an overcharge of instruction."   He also was doubtful of the effectiveness of didactic literature: one of the concerns he expressed about popular plays in "The Amusements of the People, I" was that, after seeing a melodrama of astonishing representations of virtue and evil, Joe Whelks (the common man) might be left with a "confusion between right and wrong. . . ."[65]

By no means was he exclusive about the good that writing could do: he did not limit it to novels, or to literature in the narrow sense.   Without all that appears in print, he asked rhetorically at a function of the Printers' Pension Society, "what would be the state of the world at large?   Why, tyrants and humbugs in all countries would have everything their own way!"   And he added that "Of all inventions, of all the discoveries in science or art, of all the great results in the wonderful progress of mechanical energy and skill, the printer is the only product of civilization necessary to the existence of free man."   But again, the principal hope of improving mankind through reading lay not in any eighteenth-century attempt to mend his manners, or utilitarian effort to fill him with information, or even in puritanic effort to dictate his morals.   Rather, as we would expect from the Dickens who inherited the Romantic tradition, improvement lay in the awakening and enriching of his imagination, thus strengthening his capacity for emotional response.   "What Dickens most valued in the literature of childhood," Harry Stone says, "was its ability to nurture the imagination.   Without imagination . . . human beings could not be truly human.   He therefore set his face against any attempt to make literature serve narrow, anti-imaginative ends."   To be truly human is to be open to feeling.   But such are the conditions of our actual lives, in which the awareness of pervasive and unavoidable suffering deadens us, in which the repetition of a pleasure dulls it, in which our own needs blunt our sensitivity to the needs of others, in which time urges us to turn from one sorrow to another, that our capacity to feel is diminished. Only in the world of imagination--and especially in dramatic fiction--are we directed to a specific sorrow, freed from our own concerns and from the press of time and from other inhibitions, enabled to be truly human in our grief for the suffering fictional character, in our delight in his or her joy. Millions who are not brought to part with a dime by the appeals of the poor at Christmas time have wept over Tiny Tim--and perhaps the tears have prompted some to contribute a coin. Dickens believed that, whatever happened to the dime, humanity was indisputably better for having felt something because of a writer's imagination. One of the words he used to express his effort to awaken imagination was, appropriately enough for a writer who felt so close to his audience, "touch"; he wrote to the Honorable Robert Lytton that one of his motives in reading his novels to the public was "the hope that I could drop into some hearts, some new expression of the meaning of my books, that would touch them in a new way." He endeavored to bring imagination as a vital force into both the private and the public life; after reading *A Christmas Carol* at Sheffield, he told his audience of his desire "to do right by my readers, and to leave our imagination and popular literature more closely associated than I found it with the private houses and public rights of the English people. . . ." Again and again the letters demonstrate the sincerity of this wish. When a boy named Hastings Hughes sent him advice on how to reward and punish characters in *Nicholas Nickleby*, Dickens wrote a carefully composed reply of five full paragraphs, explaining to what use he had put the boy's advice, and working in some touches designed to improve his judgment.[66]

IMAGINATION: THE HARLEQUIN'S WAND

Like the rest of humanity, Dickens began his love affair with imagination in his childhood, but that faculty was so strong in him, and had such reinforcement during that time, that it remained the most powerful force in his adult life. From his first consciousness, he seems to have seized upon anything that could help him to use his imagination to enhance, if not to recreate, reality; and he grew into the unshakable conviction that imagination was the greatest lever man possessed with which to lift the weary weight of the unintelligible world, and that it was his task to exert that great force on behalf of the lives of others--primarily by turning his own fancy, as he called it, into literature, but also by struggling to protect the imaginative life against the onslaught of nineteenth-century materialism, and to encourage all men and women to avail themselves of its blessings.

The illuminating "A Christmas Tree" is useful once again in listing the several things upon which the early imagination of Charles Dickens fastened: toys (which foreshadowed his imaginative life by both delighting and terrifying him), the theater, music, and pictures. But from the first, it was fiction which most frequently excited his fancy: before he could read he seized, again with both delight and terror, upon the stories told him by his paternal grandmother, Elizabeth Ball Dickens, and an early nurse, Mercy. And when he came to read nursery stories on his own, says Harry Stone, they ". . . became part of his dream of felicity. He surrounded his early reading . . . with a soft muted penumbra of golden glory. It had been a time (or so he liked to remember it) of imagination, peace, security, and innocent delight; it had been the pastoral age before the fall, before the abrupt descent into the experience of London." In the exhortations of his maturity that the world not abandon the life of the imagination, phrases referring to this early period are inevitably to be found: "our dear old nursery books," "pictures attached to childish books," "the beautiful little stories which are so tenderly and humanly useful to us"; when he was forty-four he described a felicitous state of mind to a friend by saying it was "as if I had walked (I wish to God I had) out of a fairy tale!" Throughout his life, according to Forster, "No one was more intensely fond than Dickens of old nursery tales. . . ."[67]

The Arabian Nights, especially, remained in his consciousness and was referred to frequently. Like the toys and ghost tales ("ghostly" became a term synonymous with imagination in his vocabulary: in 1851 he told a friend of "the first shadows of a new story hovering in a ghostly way about me (as they usually begin to do, when I have finished an old one. . .") of his infancy, *The Arabian Nights* possessed qualities not found in the conventional reading of nineteenth-century children.   Contrasted, as Harry Stone says, with "the smothering didacticism of *Primrose Prettyface* or *Little Goody Two-Shoes* . . . the Eastern tales were designed to entertain, to elicit amazement and wonder.   The world of *The Arabian Nights* could be cruel, even savage, but in that world birds sang,   lovers   loved,   and   the   most   magical   things   were possible"--just as they were in the theatrical land of fairy immortality described in "A Christmas Tree."   Here are the two "chords" or qualities of the Dickensian imaginative world, as Stone suggests: "wonder, delight, innocence, and freedom," and "horror, fear, and loathing."   The book title became a term for the marvelous: of Mr. Booley travelling in Egypt Dickens said that "His days were all Arabian nights, and he saw wonders without end."[68]   But the real point was that one need not go to Egypt: the value of *The Arabian Nights* lay in its capacity to show that wonders could be found anywhere: Dickens would have liked Thoreau's statement that "The Concord nights are stranger than the Arabian nights."

As Stone says, the "peace and security" in which · the infant Dickens enjoyed the pleasures and terrors of his fairy-tale world were ended when he went to London, most particularly when he descended in to the all-too-real horror of the blacking warehouse.   Here was the weary weight of the unintelligible and unimaginative world indeed, with all his story-tellers (oral and written) snatched away from him, with no haven of imagination to escape to but a rare oasis of theater now and then.   "As a toiling factory child," says Edgar Johnson, "washing and tying up bottles, he had no room in his overburdened young heart for anything but the dreadful weight of his unhappiness."   But the deprivation did not kill his imagination: like Antaeus thrown to the ground, his fancy drew strength from its fall, and Dickens could say with David Copperfield that nursery stories retained in the memory "kept alive my fancy, and my hope of something beyond that place and time . . . ." It was at this time, Edmund Wilson says, that Dickens began to employ his imagination "to give an intelligible and tolerable picture of a world in which such things could occur." But it was here, too, that he seems to have learned of the limits of the imagination: of his suffering at the warehouse he was later to say that "No man's imagination can overstep the reality."[69]   One remembers Ishmael saying, when he first saw Ahab, that "reality outstripped imagination."

The grim reality of London for the young Dickens became a wasteland separating him forever from the child-world where, as in drama, one could taste of pleasure without paying for it, and undergo horror without suffering for it: it is this that produced the Wordsworthian concept of childhood.   Harry Stone sees Dickens' work in these terms. "For Dickens the 'charmed imagination' is always circling back to a time and a place that can never be forgotten and yet can never be recovered.   He summons the sights and feeling of a distant day, but the day itself has fled, and with it a portion of the world's freshness and glory."   The definitive statement came when Dickens attacked his friend Cruikshank for his misuse of imaginative literature:

> We may assume that we are not singular in entertaining a very great tenderness for the fairy literature of our childhood. . . . It would be hard to estimate the amount of gentleness and mercy that has made its way among us thorough these slight channels.   Forbearance, courtesy, consideration for the poor and aged, kind treatment of animals, the love of nature, abhorrence of tyranny and brute force--many such good things have been first nourished in the child's heart by this powerful aid.   It has greatly helped to keep us, in some sense, ever young, by preserving through our worldly ways one slender track not overgrown with weeds, where we may walk with children, sharing their delights.

It is not the fiction only which is influenced by the

childhood reading: as Stone also notes, Dickens' editorial plans for *Master Humphrey's Clock* show him looking back to the eighteenth-century models of his childhood. "At this time (and for the next ten years) Dickens was unable to divorce his conception of what a periodical should be from his childhood introduction to that form." Imagination, well beyond those ten years, remained the key to a successful journal, as far as Dickens was concerned. "KEEP HOUSEHOLD WORDS IMAGINATIVE!" he wrote Wills from Rome in 1853. But what was good for Dickens was apparently not always as good for all his contributors: Percy Fitzgerald said that

> The writers were compelled, owing to the necessity of producing effect, to adopt a tone of exaggeration. Everything, even trivial, had to be made more comic than it really was. This was the law of the paper, and the reader is conscious of it when he takes up the journal after an interval of years. As I can testify from my own experience, this pressure became all but irresistible. A mere natural, unaffected account of any transaction, it was felt, was out of place; it would not harmonize with the brilliant, buoyant things surrounding it. I often think with some compunction of my own trespassings in this way, and of the bad habit one gradually acquired of colouring up for effect, and of magnifying the smallest trifle.

Such a method got Dickens into something like today's controversy over whether writers of purportedly factual books should invent scenes that "probably" happened, or create dialogue that is "essentially" accurate. One of the "chips" in Dickens' journal, entitled "Household Words and English Wills" (probably written by Wills but certainly expressing Dickens' own view) defended that publication against a charge that an article entitled "The Doom of English Wills" was "a little bit of fact, expanded by a good deal of fancy." "The evidence in our hands," the magazine replied, "of the material facts, is full and complete: there is nothing fictitious beyond the manner of telling the story. The tale itself is as correct as arithmetic."[70]   It sounds much like Woodward and Bernstein defending their book on the Supreme Court.

As we will see more fully in our discussion of reality, Dickens did insist on factual accuracy in all his journals: if the presentation must be imaginative, the details must be correct.   Speaking of contributors to *Household Words*, he said, ". . . Some remarkable descriptions in this Journal have come to us from wholly unaccustomed writers, who have faithfully and in thorough earnest put down what they have undergone or seen."   But reality unimaginatively viewed was for Dickens like water to the toper who, when he tasted it, said, "I don't know what it is, but it won't sell."   Rejecting a submitted story he said, "Something more is wanted in such a Narrative, than its literal Truth. . . .   It is in the nature of such Truths . . . to require to be told, artistically."   He urged a young woman writer to have "Courage to reject what comes uppermost, and to try for something better below it." It is the Wordsworthian gleam of imagination, again, playing over the facts of his articles, as well as his novels.   He liked the first piece submitted to him by George Sala, but noted that "there is little fancy in it. . . ."   Looking over back numbers, he wrote to Wills that "Wherever they fail, it is in wanting elegance of fancy.   They lapse too much into a dreary, arithmetical . . . dustiness that is powerfully depressing."[71]   "What the Xmas No. wants," he said in 1851, "is something with no detail in it, but a tender fancy that shall hit a great many people."   Early on, Wills had responded most sensibly to these complaints: if we compare *Household Words* to other journals, he said,

> We come out brilliantly. . . .   It is universally acknowledged that subjects of an uninviting nature are treated--as a rule--in HW in a more playful, ingenious and readable manner than similar subjects have been hitherto presented in other weekly periodicals; but to such a rule there must necessarily be large exceptions in all works which demand a certain space to be filled by a certain

time every week. No one, not even yourself (as
you said the other day) [in a letter (9/29/51) in
which, trying to come up with an article, Dickens
had said "The sparkling muse has not been at all
propitious!"] can sparkle to order, especially
writers who have only an occasional sparkle in
them. As to the 'Elegance of Fancy' you
desiderate, that, I apprehend, is simply impossible
as the prevailing characteristic of twenty-four
pages of print published fifty-two times a year.
Elegance of fancy cannot be thrown broadcast over
such an acreage of letter-press; although, happily
for *HW* (and for *HW* alone) it can be *sprinkled*
over its pages. If you could regularly see and go
over each sheet before it is put to press there
would be a very thick sprinkling of the excellence
in which you say *HW* is deficient.[72]

It is a beautiful bit of corrective surgery, performed by a
resident on his chief surgeon, ending with a complimentary
piece of nourishing candy (though even the candy has a
cutting edge in it: Dickens should edit more). And though
it seems to have abated Dickens' complaints not a bit, it
must have taught him something about another aspect of
reality which not even his imagination could overcome.

Dickens' comments on the uses and artistry of the
imagination are few and of surprisingly little interest, but his
recognition of the incessant struggle in him between
imagination and reality is fascinating. In Dickens, as we
shall see, the two were not always at odds: much that he
says suggests an ideal balancing or even symbiosis, rather
like Pope's arrangement of reason and self-interest in his
Essay on Man--indeed, he used language similar to that of
Pope in describing the need to harness imagination, as Pope
did self-love: "I work slowly and with great care, and never
give way to my invention recklessly, but constantly restrain
it. . . ." With but a few exceptions Dickens argued that
imagination need not seek to efface reality, replacing it with
another kind of truth; rather, the task of fancy is to play
over its antithesis such a light as (to use Wordsworth's

imagery and Wilson's word one last time) may make it tolerable. In his "A Preliminary Word" Dickens began like an enemy of reality, promising to subject his reader to "no mere utilitarian spirit, no iron binding of the mind to grim realities." But then he adopted a more conciliatory tone, saying that he would "show to all, that in all familiar things, even in those which are repellant [sic] on the surface, there is Romance enough, if we will find it out." In a handbill introducing *All the Year Round*, he spoke of "that fusion of the graces of the imagination with the realities of life, which is vital to the welfare of any community, and for which I have striven . . . as honestly as I could. . . ."[73] Looking for a unique formula for what was to become *Household Words*, he ruminated in a letter to Forster on the idea of a "Shadow," a kind of spirit observing and reporting to his readers on all things, speculating that it was a technique "which is just mysterious and quaint enough to have a sort of charm for their imagination, while it will represent common-sense and humanity." Such remarks suggest that, in much of his thinking, Dickens would have agreed with Bulwer's assertion (as paraphrased by Forster) that "the happiest effort of imagination, however lofty it may be, is that which enables it to be cheerfully at home with the real." Speaking at the annual meeting of the Birmingham and Midland Institute, Dickens said, "My own invention or imagination, such as it is, I can most truthfully assure you, would never have served me as it has, but for the habit of commonplace, humble, patient, daily, toiling, drudging attention."[74] He was aware of the danger of overbalancing the equation between reality and imagination: in his Preface to the third volume of *Master Humphrey's Clock*, he confessed that, in creating Master Humphrey and his three friends to tell tales, he had "insensibly fallen into the belief that they are present to his readers as they are to him, and has forgotten that, like one whose vision is disordered, he may be conjuring up bright figures when there is nothing but empty space."

This happy cooperation of fact and fancy has been discovered by many scholars in Dickens' work. While rightly emphasizing the power of imagination, Harry Stone recognizes the importance of experience: though all Dickens' writings are "rich with nostalgic allusions to the childhood literature that soothed and sustained him," by the time of *David Copperfield* he "turned his own experiences into articles of faith." Denis Donahue establishes the balance still more firmly: ". . . Dickens is not a fabulist, he does not insist upon the claims of the imagination over and against every claim of fact or time. . . . In the relation between imagination and reality he does not think of imagination as the senior or the greater term." Dickens himself, in response to a query from a reader, said "I presume most writers of fiction write, partly from their experience, and partly from their imagination. . . ."[75]

For critical readers of Dickens' time, and for more than a few in ours, this balance has posed a problem, for realism dominated fiction then and, as Northrop Frye has said, still colors our way of understanding it:

> The great Victorian realists subordinate their storytelling skill to the representational skill. Theirs is a dignified, leisurely vehicle that gives us time to look at the scenery. They have formed our stock responses to fiction, so that even when traveling at the much higher speed of drama, romance, or epic we still keep trying to focus our eyes on the incidental and transient. Most of us feel that there is something else in Dickens, something elemental, yet unconnected with either realistic clarity or philosophical profundity. What it is connected with is a kind of story that fully gratifies the hope expressed, according to Lewis Carrol, by the original of Alice, that "there will be nonsense in it." The silliest character in *Nicholas Nickleby* is the hero's mother, a romancer who keeps dreaming of impossible happy endings for her children. But the story itself follows her specifications and not those of the sensible people. The obstructing humors [characters] in Dickens are absurd because they have overdesigned their lives. But the kind of design that they parody is

> produced by another kind of energy, and one
> which insists, absurdly and yet irresistibly, that
> what is must never take final precedence over
> what ought to be.

"What ought to be" is difficult to define, but if it competes
with "what is," perhaps it is comparable to the Keatsian
truth that only the imagination can seize upon. Frye's last
sentence only partly supports Donahue's assertion that reality
and imagination are balanced in Dickens, because it somewhat
shifts emphasis: Donahue says that imagination is never
greater, while Frye argues that reality must not take
precedence. Coming from each side, they meet in the center,
but Frye's emphasis is, I think, the more crucial: what makes
Dickens different from (by implication better than) his
contemporaries is the presence of imaginative power far less
restrained by reality than in the other Victorians. The
contrived fairy-tale plots grown out of Dickens' first literary
love are not, Frye says, weaknesses or careless flaws
unnoticed by Dickens, as some critics have thought, but "an
essential part of his novels." If they are equal with reality
in his stories, as Donahue rightly argues, yet they are also
the part that is more equal: Dickens writes "not realistic
novels but fairy tales in the low mimetic displacement. . . ."
The balance is, in one sense, unbalanced, and imagination, if
it does not rule, speaks louder. As Chesterton said, "Dickens
. . . had common sense and uncommon sensibility." Dickens
himself used the phrase "fantastic fidelity" to describe what
he attempted in his combination of imagination and reality--
"consciously using distortion and fantasy" to present the
truth that lies beneath appearance, as Richard Stang says.
"It does not seem to me to be enough," Dickens said,

> to say of any description that it is the exact
> truth. The exact truth must be there; but the
> merit of art in the narrator, is the manner of
> stating the truth. As to which thing is literature,
> it always seems to me that there is a world to be
> done. And in these times, when the tendency is
> to be frightfully literal and catalog-like,--to make

> the thing, in short, a sort of sum in reduction that
> any miserable creature can do in that way--I have
> an idea (really founded on the love of what I
> profess), that the very holding of popular
> literature through a kind of popular dark age, may
> depend on such fanciful treatment.

It was in the manner of stating the truth that Dickens'
drama-dream of, as he put it in "A Christmas Tree," making
"all common things" become "uncommon and enchanted" was
to be effected. Rejecting a story submitted to his journal,
he complained of one of the characters in it that there was
no "quaint touch of observation or imagination to single him
out from the rest who have been doing literary duty these
forty years." In one instance, he even suggested that writing
down an experience, factually, could inhibit the imaginative
use of it later: writing to his friend Thomas Mitton of an
interview he had conducted, he said, "As I *must* use the
interview in a book, I can't weaken it by writing it down."[76]
    To cover a possible error about the date of a departing
ship, Dickens jokingly wrote to a friend that "any impression
of mine is, I need not say, much better than a fact." Taking
it for granted that an American friend, Jonathan Chapman,
would soon come to England, he said, "There is nothing like
assuming a fact stoutly in such a case as this. The comfort
is unspeakable." What was a joke for travel was a sober
truth for much of his life. Remembering happy moments with
friends in Switzerland, Dickens wrote to one of them, "I
don't know how it is, but the ideal world in which my lot is
cast, has an odd effect on the real one, and makes it chiefly
precious for such remembrances." According to George
Dolby, James Fields said that Dickens liked "to dilate in
imagination over the brewing of a bowl of punch, but . . . he
drank less of it than anyone who might be present. It was
the sentiment of the thing, and not the thing itself, that
engaged his attention." Certainly reality failed often enough
to live up to his imagination, even in mundane matters like
travel. He contrasted the stateroom on his ship to America
with "that snug chamber of the imagination" in which he had
dwelt before seeing it. Of a woman who had told him that

the sea voyage would be better than it was, he said, "God
bless that stewardess for her piously fraudulent account . . .
for her predictions . . . (all wrong, or I shouldn't be half so
fond of her). . . ."[77] In certain moods, imagination insisted
on reshaping reality: the first night out, even though objects
on board had become familiar, it became "difficult, alone and
thoughtful, to hold them to their proper shapes and forms.
They change with the wandering fancy."   His objection to
the prairie view west of St. Louis was that it "left nothing
to the imagination. . ."; he obviously much preferred a
journey by coach through a wood, in which he became
fascinated by the shapes stumps assumed in the growing dark:

> Now there is a Grecian urn erected in the centre
> of a lonely field; now there is a woman weeping at
> a tomb; now a very commonplace old gentleman in
> a white waistcoat, with a thumb thrust into each
> armpit of his coat; now a student poring on a
> book; now a crouching negro; now, a horse, a dog,
> a cannon, an armed man; a hunch-back throwing
> off his cloak and stepping forth into the light.
> They were often as entertaining to me as so many
> glasses in a magic lantern, and never took their
> shape at my bidding, but seemed to force
> themselves upon me, whether I would or no; and
> strange to say, I sometimes recognized in them
> counterparts of figures once familiar to me in
> pictures attached to childish books, forgotten long
> ago.[78]

This, surely, is the creative mind of Dickens at work, far
more clearly seen than in anything Butt and Tillotson can
show, excellent as their study is.   Dickens looks at reality
like a modern painter: what he sees is not just what is there
but, as I have elsewhere suggested he saw in the best
portraits, something more, something seen when one mixes
memory and desire, and this he sees so clearly that he feels
himself seeing without volition, without as it were even
looking, as he said to Forster:

> . . . When . . . I sit down to my book, some
> beneficent power shows it all to me, and tempts
> me to be interested, and I don't invent it--really
> do not--but *see* it, and write it down.

The Dickens for whom a beneficent power turns stumps into Grecian urns (an appropriate beginning of the list) and dogs and cannons is the same Dickens of the early sketches who, staring into a store window full of shoes, saw people standing in them, and wrote about them; it is the Dickens who, much as he insisted upon verisimilitude in painting, disliked that which showed only what was there; it is the Dickens who sought in the theater a fairy immortality far better than the facts upon which it was based--"a bright magical untrammeled world that is superior to life," as Harry Stone put it.   In his "Prologue" to *The Lighthouse*, he advised his audience to leave "the real world" for a time, adding, "Return is easy.   It will have ye back / Too soon to the old, beaten, dusty track; . . ."   And the great tragedy of life is that at last we are forced to return, for reality in the end must triumph.   When he was a child, Dickens said, he had been given a "Harlequin's Wand," but had found that it could not change a growling Mrs. Pipchin into a pleasant woman, or work any other miracles: "I had, by many trials, proved the wand's total incapacity."

". . . Other wands have failed me since. . . ."[79]

The wand did not often fail him as artist, but even there it occasionally lost its magic power.   Describing himself in a public house in one of the early sketches, he anticipates the usual dreamy state in which the pewter pot will come alive and tell him the story of the room's past: "a romantic humour" which will bring all to life again.   But a choleric orator has just been speaking in the room, and the thought of the ill such men do defeats the Dickensian necromancy, and the inanimate pot does not, like Keats's urn, break its silence to tell him that beauty is truth, truth beauty, and that he need know nothing else.[80]

Still, he continued to wave the wand, to urge others to procure one for themselves, and to oppose all who wanted to break wands.   In a speech at the Royal General Theatrical

Fund, he said,

> . . . We have schoolmasters going about like those
> horrible old women of whom we read in the public
> reports, perpetually flaying Whittington's cat alive;
> we have schoolmasters constantly demonstrating on
> blackboards to infant minds the utter impossibility
> of Puss in Boots; we have all the giants utterly
> dead and gone, with half the Jacks passing
> examinations every day in mental arithmetic; and
> with Tom Thumb really only known in these times
> as the gallant general seeking kisses of the ladies
> at 6 d. a head in the American market; . . . In
> these times when we have torn so many leaves out
> of our dear old nursery books, I hold it to be
> more than ever essential to the character of a
> great people that the imagination, with all its
> innumerable graces and charities, should be
> tenderly nourished. . . ."

In another speech, after commending students for their
accomplishments in mathematics and chemistry, he said,

> Do not let us, in the midst of the visible objects
> of nature, whose workings we can tell off in
> figures, surrounded by machines that can be made
> to the ten thousandth part of an inch, acquiring
> every day knowledge which can be proved upon a
> slate or demonstrated by a microscope--do not let
> us, in the laudable pursuit of the facts that
> surround us, neglect the fancy and the imagination
> which equally surround us as part of the great
> scheme. Let the child have its fable; let the man
> or woman into which it changes, always remember
> those fables tenderly. Let numerous graces and
> ornaments that cannot be weighed and measured,
> and that seem at first sight idle enough, continue
> to have their places about us, be we never so
> wise. The hardest head may co-exist with the
> softest heart. The union and just balance of those

two is always a blessing to the possessor, and always a blessing to mankind.

"It would be a great thing for all of us," he wrote to Angela Burdett Coutts, who was active in providing education for the poor, "if more who are powerfully concerned with Education, thought as you do, of the imaginative faculty."[81]

Thus for Dickens' insistence upon the value of imagination for others. For his own consciousness, often, the fancy could do more than cast a beneficent light upon reality; it could create for him another kind of reality, almost like science fiction's parallel existence, identical point by point with ours yet with a fundamental difference. The only evidence Dickens ever gave of the *un*reality of his fictional world came from that other level of imaginative existence which fascinated him and about which he constantly speculated: dreams. ". . . Is it not a strange thing," he wrote Felton, "if writers of fiction never dream of their own creations: recollecting I suppose, even in their dreams, that they have no real existence? I never dreamed of any of my characters. . . ." In all other ways, his characters were as real to him as living people: the deaths of Little Nell and Paul Dombey seem to have affected him as strongly as the loss of his own baby Dora. When he finished the death scene in *Dombey and Son* he wrote, ". . . Paul is dead. He died on Friday night about 10 o'clock; and as I had no hope of getting to sleep afterwards, I went out, and walked about Paris until breakfast-time next morning." Writing of *The Chimes* he said, "Since I conceived, at the beginning of the second part, what must happen in the third, I have undergone as much sorrow and agitation as if the thing were real; and have wakened up with it at night."[82] (Note the word "must"; Dickens indeed has no control over his story, but simply sees what is, and writes it down.) Gladys Storey said that "There is no doubt that the children of his imagination came before his children of the flesh, which may have accounted for Mrs. Perugini saying: 'The only fault I found with my father was that he had too many children.'" Perhaps he loved his fictional children so much because they took him beyond his own experience, as his physical children could never do. Writing to Forster about some characters in *Martin Chuzzlewit*, probably Pecksniff and Tom Pinch, he said, "As to the way in which these characters have opened out, that is, to me, one of the most surprising processes of the mind in this sort of invention. Given what one knows, what one does not know springs up. . . ."[83] Clearly, much of what Dickens wrote was not upon Locke's white sheet of paper.

At times, Dickens seems to have gone even farther, conceiving his imagined world not as an alternative or parallel to reality, but as a replacement for it. In a discussion of his dramatic readings I have noted his fascination with a remark made by a Spanish monk who showed to Sir David Wilkie Titian's painting of the Last Supper, and said that he often thought that the figures in it were "in truth the Substance, we the Shadows"; at times Dickens came to feel his fiction to be "the only reality in life and to mistake all the realities for short-lived shadows." A remark he made about a prisoner entering jail suggests that reality, for the mind, is no constant thing: "His confinement is a hideous vision; and his old life a reality." But as time passes, ". . . the world without, has come to be the vision, and this solitary life, the sad reality." (I promised not to mention Wordsworth again, but here is his prison-house of earth, closing about us as we grow, forcing us to lose our sense of the bright world we came from, trailing clouds of glory.) Reflecting in a letter to Mrs. Watson on the misfortunes of William Haldimand, a common friend, Dickens said, ". . . What a dream we live in. . . ." And referring to a story told about a madwoman in the streets of London, he commented, "A story, alas! all likely enough; but, likely or unlikely, true or untrue, never to take other shape in our mind."[84]

The last sentence again illustrates the difficulty of sorting out Dickens' literary aesthetic from the scattered comments with which we must work. Here "true" means "historically verifiable," but what is really truth for Dickens is what takes shape in the mind. And so it is not the experience of the woman, but rather the story about her, that makes truth.   As the "alas!" suggests, the story here is sad, but one guesses that it is not, like reality, crushing, for however dark and sad a story may be--like Dickens' own "dark" novels--it remains for him, Stone said, "a sort of beneficent amulet" which had saved him as a child, which he could use to save others, which we all can use to save ourselves from defeating reality.   Dickens did not explain why the man in jail did not avail himself of the amulet to deal with his sad reality, but merely traded realities: perhaps the point is that prisoners are people who lack imagination. (Perhaps, of course, Dickens had no such thoughts in his mind, but one of the things I hope this study shows is that many of his seemingly casual references to imagination and reality form a fairly coherent pattern, just as do some of his figures of speech.)   Certainly Dickens expected that sensitive sufferers would have the amulet, and use it: speaking of Robinson Crusoe's agonies of solitude, he wondered that they "never involved any ghostly fancies; a circumstance so very remarkable, that perhaps he left out something in writing his record?"   Imaginative literature could relieve the pain of the man isolated for years on an island or for hours on a train: in "By Rail to Parnassus" a passenger escapes dullness by reading a poem.   According to Forster, what reading did for others, writing did for Dickens: ". . . Whatever might befall he had a set-off in his imaginative creations, a compensation derived from his art that never failed him, because there he was supreme.   It was the world he could bend to his will, and make subservient to all his desires."   Well, not quite, as we have seen: the wand did not work quite so well as it was famed to do, and just two pages later, Forster recognizes the limitations of the imaginative life, speaking of "the so happy and yet so unhappy existence which seeks its realities in unrealities. . . ."   Still, Dickens could say to Wills about his state of health that "my habit of easy self-abstraction and withdrawal into fancies, has always refreshed and strengthened me. . . ."   Those who would live without the wand always drew his condemnation, especially when they pushed their restrictions on others.   Of the Shakers he met in America he said,

I so abhor, and from my soul detest that bad
spirit, no matter by what class or sect it may be
entertained, which would strip life of its healthful
graces, rob youth of its innocent pleasures, pluck
from maturity and old age their pleasant
ornaments, and make existence but a narrow path
towards the grave: that odious spirit which, if it
could have had full scope and sway upon the
earth, must have blasted and made barren the
imaginations of the greatest men . . . that, in
these [Shakers] . . . I recognize the worst among
the enemies of Heaven and Earth. . . .[85]

Richard Stang argued that "Dickens never would have
subscribed to any theory that considered art as escape," but
some things Dickens said suggest that he considered
imaginative literature to be what drama had been for him: if
not escapism, certainly a haven from weary reality. In a
letter intended for the *Daily News* he said of himself and his
fellow novelists that "we had sometimes reason to hope that
our imaginary worlds afforded an occasional refuge to men
engaged in the toils of life, from which they came forth
none the worse to a renewal of its strivings. . . ." At his
greatest, Dickens did not think of literature as mere
escapism, as mindless distraction from reality; indeed, as
Stang says, his early concept of art as a reformer of abuses,
as in the work of Charles Reade, changed as he gradually
came to see that the artist must use imagination to penetrate
the apparent surface reality to reveal the deeper truth, and
communicate this imaginative vision to his reader. By the
time of *Bleak House*, says Stang, Dickens was no longer
willing merely to identify social wrong; he gave his reader a
unifying vision, the vision which decent but flawed
characters like Gradgrind of *Hard Times* so clearly lacked.
Certainly the imaginative vision perceived, as in the
madwoman's story, more than the merely light and joyous;
long before most readers, Carlyle saw beneath Dickens'
"bright and joyful sympathy with everything around him"
something else: "deeper than all, if one has the eye to see
deep enough, dark, fateful, silent elements, tragical to look

upon, and hiding, amid dazzling radiances as of the sun, the elements of death itself."[86]   As with the toys and nursery tales, so with adult life: imagination responds both to joy and to terror.

In the great novels, even the darkest ones, the tragical elements were subsumed into a unifying vision that enabled the reader to bear them, but in other places Dickens' imaginative act comes closer to an escapism that is a kind of admission of defeat before reality.   One of these is to be found in, of all places, a Christmas tale: "The Poor Relation's Story," as dark and grim a representation of the imagination as Dickens ever wrote.   In this bitter narrative a poor relation, betrayed by his business partner and disinherited by an uncle for falling in love with a woman who, when she hears of the disinheritance, abandons him, tells of the happy life he leads in his "castle."   The castle is in the air, he admits: "the precepts of the season seem to teach me that it is well to be there."   The amulet works fitfully here, if at all: the man's castle-fantasies are mere airy escapism, and help him only to avoid, not deal with, reality.   And the same castle image, applied by Dickens to himself, suggested that at times he too could lose the childhood amulet.   At "nineteen years of age," Dickens wrote of himself in "Gone to the Dogs," his only inheritance had been

> A shining castle (in the air) with young Love looking out of window, perfect contentment and repose of spirit standing with ethereal aspect in the porch, visions surrounding it by night and day with an atmosphere of pure gold. . . .   Where is that castle now, with all its magic furniture? Gone to the Dogs.   Canine possession was taken of the whole of that estate, about a quarter of a century ago.

Not even the dreams that were the fictional character's only compensation for the misery of his life are, Dickens seems to be saying, any longer available to his creator.   And they are unavailable, he suggests, to many others: in "Nobody's Story" Nobody can find among the honored people of society those "whose wise fairy had opened a new and high existence to the humblest. . . ."[87]   In *A Christmas Carol* Bob Crachit wants such a fairy: he fails to warm himself at his small candle because he lacks "a strong imagination."

A most interesting combination of "castles in air" and "gone to the dogs," along with several other words Dickens used in connection with the imagination, occurs in chapter 22 of *David Copperfield*.   David, building castles as he imagines a happy future for himself, encounters Steerforth, who has also been daydreaming, but not happily.   David asks if he has been above among the stars in his reverie; Steerforth answers, "No," twice.   David asks if he has been below, then, and Steerforth gives a noncommital answer, but is described as staring into the fire, which is hint enough.   Nursery tales have come into his mind, says Steerforth, especially one about a boy who did not learn to care, and so was eaten by lions--a larger kind of "going to the dogs," he says.   The realization that he is that boy, who has not learned enough from nursery tales to keep him from visiting harm upon the Peggoty family, is obviously what Steerforth is thinking, and it has given him "what old women" (who tell nursery stories) call "the horrors."[88]

The episode is interesting for a number of reasons.   It sets a pleasurable imagining in the future--David's castles in the air, which may become a reality (and do, after some suffering)--over against a melancholy reworking of imaginative tales of the past which predicts an unhappy future--a going to the dogs.   This last, furthermore, would seem to use nursery tales as did Mr. Barlow, whom Dickens hated so much, or as George Cruikshank planned to do in *Hop o' my Thumb*, to which he objected so strongly: to inculcate a moral.   But there are instructive differences. First, the recipient of the lesson is an adult, not a child. Second, he remembers the tale, and applies its moral, himself: it is not thrust upon him.   Under these circumstances, the nursery tale is doing exactly--or at least is trying to do-- what Dickens felt it could do: soften the heart of the hardened adult by re-establishing contact with the better world of the child, that world lost by each of us on the other side of our own blacking warehouses.   Dickens is painting the scene in which the adult with imagination can reach back for the child's amulet, and be saved from the grown-up's agonies, including those he brings upon himself. Steerforth does not reach back well enough; he does not regain the amulet, and harms himself and others--he does indeed go to the dogs, just as Dickens was to do in some sad episodes of his own life, perhaps not too different from those of Steerforth. But one thinks better of Steerforth for this momentary reaching back, and no doubt in our present spreading assessment of the sins and failures of his creator, we should remember how desperately he reached back, and how sincerely he lamented when the amulet failed him, or when he failed it.

The dog and castle imagery explores the possibilities of the failure of the imagination, and the suffering that results. The man in the jail, the poor relation, Steerforth, and Dickens himself--all fail, to a greater or lesser extent, to use imagination to make life intelligible, bearable. We pity the convict, sympathize with the relation's escape into airy castles, and feel that Steerforth's regret that fairy tales have not kept him from the dogs is perhaps his best feeling in the novel. As for Dickens, at the least, we must applaud the fact that the failures of his own life did not deter him from continuing to wave his harlequin's wand. It was not possible that he should stop when, as Angus Wilson said, "His favourite moral was that in an increasingly utilitarian, industrial world we needed to cultivate the imagination, the fancy of childhood. . . ."[89]

Among other things Dickens had to say about imagination was the suggestion that at times it was the only way in which some things could get said. Trying to thank T. J. Thompson for the gift of an inkpot and pen, he wrote, "I know not how to thank you. . . . If I could imagine such a case in a work of fiction I might perhaps do justice to the feelings of the receiver, but when it comes home to myself I am quite powerless and have no words to use." He sounds like a character in a Vonnegut short story ("Who Am I This Time?"), who cannot in his own person do anything, and is obliged to make love by acting the character of Romeo. Dickens was also aware of the need to carry his readers carefully from their real world into his fictional one, making the transition gradual and convincing. He defended the opening of *The Haunted Man* against a charge of too much fancy by saying

> . . . The heaping up of that quantity of shadows, I hold to be absolutely necessary, as a preparation for the appearance of the dark shadow of the Chemist. People will take anything for granted, in the Arabian Nights or the Persian Tales, but they won't walk out of Oxford Street, or the Market place of a country town, directly into the presence of a Phantom, albeit an allegorical one. And I believe it to be as essential that they come at that spectre through such a preparation of gathering gloom and darkness, as it would be for them to go through some such ordeal, in reality, before they could get up a private Ghost of their own.[90]

Beyond this, Dickens said nothing about the artistry of utilizing the imagination. Forster too, in his comments on his friend's art, offered little help in describing the uses of his fancy, but he did mention two things. First, he defended Dickens against the charge that he did not present ideal characters (again, poor Dickens was attacked on both sides of the imagination-reality issue: he wasn't realistic enough, and he wasn't ideal enough) by explaining that in his work "the best ideals . . . are obtained, not by presenting with added comeliness or grace the figures which life is ever eager to present as of its best, but by connecting the singularities and eccentricities which ordinary life is apt to reject or overlook, with the appreciation that is deepest and the laws of insight that are most universal." It is as it was in the best portrait painting, once again: the true artist does not distort reality, but perceives and renders the reality which others fail to see. Second, Forster suggested that upon occasion the harlequin wand, if it did not fail Dickens in literature as it had in life, at least worked its magic fitfully. The manuscript sheets of the early novels, Butt and Tillotson show us, reveal "a hand racing to keep pace with the mind's conceptions." To use Dickens' own expression, he was "seeing" so fast that he hardly had time to "write it down," it would seem. In 1846, while writing *Dombey and Son*, he told Forster that "Invention, thank God, seems the easiest thing in the world. . . ."[91] But by the time of *Little Dorrit*, Forster says, things had changed: his discussion with Dickens of a proposed alteration of the beginning of the novel led him to conclude that "the old, unrestrained, irrepressible flow of fancy had received temporary check." In part, it seems, the restraint was self-imposed: it is the mature Dickens who told Forster that "I work slowly and with great care, and never give way to my invention recklessly, but constantly restrain it. . . ." But by *Our Mutual Friend*, if not before, the check to imagination seems to have been neither temporary nor voluntary: "I have been wanting in invention," Dickens wrote.[92]

Were the fairy tales receding out of memory? Was Dickens beginning to ask himself, like the aging Wordworth, where the vision and the gleam had fled? *Our Mutual Friend* gives evidence of no such thing (while Wordsworth wrote nothing of comparable greatness after the "Ode"), but some might say that *The Mystery of Edwin Drood* does. Still, if the wand at times faltered in his last novel, Dickens but grasped it the more firmly, and waved it again.

REALITY: HELPS TO MY FANCY

In our discussion of imagination, we found Dickens speaking for a balance between the fancy and reality, but stressing the necessity of the imagination. We did not pause to attempt a definition of reality, because Dickens does not say enough to help us work with the complex terms of modern definitions of the entity; none of his commentary justifies reference to Lukacs and Wellek and Barthes, or to help us agree or disagree with or modify such contemporary assessments as John Romano's assertion that Dickens "is one of the company of realists, because the form of his novels protests against their confinement and distortion of reality."[93] But we can note that Romano sees Dickens as a realist (at least, in their company), while Northrop Frye works to distinguish him from his contemporaries in that regard. With such apparently divergent views in mind, it may be worth our while to examine more closely what Dickens did say about reality, though this may take us over ground partially covered in our discussion of imagination.

We have concluded from what we have heard him say so far that while he thought it his task never to settle for the mere representation of reality, he also insisted on beginning with it, and never merely flaunting it. Reality was the necessary raw material without which imagination could not work. What, then, in the relatively simple terms of his own time and usage, did he consider reality to be, and what-- more than a beginning--was its use to fiction?

Whatever Dickens considered the relation of reality to fiction to be, he assuredly did not think of it as a lawyer in one of his short stories did. This Jaggers-like figure, about to narrate an event, begins thus:

> Now, I absolutely decline to tell you a story. But, though I won't tell a story, I am ready to make a statement. A statement is a matter of fact; therefore the exact opposite of a story, which is a matter of fiction. What I am now going to tell you really happened to me.

The passage is fascinating because in it Dickens does two things at the same time: he mocks the Gradgrindist notion that truth resides only in fact, yet he conveys to his reader a strong sense that what follows in the story did in fact "really" happen; it reminds one of the dialogue in the postscript to "The Legend of Sleepy Hollow," in which the narrator of the tale and a grave gentleman discuss how much of the story is to be believed. But for our purposes the importance of the passage lies in the fact that the lawyer is wrong: he *is* going to tell us a story, whether the basis is fact or not. Dickens' reply to the lawyer is contained in a comment he made to Forster: "Fiction cannot prove a case, but it can forcibly represent a righteous sentiment. . . ."[94]

On another occasion, Dickens seized upon an opportunity to laugh at a living version of the lawyer in the person of Sir Peter Laurie, one of his oldest enemies on the matter of reform, when he caught that individual assuming that anything which appeared in a work of fiction could not be real. Having found "Jacob's Island" in *Oliver Twist*, Laurie assumed that it was a fictional place, and attacked Charles Blomfield, Bishop of London, for believing it to be real, and in need of improvement for its poor. Laurie's error (there *was* a Jacob's Island) was uncovered within a week, and Dickens used the occasion of his preface to the Cheap Edition of *Oliver Twist* to rub Laurie's nose in his mistake:

> . . . Reflecting upon this logic, and its universal application; remembering that when Fielding described Newgate, the prison immediately ceased to exist; that when Smollett took Roderick Random to Bath, that city instantly sank into the earth . . . I was inclined to make this preface the vehicle of my humble tribute to SIR PETER LAURIE. But I am restrained . . . by no less a consideration than the impossibility of his existence. For SIR PETER LAURIE having been himself described in a book (as I understand he was, one Christmas time, for his conduct on the seat of justice), it is but too clear that there CAN be no such man.

In his own writing about fiction, Dickens showed what Laurie had failed to understand: Sir Peter would allow no fact in fiction, but Dickens spoke of the need to use fact as help to fiction: we are, he said, "in the habit of allowing impressions to be made upon us by external objects, which should be produced by reflection alone, but which, without such visible aids, often escape us. . . ." Speaking here as Master Humphrey, he continued that the condition of Little Nell was only brought "palpably before me" by the objects he saw in her grandfather's warehouse. He would probably have not been impressed with her unusual state had he not had these "helps to my fancy." "What Dickens argues here," John Romano says, ". . . is that the verisimilitudinous is not the realistic. The real is only apprehended by art where its actuality is not diminished or swallowed up by a tedious

exactitude of imitation. . . ."[95]   Romano and Frye, then, are
not so very much apart: Dickens is "realist" only by
stipulative definition.

Much that Dickens said bears out this interpretation.
He wrote to George Beadnell to say that he had put one "Mr.
Clarke's own story" into *Pickwick Papers*, but added,

> . . . This is the only reality in the whole business
> of and concerning the Fleet.   Fictitious narratives
> place the enormities of the system in a much
> stronger point of view, and they enable one to
> escape the personalities and endless absurdities
> into which there is a certainty of rushing if you
> take any man's account of his own grievances.

When offered information about General Gordon for *Barnaby
Rudge* he replied, "As to the Riot, I am going to try if I
can't make a better one than he did."   To another man who
offered him similar information he replied that he had
completed the part of the novel dealing with the riots, and
added, "you will readily understand that in using them for
purposes of fiction, it has been necessary--quite indispensable
to the Progress of the Story--to reject many circumstances
growing out of them. . . ."   Clearly, he felt--much as did
Henry James--that fact could be a burden to the novelist,
could bury his imagination.   Northrop Frye said that Dickens
saw "in the cult of facts and statistics a threat, not to the
realistic novelist, and not only to a life based on concrete
and personal relations, but to the unfettered imagination, the
mind that can respond to fairy tales and fantasy and
understand their relevance to reality."[96]   I find no record
of Dickensian comment on Ichabod Crane or Hawthorne's
Judge Pyncheon, but if he knew these American characters
he must have been interested in their inability to distinguish
between fantasy and reality, or to use the first to understand
the second.

Certainly Dickens' refusal to paint the world exactly as
it is in his fiction is also owing to his desire to protect his
readers against what he considered to be the harmful effects
of reality when thrust in ugly detail before them.   Angus

Wilson says that two factors diverted Dickens from reality: "the necessity to sustain a central hopeful chord in the human heart and some concern for contemporary sexual conventions. . . ." This makes Dickens sound merely idealistic and prim, but he had other reasons for avoiding strict mimesis. Writing which insisted on unvarnished reality, he believed, was doubly dangerous: it could harm the reader, and it could turn him away from truths he ought to face. Discussing the terrible treatment of discharged soldiers in an article in *The Uncommercial Traveller*, he wrote, "I find it very difficult to indicate what a shocking sight I saw in them, without frightening the reader from the perusal of these lines, and defeating my object of making it known." And if as Wilson says he desired to strike a hopeful chord, he did not see such an effort as distortion of reality, but as interpretation of it. In one of his journals he spoke of "the intimate connexion between the facts and realities of the time, and the means by which we aim, in Household Words, to soften what is hard in them, to exalt what is held in little consideration, and to show the latent hope there is in what may seem unpromising."[97] The passage does not promise to make bad things nice; it offers to penetrate beyond slight consideration and inaccurate seeming--the delusions of reality--to bring forth deeper truth.

Where factual detail could be given without turning away the reader, he approved of it: despite his reservations about the all-good blacks and all-bad whites of *Uncle Tom's Cabin*, he admired the fact that "the details of the slave system . . . have been carefully collected, and are represented, bright or black, fairly and with all due variety, so that they may be generally accepted as remarkable pictures of the every day truth."[98] In his Preface to *Barnaby Rudge* he assured his readers that "in the description of the principal outrages, reference has been had to the best authorities of that time, such as they are; and that the account given in this Tale, of all the main features of the Riots, is substantially correct." Defense of his fiction against charges of exaggeration, extravagance, and "preposterous fancy" is found in several of his prefaces; perhaps the best known is that in which he argues the possibility of spontaneous human combustion in *Bleak House*, in which he said that "I do not wilfully or negligently mislead my readers. . . ." He believed that the avoidance of certain kinds of reality so common in his time--especially "low" reality--was a mistake. In the Preface to *Oliver Twist* Dickens defended his use of characters from among "the most criminal and degraded of London's population," saying that "I have yet to learn that a lesson of the purest good may not be drawn from the vilest evil," and adding that

> I saw no reason, when I wrote this book, why the dregs of life, so long as their speech did not offend the ears, should not serve the purpose of a moral, at least as well as its froth and cream. Nor did I doubt that there lay festering in St. Giles's, as good materials toward the truth as any to be found in St. James.

He had read, he said, of dozens of charming, well-dressed thieves, but "had never met (except in Hogarth) with the miserable reality," and so decided that to present a thief as he was "would be a service to society." "It is wonderful how Virtue turns from dirty stockings, and how Vice, married to ribbons and a little gay attire, changes her name, as married ladies do, and becomes Romance."

It is well documented that Dickens on several occasions carefully studied some actuality before representing it in his novels: probably the best-known instances are the Yorkshire schools in *Nicholas Nickleby* and the strike in *Hard Times*. Close observation of the world he lived in was a key to his greatness; the letters show him at work in this way. From Boston he wrote that "There is a great deal afloat here, in the way of subjects for description. I keep my eyes open, pretty wide, and hope to have done so to some purpose, by the time I come home." In 1843 he told Forster that he would like to stop writing for a time and "enlarge my stock of description and observation by seeing countries new to me." In 1847 he wrote to Augustus Tracey saying that he wanted "to ask you a question on one or two little nautical points, in order that I may be quite right in Dombey."

Similar concern for veracity may be seen in many other letters. The final test of imagination was to compare it to reality: discussing kinds of articles for *Household Words*, he suggested a typical one might be "A history of remarkable characters, good and bad, in history; to assist the reader's judgement in his observation of men, and in his estimates of the truth of many characters in fiction."[99]

He compared his observation to taking photographs: while on a reading tour he "walked from Durham to Sunderland, and made a little fanciful photograph in my mind of Pit Country, which will come well into *H. W.* one day. I couldn't help looking upon my mind as I was doing it, as a sort of capitally prepared and highly sensitive plate. And I said, without the least conceit (as Watkins might have said of a plate of his) 'it really is a pleasure to work with you, you receive the impression so nicely.'" Such photographic impression, it was clear, was the basis upon which any ideality of art was based: he assured Joshua Fayle, a Quaker schoolmaster, that ". . . The descriptions in Oliver Twist and Barnaby Rudge are ideal, but are founded on close observation and reflection." Founded upon, but not limited to: the photographer lent meaning to what he represented by the way he took his picture. Dickens did not record experience, but his experience of experience: in his Preface to *A Tale of Two Cities* he said that "I have so far verified what is done and suffered in these pages, as that I have certainly done and suffered it all myself." Observing him at work, his daughter Mary described him thus:

> . . . He had thrown himself completely into the character he was creating, [so] that for the time being he had not only lost sight of his surroundings, but had actually become in action, as in imagination, the creature of his pen.[100]

It was the seeing, not the thing seen, that made the artist: ". . . There is potential interest in everything we see, if we have the power properly to see it. . . ." Still, he was capable of agreeing that in some instances fact could replace imagination, bringing us equal wonder and delight. If scientific knowledge could not quite compensate for Keats's "awful rainbow," reduced from its mysterious beauty by hard understanding, it could, as he said in a review of a book called *The Poetry of Science*, replace something of our poetic feeling about nature with a new sense of wonder in nature by what it revealed to us--"ample compensation," he called it. One of the strongest pieces of evidence of his regard for reality lies in the hilarity with which he responded to anything which violated it--beginning perhaps as early as his huge enjoyment of "the absurd improbability of his nurse's tales." He urged reality upon a young Danish friend, Emmely Gotschalk: "The world is not a dream, but a reality, of which we are the chief part. . . . Be earnest--earnest--in life's reality."[101]

Faced with a choice between reality and imagination, Dickens usually chose the latter, but he distinguished between the imaginative and the ideal; obliged to choose between reality and unfounded ideality, he chose the real. He did not totally reject ideality. "I think it would be well . . . for the American people," he wrote in *American Notes*, ". . . if they loved the Real less, and the Ideal somewhat more." But Forster makes it clear that for Dickens the ideal was rooted in the actual. "Not his genius only, but his whole nature, was . . . exclusively made up of sympathy for, and with, the real in its most intense form. . . . There was for him no 'city of the mind' against outward ills, for inner consolation and shelter. It was in and from the actual he still stretched forward to find the freedoms and satisfaction of an ideal. . . ." He objected, it goes without saying, to fictional devices which disguise the truth, which make it pretty not only to make it palatable but to conceal it. Constance Cross said that, unlike Bulwer, Dickens "offered no ideals for my contemplation. Human nature as we found it, he said, should be the model of all good work; there must be no painting men as they ought to be."[102] Dickens' defense of one of his first heroes, in the Preface to *Nicholas Nickleby*, supports the statement: "If Nicholas be not always found to be blameless or agreeable, he is not always intended to appear so. He is a young man of an impetuous temper and of little or no experience; and I saw no reason why such

a hero should be lifted out of nature." That Dickens felt
impelled to defend Nicholas against a charge of not being
nice enough says volumes about the difference between his
and our century.

He took strong exception to the fictional form an
English town would so often assume when visited by the
Queen:

> Does it not clumsily try, at considerable expense,
> to make itself look as like a bad travelling circus
> as possible? Does it not stick up, in honour of
> the occasion, theatrical canvas arches, and absurd
> flags that are no flags, and pretended drab statues
> in pretended drab niches that are not statues and
> not niches, and lamentable dead boughs that are a
> ghastly parody on living and growing trees? Does
> it not commit every sort of unpardonable offense
> against Taste, and make itself as ridiculously
> unreal as possible in the broad, truth-telling
> daylight?

It is significant that Dickens mentions in the passage two
things he loved: circuses, and the theatrical. He liked both
even when they were bad, apparently feeling that, as
undisguised fancy, they offered no danger to the
understanding, whatever they might do to taste; but when
reality masqueraded as such things, the case was different.
The town, Dickens went on, should present its own face to
the Queen:

> . . . Let it say to the Queen, in effect:--Please,
> your Majesty, there are my plain stone-paved
> streets, where so many thousand people in
> Lancashire and Yorkshire clogs, wake my echoes as
> they go to their work at five or six in the
> morning. Please your Majesty, these are my great
> chimneys, always vomiting smoke when your
> Majesty is not here; smoke which is very ugly to
> look at and very unpleasant to smell, which is also
> inseparable from many of the most beautiful and

useful works in you Majesty's kingdom. Please your Majesty, this concourse of inhabitants, in clean plain clothes, that lines both sides of your way, is a striving, loyal respectful, good-humoured, long-suffering specimen of your Majesty's working subjects. It is my opinion that I can show your Majesty nothing better or more interesting than this. . . .[103]

Perhaps the closest Dickens ever came to saying the same thing about literature itself was in a letter to Wilkie Collins, in which he argued "that you can't shut out the world; that you are in it, to be of it; that you get into a false position the moment you try to sever yourself from it; and that you must mingle with it, and make the best of it, and make the best of yourself into the bargain."[104] On several occasions he made it plain that he thought the artist's job was to use fancy only in combination with reality: Master Humphrey, speaking of *Barnaby Rudge*, speculates "that the writer of this tale--which is not impossible, for men are apt to do so when they write--has actually mingled with it something of his own experience and endurance." It was in "the way he used his experience," he believed, that "the merit and art in the novelist lay. . . ." In a short work, Dickens felt, the author could afford to separate himself for a time from the world: in *The Haunted Man*, he said, "I think a little dreaminess and vagueness essential. . . . But the introduction of such a quality into any of my longer books, is what I never thought of. . . ."[105] Again and again Forster praises Dickens' "art of copying from nature as it really exists," but he makes it clear that by "copying" he does not mean mere reproduction: Dickens "had given new beauty to the commonest forms of life. . . ." If fiction should never prettify reality, neither should reality constrain fiction: when the actual was not vital, it should give way to the needs of the imaginative--especially when the imaginative was dramatic. Writing to Collins about *No Thoroughfare*, Dickens advised, "Whatever is most dramatic in such a thing as the Clock Lock I think the best for the stage, without reference to the nicety of the real mechanism."   Answering   an   aspiring   author   who   had apparently pleaded his case with the argument that his story was good because it was based on fact, Dickens said,

> Whether the substance of your book be true
> or fictitious, is nothing to the purpose. If you
> cannot grace truth in the narration, and have not
> the faculty of telling it in writing, you should
> either leave it untold, or leave it to the chance of
> being told by some one else. If it were a reason
> for writing, that what is written is true, surely
> there is nothing to prevent the whole civilized
> world from becoming authors, in as much as every
> man, woman, and child, has some truthful
> experience and might, on such a plea, rush into
> print with it.[106]

Mark Twain's remark that fiction could not afford to be as strange as truth was something with which Dickens would have agreed, though with some qualification. He wrote to Forster of a "strange story" told him by a friend, "belonging," said Forster, "to that wildly improbable class of realities which Dickens always held, with Fielding, to be (properly) closed to fiction. Only, he would add, critics should not be so eager to assume that what had never happened to themselves could not, by any human possibility, ever be supposed to have happened to anyone else." The "only" here was no doubt what Dickens had in mind when he defended the spontaneous combustion in *Bleak House* against charges of impossibility; thanking a correspondent for evidence supporting the incident, he said, "It is inconceivable to me how people can reject such evidence, supported by so much familiar knowledge, and such reasonable analogy." Against another charge of improbability, that of the means by which Madame Defarge meets her death in *A Tale of Two Cities*, he entered another defense, a mixture of artistic unity, symbolic significance, and *deus ex machina*:

> I am not clear, and I never have been clear,
> respecting the canon of fiction which forbids the

interposition of accident in such a case as Madame
Defarge's death. Where the accident is inseparable
from the passion and action of the character;
where it is strictly consistent with the entire
design, and arises out of some culminating
proceeding on the part of the individual which the
story has led up to; it seems to me to become, as
it were, an act of divine justice. And when I use
Miss Pross (though this is quite another question)
to bring about such a catastrophe, I have the
positive intention of making that half-comic
intervention a part of the desperate woman's
failure; and of opposing that mean death, instead
of a desperate one in the streets which she
wouldn't have minded, to the dignity of
Carton's.[107]

He also defended his characters against the charge of
improbability. Already in his time his people had been
criticized as exaggerations, but Dickens answered in his
Preface to the "Charles Dickens" edition of *Martin
Chuzzlewit* that

What is exaggeration to one class of minds and
perceptions, is plain truth to another. . . . I
sometimes ask myself whether there may
occasionally be a difference of this kind between
some writers and some readers; whether it is
always the writer who colours highly, or whether
it is now and then the reader whose eye for
colour is a little dull?
. . . I have never touched a character
precisely from the life, but some counterpart of
that character has incredulously asked me: "Now
really, did I ever really, see one like it?"

One such character was Dickens' own mother, who expressed
her disbelief that such a person as Mrs. Nickleby--whom
Dickens drew after her--could ever exist. His reply in the
Preface of *Pickwick Papers* to the criticism that Pickwick's

nature changes improbably was no doubt reached after he wrote the novel, and is not convincing, but it expresses a sincere aesthetic conviction:

> I do not think this change will appear forced or unnatural to my readers, if they will reflect that in real life the peculiarities and oddities of a man who had anythng whimsical about him, generally impress us first, and that it is not until we are better acquainted with him that we usually begin to look below these superficial traits, and to know the better part of him.

Perhaps the most interesting thing one finds in Dickens' relation to reality is that he, even he, found something he despaired of capturing in language. It was Venice. He thought "the reality itself, beyond all pen or pencil. I never saw the thing before that I should be afraid to describe. But to tell what Venice is, I feel to be an impossibility." Was it following this, when he looked at the paintings of Venice by Stanfield and Canaletto and found them "miraculous in their truth," that he began to think of illustrations as a way of extending the truth of his novels? Certainly he had worked with illustrators before this time, but if Venice did not awaken in him the sense of what art could do that words could not, it surely must have augmented it. Another piece of reality also stunned him: when he learned of the continuing regard and respect a man named Frederick Maynard had for his sister, though she had lived for some years with a man to whom she was not married, he said it was "a romance so astonishing yet so intelligible as I never had the boldness to think of."[108]

But of almost equal interest is the sense, running through some of his comments, that Dickens found himself remarkably divided between the worlds of fancy and of reality. Writing from Brighton, he said that ". . . When one laughs, and cries, and suffers the agitation that some men experience over their books, it's a bright change to look out of window and see the gilt little toys on horseback going up and down before the mighty sea and thinking nothing of

it."[109]   What a statement that is. It begins by reversing the
usual attitude of Dickens and most of us, and ends by
mocking those in that reality who stand in unthinking
proximity to what was for Dickens the symbol of the ultimate
reality, and so it brings us back to literature again as a way
of understanding.   (It also makes us think of Wordsworth's
sonnet, "It Is a Beauteous Evening.")

CHARACTER: TUGGING AT HIS SLEEVE

Speaking in company one day, Dickens took up a wine
glass and said,

> Suppose I choose to call this a *character*, fancy it
> a man, endue it with certain qualities; and soon
> the fine filmy webs of thought, almost impalpable,
> coming from every direction, we know not whence,
> spin and weave about it, until it assumes form and
> beauty, and becomes instinct with life.[110]

The picture is compelling: it images its speaker's mind in
the act of creating, as that mind in a myriad of instances
replaced the glass now with a pair of shoes in a store
window, now with a drawing of a figure, again with the face
of an acquaintance, neighbor, or public person--all spun by
Dickens, he knew not how, into a life they never possessed
before he touched them.
    At other times, he described the making of a character
in more detail.   "It is difficult always to tell where a
particular character, as it is finally left, comes from.   Of
course it must be suggested by something seen, met or read
of; but in passing through the mental laboratory, its
constituents are put together and coloured so subtly and
curiously that it is difficult to decompose the various
elements."   Asked if his characters were "mere fancies," he
replied, "No. . . .   They are copies . . . not . . . true
histories in all respects, but they are likenesses, nor have I
in any of my works attempted anything more than to
arrange my story as well as I could, and give a true picture
of scenes I have witnessed."   But the kind of character he

created clearly indicates what he meant here by "true." Walter Phillips defined his use of character in 1919: "In a notable degree the persons of the story are to be made to talk, to act in their proper person, and thus to develop a story.   Dissection and analysis of character by the novelist to Dickens spells futile narrative art."   Forty-eight years later, working with Dickens' nonfictional writing, Richard Stang reached the same conclusion, pointing out that Dickens would have characters understood--inner as well as outer--by action, not analysis.   "Formal psychological analysis of the states of mind of his people were out of the question in a novel what was meant to be dramatic. . . . .   Such analysis he called dissection. . . ."   No doubt this is why Dickens felt that "The psychological part of" *The Scarlet Letter* was "very much overdone. . . ."[111]

Stang has given us the key word--the keystone of Dickens' aesthetic for character as for all else: dramatic. Characters in a story should function as do characters in a play, always remembering that for Dickens good drama depended more upon dialogue than upon incident.   He was aware of the danger of such dependence: he once wrote that he found some books "so infernally conversational, that I forget who the people are before they have done talking, and don't in the least remember what they talked about before when they begin talking again!"   But his own best method lay in the conversation of his characters.   Forster attributed the limited success of *A Tale of Two Cities* to an uncharacteristic shift from dialogue to action:

> . . . There is no instance in his novels, excepting this, of a deliberate and planned departure from the method of treatment which had been pre-eminently the source of his popularity as a novelist.   To rely less upon character than upon incident, and to resolve that his actors should be expressed by the story more than they should express themselves by dialogue, was for him a hazardous, and can hardly be called an entirely successful, experiment.

Speaking himself of *A Tale of Two Cities*, Dickens said,

> I set myself the task of making *a picturesque
> story*, rising in every chapter, with characters
> true to nature, but whom the story should express
> more than they should express themselves by
> dialogue. I mean in other words, that I fancied a
> story of incident might be written, (in place of the
> odious stuff that *is* written under that pretence),
> pounding the character in its own mortar, and
> beating their interest out of them.

The wording suggests that Dickens agreed with Forster; if
he did not argue that all character in fiction should be
realized through dialogue, at least he may have decided that
such a method was best for him.   Forster also connected
Dickens' characterization with his love of drama.
Remembering that he at one time thought of becoming an
actor, Forster said,

> He took to a higher calling, but it included the
> lower.   There was no character created by him
> into which life and reality were not thrown with
> such vividness, that to his readers the thing
> written did not seem the thing actually done. . . .
> He had the power of projecting himself into
> shapes and suggestions of his fancy which is one
> of the marvels of creative imagination, and what
> he desired to express he became.   The assumptions
> of the theatre have the same methods at a lower
> pitch. . . .[112]

Vividness, Monroe Engel was to say almost a hundred years
later, became for Dickens "a matter of literary principle."
Dickens' own words for the quality of drama in fiction
(though he sometimes also used *vividness*) were *force* and
power: George Eliot's *Adam Bede* was greater than her
Scenes from Clerical Life because it had "a World of Power
added thereunto."   The ability to make the reader of a page
respond to its characters as alertly and emotionally as he or

she would to actors on a stage was for Dickens a crucial test of fiction. But he guarded against striving for more emotional impact than a character could legitimately deliver: in describing his characters, he said, "I aim no higher than to feel in writing as they seemed to feel themselves."[113]

In the above quotation, Forster also uses the word *reality*: the concept was an important part of Dickens' theory of characterization--the only one about which he wrote to any considerable extent. His greatest compliment to a fictional character was that it was "true": if *Adam Bede* was admirable for its power, it was also excellent because such a character as Hetty was "so extraordinary [sic] subtle and true, that I laid the book down fifty times, to shut my eyes and think about it." It is prudent, however, to beware the mere equation of *true* with *real*, for *true* seems to have meant three different things to Dickens, and it is difficult at times to be certain which meaning he intends in a particular case, though often the best guess is that he meant all three: 1) true to life; 2) alive, vital; 3) representing a value of life that penetrates beneath mere appearance. When he said in his Preface to *Oliver Twist* that there was no point in discussing whether the prostitute Nancy was realistically portrayed or not, because she was *true*, he surely used the word in its third sense. When he said that Eliot's Hetty Sorrel was true, he may have meant all three. But the second meaning, as distinct from the other two, was important to him: to create truth, the marks in a book had to make something come alive, magically creating breath and blood and passion. Where this did not happen, Dickens felt the writing was beyond help. When his subeditor Wills sent him a story he had written, Dickens replied,

> It has interest, but it seems to me to have one great want which I cannot overcome. It is all one working machinery, and the people are not alive. I see the wheels going and hear them going, and the people are as like life as machinery can make them--but they don't get beyond the point of the moving waxwork. It is

very difficult to explain how this is, because it is
a matter of intuitive perception and feeling; but
perhaps I may give two slight examples. If the
scene, where the woman who dies is lying in bed,
were truly done, the conversation between the
heroine and the boy would belong to it--*could* do
no violence to it--and whatever it might be
about, *would* inevitably associate itself in the
reader's mind with the figure on the bed, and
would lead up to the catastrophe that soon
happens. If the boy on the outside of the Coach
were naturally done, his illness would be a
natural thing and one would receive it
accordingly. Now, the conversation by the bed is
an interruption to the idea of the dying woman,
and the dying woman is an interruption to the
conversation, and *they don't fit.* And it is plain
that you, the author, make the boy ill because you
want him to be ill--for, if the few closing lines of
the chapter, referring to him, were taken away,
the reader would have no reason whatsoever to
suppose that anything was the matter with him.

The intuitive artistry which changes characters from wax
figures (or wine glasses) into real people, "truly done," is the
key not only to effective characterization but to making the
reader accept what the writer wants to do. Later in the
same letter Dickens advises Wills to get this effect by
treating the scene as the product of a kind of imagined
memory:

> The scene outside the Coach has a good deal
> of merit in it, but the same direful want.
> Consider if you had been outside the coach, and
> had been suddenly carried into the midst of a
> Torchlight meeting of that time, whether you
> would have brought away no other impression of it
> than you give the reader. Imagine it a
> remembrance of your own, and look at the passage.
> And exactly because that is not true, the conduct

of the men who clamber up is in the last degree improbable. Whereas if the scene were truly and powerfully rendered, the improbability more or less necessary to all tales and allowable in them, would became a part of a thing so true and vivid, that the reader must accept it whether he likes it or not.

Dickens gave similar advice to others: make your story real by imagining yourself living it, by making it as close to an actual experience as you can, and then by telling your reader what you have seen. No doubt he is thinking in the above passage of other things as well as character that help create reality, but character is the most important; though he goes on to praise other things in Wills's story, he concludes "--but I still feel that Frankenstein has made the people." And of another story he said, "It seems to me as if it were written by somebody who lived next door to the people rather than inside of 'em."[114]

But truths two and three are not advocated at the expense of truth one: truth to life. It is the character "drawn to the life" that merits Dickens' constant approval. Scott's characters were great because they were "real." As for his own writing, Forster tells us, Dickens far preferred to praise of any of his "merely literary"--by which one supposes he meant craftsmanlike--accomplishments, admiration for his stories as "bits of actual life, with the meaning and purpose on their part, and the responsibility on his, of realities rather than creatures of fancy." And Forster quotes from a letter to him from Dickens thanking him for his review of *Oliver Twist*: ". . . the sense of poor Oliver's reality which I know you have had from the first, has been the highest of all praise to me. None that has been lavished upon me have I felt half so much as that appreciation of my interest and meaning. You know I have ever done so. . . ." ". . . There is scarcely a character of description, the nucleus and substantial body of which was not furnished from reality," he said. I have found but one instance in which Dickens' sense of the reality of his character was less than complete. Marcus Stone, the illustrator of *Our Mutual*

Friend, asked him which of Silas Wegg's legs was false. "To my surprise, Dickens said: 'I do not know. I do not think I had identified the leg.' That was the only time I ever knew him to be at fault on a point of this kind, for as a rule he was ready to describe down to the minutest details the personal characteristics, and I might add, the life-history of the creations of his fancy." Further, as we have seen it to be with incident, so it was with character: Dickens did not hold "true to life" to mean "ordinary," "commonplace." He told Grace Greenwood that a kind of reverse law applied to many of his characters:

> . . . He said explicitly that the most fantastic and terrible of his characters were the most real--the "unnatural" were the natural--the "exaggerations" were just those strange growths, those actual human traits he had copied most faithfully from life.[115]

It was never enough to make a character merely believable; for Dickens *real* meant *distinct*, meant *individual*. In a letter to R. H. Mason he urged Mason to develop "interest" in the separate characters.

> . . . They come to nothing. The very circumstance of a Slave Dealer wanting to buy a slave, and his master refusing to sell him, is not enough. To make that dramatic (I don't mean in the Theatrical sense, but as a piece of art) the slave should be in doubt about his destiny, and the master should draw the Slave-Dealer out, by asking questions, as if he were undecided. Then, the landlord should have something about him, in his way of thinking and expressing himself, *like* a landlord, and a collector of curiosities. And the good-natured gambler ought to have something about *him*, expressive of *his* character and pursuits. It is not enough to say that they were this, or that. They must shew it for themselves, and have it in their grain.

Of the narrator in a story sent him he complained that "There is no individuality about M. Noel, no quaint touch of observation or imagination to single him out from the rest who have been doing literary duty these forty years."[116]

Individual touches, speech which separates one character from another, the avoidance of stereotype--these are the Dickensian specifics. Occasionally he gives us glimpses of how such touches came to him. Writing to Forster while *David Copperfield* was gestating, he asked,

> What should you think of this for a notion of a character? "Yes, that is very true: but now, *What's his Motive?*" I fancy I could make something like it into a kind of amusing and more innocent Pecksniff. "Well now, yes--no doubt that was a fine thing to do! But now, stop a moment, let us see--*What's his motive?*"

(The editors of Pilgrim Edition *Letters* point out that Mr. Wickfield often asks this question.) For some critics, such individual touches--at least as they became catchphrases, or made Dickens' characters into something like the old humours characters of drama--removed Dickensian figures from reality, instead of making them lifelike. Northrop Frye argues that Dickens' characters are not realistic: "there has grown up an assumption that, if we are to take Dickens seriously, we must emphasize the lifelikeness of his characters. . . ." But Dickens follows the humours practice of Plautus and Terence, Frye says, not the "customary form of Victorian seriousness--realism." Dickens' own comments on character indicate that he would not agree, but certainly his critical if not his popular reputation suffered as the taste for realism--for character which "conforms to the normal patterns and motivations of everyday life" grew in the third quarter of the nineteenth century. Kenneth Graham tells us how Dickens' characters were "criticized as 'speaking abstractions or animated machines,'"[117] criticisms which, considering his own strictures on the mechanical nature of characters in Will's story, must have been painful to him.

Perhaps the reason that Dickens' characters seemed

real to him yet abstract to others can best be explained by two things: the set of obligations to his reader we have examined, and his third meaning of the word *true*. We may take one more look at his prostitutes as an example of the first point. Dickens' prostitutes are always under attack as improbable--"the most unreal of his characters," Angus Wilson says. "Prostitutes in Dickens's fiction are not only not of the real world, but they are somehow not really even of his own strange world--they merely cross the stage, delicate-speaking allegories of Woman made Victim." Why is this so, in a novelist who counseled almost everyone who ever consulted him about writing to draw his characters "from the life"? Wilson's conclusion that "perhaps it is only an extreme example of the general denial of real humanity to young women,"[118] may have its share of truth, but I believe a better explanation is found both in Dickens' concern to protect his reader, which outweighed his need to create believable streetwalkers, and his conviction that truth was only to be conveyed by penetrating beyond mere surface reality, which could work to obfuscate it. How does one please, protect, and improve a reader by offering him a realistic, offensive, unrepentant whore? Other writers have found answers to such a question--not always good answers-- but Dickens did not; his principle that character should be drawn from life was subject to the (for him) higher principle of reader protection. Perhaps this was, as Engel posits, a curb on his art; certainly it cost him critical approval. Still, Nancy is remembered, while more lifelike prostitutes are forgotten, just because, perhaps, in her Dickens managed both to eschew seamy reality and yet, as he argued in his Preface, to offer something in her that touches a deeper reality, something that is "true."

But when a character could be made real and meaningful without danger to his reader, and with good aesthetic effect, he tried to make it so, and showed awareness of things which could damage its credibility. Certainly he would have agreed, for example, that there was a danger in building a character too completely around a single quality, however "real" the quality might be. Catchphrases, we have heard him admit to the Earl of Carlyle, were chancey. And he said that characters so dominated by a single quality that they approached stereotype were not realistic, and not good fiction. A play submitted to him by John Overs was "incurable," he said, because--among other things--

> the father is such a dolt, and the villain such a villain, the girl so especially credulous and the means used to deceive them so very slight and transparent, that the reader *cannot* sympathize with their distress. . . . The characters not being strongly marked (except in improbabilities) the dialogues grow tedious and wearisome. . . . I don't remember . . . any difference in the mode or matter of their speech which enables me to distinguish . . . one character from the other. . . .

But type, as distinguished from stereotype, could be useful: criticizing a story submitted for *All the Year Round*, Dickens advised Wilkie Collins' brother to give play to his humor and observation:

> As, for instance, by making the sister who writes to the Sailor, some recognizable type of woman. A wolfish kind of thing like the Italian, requires a Red Riding Hood, or a grandmother. I feel after reading the story, exactly as if it had been told me by somebody who couldn't tell it; and as if I had to fill in all the things to make it life-like, myself.[119]

Type is natural, and stereotype is artificial. The characters in Charlotte M. Yonge's *The Heir of Redclyffe* "are simply impossible" because "They have no types in nature, they never did have types in nature, and they never will have types in nature. . . ." Anything smacking of the artificial, the methodical, hurts: writing to Wilkie Collins about *No Name*, Dickens drew his attention to "the scene when Magdalen, in Mr. Pendril's presence and that of Frank's father (who is excellent), checks off the items of the position one by one. She strikes me as doing this in too business-like and clerkly a way." Character should be natural, familiar: one advantage to changing their plan for an opera from Italian to English locale, Dickens told his composer John Pyke Hullah, was that "the characters would act and talk like people we see and hear of every day. . . ." Like people we see every day, fictional characters should, says the creator of Rose Maylie, Nicholas Nickleby, Daniel Quilp, and Little Nell, be combinations of good and bad qualities: "I always seek, in drawing characters, for a mixture of Good and Evil, as the Almighty has created human character after that fashion."[120]   This was written in 1842, when, with *Martin Chuzzlewit* and later novels, Dickens was indeed moving away from allegorical figures of Virtue and Wickedness: perhaps his "always" was intended not to include past performance but to define present and future intentions. Earlier, his advice had concentrated not upon mixture, but upon making characters either attractive or repulsive to the reader.   "You cannot interest your readers in any character unless you have first made them hate, or like him," he told John Overs two years before the above letter.   Even later, though, Dickens was not opposed to unmixed wickedness in a character; he did, however, advise offering the reader something pleasant with which to swallow it.   He told Percy Fitzgerald that one of his characters "wants relief":

> It is a disagreeable character, as you mean it to be, and I should be afraid to do so much with him, if the case were mine, without taking the taste of him, here and there, out of the reader's mouth. It is remarkable that if you do not administer a disagreeable character carefully, the public have a decided tendency to think that the *story* is disagreeable, and not merely the fictitious person.

Dickens was right to think so: his own biographer and friend Forster objected that the wickedness of *Bleak House* was "too little relieved, and all-pervading." (Again, poor Dickens: for many readers of his own time he was either not real enough, or too real).   On several occasions in addition to the one already cited, he complained humorously that the readers least likely to believe in his characters were those upon whom he had based them. To Richard Lane, who had given him a description of a terrible parent, he wrote,

> if I were to put such a father as he into a book all the fathers going (and especially the bad ones) would hold up their hands and protest against the unnatural caricature. I find that a great many people (particularly those who might have sat for the character) consider, even Mr. Pecksniff, a grotesque impossibility.[121]

The advice to "administer a disagreeable character carefully" is a part of that conviction that the reader should be protected against the unpleasant which we saw in Dickens' comments on his relationship with his readers, but it is accompanied by the conviction that the reader will also not enjoy that in which he does not believe. Reading something about the Girondist Mme. Roland, Dickens said, "I derived, as I always do, great pleasure from that spiritual woman's society, and the charms of her brain and engaging conversation. I must confess that if she had only some more faults, only a few more passionate failings of any kind, I might love her better; but I am content to believe that the deficiency is in me, and not in her."[122] Chances are he believed no such thing, or he would have said nothing--but certain it is that he expected readers to find no such deficiency in themselves: "unmixed" characters could not help them accept that improbability inescapable in fiction.

An interesting feature of Dickens' own creation of character was his need for crowds. When he left England to write *Dombey and Son*, he wrote to Forster that the writing was going unusually slowly, the effect

> partly of the absence of streets and numbers of figures. I can't express how much I want these. It seems as if they supplied something to my brain, which it cannot bear, when busy, to lose.

> For a week or a fortnight I can write
> prodigiously in a retired place. . . . But the toil
> and labor of writing, day after day, without
> [crowds] is immense! . . . My figures seem
> disposed to stagnate without crowds about
> them.[123]

Dickens commented on the need to keep characters distinct from their creator, as well as from each other, especially when they narrated their own story. Neither character nor author should speak for the other. He wrote to George H. Lewes in admiration of his novel, *Ranthorpe*, but added that "the characters were, sometimes, not sufficiently distinct from each other, and that instead of your being metaphysical for them, they are a little too metaphysical for themselves." In several passages he demonstrated concern that characters in fiction should be offered, as Walter Phillips put it, "not as the marionettes of a show-master," which is precisely the image with which Thackeray closes *Vanity Fair*. Reviewing the manuscript of one writer, he said

> It strikes me that you constantly hurry your
> narrative (and yet without getting on) *by telling
> it, in a sort of impetuous breathless way, in your
> own person, when the people should tell it and act
> it for themselves.* My notion always is, that
> when I have made the people to play out the
> play, it is, as it were, their business to do it, and
> not mine.

And of the story submitted to *All the Year Round* by Charles Collins, he said, "there is too much of the narrator in it-- the narrator not being an actor. The result is, that I can not see the people, or the place, or believe in the fiction."[124] Again we see the play as standard for good fiction: dramatists do not--cannot--tell their own tales; the people in the play must do for themselves.

Except for such few comments, Dickens spoke hardly at all of such technical matters as point of view and narrative

voice.   Whatever the reason my be for his reticence in art
and other aesthetic areas, it must be obvious that here the
cause of his silence is not inability to speak.   The little he
did say is enough to show his awareness of and involvement
in the problems of narration.   Richard Stang mentions
"Dickens' insistence throughout his correspondence on the
need for impersonality in novel writing," calling it "Dickens'
canon of dramatic presentation."   Dickens did not dislike
first-person narrative, but he saw the obvious dangers in it.
One of these was that too much exposure to it produced a
negative effect.   Writing to Wills about material to be used
in *All the Year Round*, he urged him to "Keep articles which
will have the first person singular, inveterately, as wide
asunder as you can."   He carefully altered first- and third-
person voices in *Bleak House*, the only non-autobiographical
novel in which he used the first person at length.   And
first-person narrative, obviously, could also inhibit suspense:
speaking at a banquet in his honor at Liverpool he said,
"there is this objection, in writing fiction, to giving the
story an autobiographical form: that through whatever
dangers the narrator may pass, it is clear unfortunately to
the reader beforehand that he must come through them
somehow, else he could not have lived to tell the tale."[125]
Good point.
      But Dickens was also aware of the advantages of the
first person.   One of these was variety in a collection of
stories: of *A House to Let*, the Christmas Number for 1858,
he wrote, "I *think* I had best write the framework in the
first person. . . .   I will certainly avoid the plain third
person in which the stories will be narrated."   Forster
records that it was he who suggested first-person narration
to Dickens for *David Copperfield*, "by way of change," a
suggestion which Dickens took "at once very gravely"[126]--
thinking about more than change, surely.
      He advised writers about details of handling
information supplied by characters in the story: writing to
an author about something called "the Trenchard story," he
said,

      It is an old one, perfectly well known as a story.

> *You* cannot tell it on the first hand testimony of
> an eye-witness. You only tell about your daughter
> being disturbed in the night, which might happen
> anywhere. Again, "Mr. B. told me of a house."
> Mr. Any-letter-in-the-alphabet can tell you of a
> house. Does Mr. B. mean to say that he saw[127]

--saw, the letter continues, the action that went on in the
house, or did he take part in it? Similar concern for
probability of information supplied by the narrator is seen
in other letters.

As we have noted, Dickens found great difficulty in
developing character within a small space, a fact which does
much to explain his lack of success in short fiction. "The
narrow space within which it was necessary to confine these
Christmas Stories," he wrote in his Preface to the collected
edition of them,

> when they were originally published, rendered
> their construction a matter of some difficulty, and
> almost necessitated what is peculiar in their
> machinery. I never attempted great elaboration
> of detail in the working out of character within
> such limits, believing that it could not succeed.

This is hindsight, probably; whether Dickens was conscious
of the problem of space when he wrote the stories, or
whether he simply did not elaborate detail of character
because at that point in his career he did not care to, is a
matter of conjecture. But when he wrote the Preface,
obviously he was aware of the problem. We have already
heard him admit to the Earl of Carlisle that the temptation
to use shortcuts to individualize characters in short works "is
great."

Essential to Dickens' concept of fictional character was
identification. A good character not only came alive; he
became part of the reader. When Dickens read a narrative
by Lady De Lancey (the sister of his friend Basil Hall, who
sent it to him) of her experiences with her husband at
Waterloo, he wrote, "I am husband and wife, dead man and

living woman, Emma and General Dundas, doctor and bedstead--everything and everybody (but the Prussian officer--damn him) all in one. . . . I shall dream of it every now and then from this hour. . . ." Perhaps Dickens felt this so strongly because of his own conviction of the reality of his own characters, often to be identified with, always to be considered as existing entities. They so overwhelmed him that, as J. T. Fields reports,

> he said . . . that during the composition of his first stories he could never entirely dismiss the characters about whom he happened to be writing . . . that at midnight and in the morning, on the sea and on the land, Tiny Tim and Little Bob Crachit were ever tugging at his coat-sleeve, as if impatient for him to get back to his desk and continue the story of their lives.

Fields said that Dickens taught himself to shut his characters away when he shut his study door, "and only meet them again when he came back to resume his task." But Dickens' son Charley said that he often carried his task outside of the study:

> When he was writing one of his long stories and had become deeply interested in the working-out of his plot and the evolution of his characters, he lived, I am sure, two lives, one with us and one with his fictitious people, and I am equally certain that the children of his brain were much more real to him at times than we were. I have, often, and often, heard him complain that he *could not* get the people of his imagination to do what he wanted, and that they would insist on working out their histories in *their* way and not *his*. I can very well remember his describing their flocking around his table in the quiet hours of a summer morning when he was--an unusual circumstance with him--at work very early, each one of them claiming and demanding instant

personal attention.   And at such times he would
often fall to consider the matter in hand even
during his walks.   There was no mistaking the
silence into which he fell on such occasions.   It
was not the silence only of a pause in
conversation, but the silence of engrossing
thought, not, one felt, to be broken or lightly
interrupted.   Many a mile have I walked with him
thus--he striding along with his regular four-
mile-an-hour swing; his eyes looking straight
before him, his lips slightly working, as they
generally did when he sat thinking and writing;
almost unconscious of companionship, and keeping
half a pace or so ahead.   When he had worked out
what had come into his mind he would drop back
again into line--again, I am sure, almost
unconsciously--and the conversation would be
resumed, as if there had been no appreciable
break or interval at all.

Forster quotes G. H. Lewes as saying that "Dickens once
declared to me . . . that every word said by his characters
was distinctly *heard* by him. . . ." Forster himself says that

He had his own creations always by his side.   They
were living, speaking companions.   With them only
he was everywhere thoroughly identified.   He
laughed and wept with them; was as much elated
by their fun as cast down by their grief, and
brought to the consideration of them a belief in
their reality as well as in the influence they were
meant to exercise, which in every circumstance
sustained him.[128]

His daughter Mary supports this:

When my father was arranging and rehearsing his
readings from "Dombey," the death of "little Paul"
caused him such real anguish, the reading being so
difficult to him, that he told us he could only

master his intense emotion by keeping the picture of Plorn, well, strong and hearty, before his eyes.

Here is another fascinating instance of Dickens' use of fiction, as he relieves its pain by reference to reality, a reverse of the usual order. Leaving his characters as he finished a novel was like losing friends: Forster tells of "the suffering it gave" Dickens "to separate from the people who for twenty months had been a part of himself." When he finished *David Copperfield* he wrote in its Preface that "the Author feels as if he were dismissing some portion of himself into the shadowy world, where a crowd of the creatures of his brain are going forever." Often Dickens referred to his creations as "children," at times barely distinguishing between them and his physical offspring: "I am at Broadstairs with my various children--real and imaginary. . . ." Sometimes, Forster thought, the fictional offspring were too real: he felt that in *Bleak House* the characters "are much too real to be pleasant."[129] as opposed to earlier novels in which Dickens had, as we have heard him say, carefully controlled all realistic ugliness by the use of balancing humor. But in the end, perhaps even this great concession to the contentment of his readers was overcome by Dickens' feeling that, to reach his reader, especially perhaps to affect him with the message of his novels, he must use undiminished reality. Certainly, at least in characterization, reality--as he understood it--became one of the dominant forces in his aesthetic.

PRECIOUS UNDERSTANDING

The one more thing to remember about Dickens' concept of the writer-reader relationship is that which appears so tellingly in his use of illustrations and readings. Strong as was Dickens' desire to please, to protect, and to improve, the most powerful drive was the simple and insatiable urge to communicate his imagined reality. When the American pastor, G. D. Carrow, complimented him on his female characters, Dickens was understandably (since his women were so often criticized) surprised, and asked for an example of what

Carrow liked.   Carrow talked of the scene in which Esther
Summerson accepts a proposal of marriage from her guardian,
and Dickens responded, "I see you understand me!   I see you
understand me!   And that is more precious to an author than
fame or gold."   As much that we have seen demonstrates,
while Dickens was in the act of writing he lived what he
"saw," to the extent that he felt some part of himself to be
lost when he stopped writing.   He desired intensely not
merely to write, or even convey to his reader this imagined
actuality, but to share it with him, perhaps as a means of
saving it from the oblivion of the "shadowy world," certainly
as a way of benefiting the reader whom he loved.   Many
authors have expressed the frustration stemming from the
fact that, as James said in his *Notebooks*, "the whole of
everything is never told"; the dying Ippolit, in Dostoyevsky's
The Idiot, lamented that

> in every idea of genius or in every new human
> idea, or, more simply still, in every serious human
> idea born in anyone's brain, there is something
> that cannot possibly be conveyed to others, though
> you wrote volumes about it and spent thirty-five
> years in explaining your idea; something will
> always be left that will obstinately refuse to
> emerge from your head and that will remain with
> you forever; and you will die without having
> conveyed to anyone what is perhaps the most vital
> point of your idea.[130]

But if Dickens is merely expressing what many authors have
felt, he has demonstrated in his strict control over the
illustrations of his novels, and in his dramatic readings from
them--and again and again in his comments on his own
writing--that no author ever felt more powerfully the
compulsion fully to communicate what he meant.

We have suggested that Dickens was unRomantic in his
attitude toward the reader, but in one sense he was a
Romantic here, as he was so often elsewhere.   Passages in
his letters indicate as much of a "need to tell" the reader as
Rousseau ever possessed, though others convey what perhaps

appealed less to Rousseau, an equal need to listen. Three times in his correspondence Dickens mentions dreams about communication; in two of these he is like a reader who cannot understand what others would tell him, and in the third he is the writer who vents his subconscious frustration at not being able to make others understand. In the first letter, writing to William Russell, a doctor in attendance upon Douglas Jerrold at his death, he tells of a dream in which Jerrold "came and showed me a writing (but not in his hand) which he was pressingly anxious I should read for my own information, but I could not make out a word of it." In the second, he says, "I am in a strange country and want to read important notices on the walls and buildings, but they are all in an unknown character." In the third dream, Dickens displays his own problems with communicating:

> If I have been perplexed during the day in bringing out the incidents of a story as I wish, I find that I dream at night, never by any chance of the story itself, but perhaps of trying to shut a door that *will* fly open, or to screw something tight that *will* be let loose, or to drive a horse on some very important journey, who unaccountably becomes a dog and can't be urged along, or to find my way out of a series of chambers that appears to have no end. I sometimes think that the origin of all fable and allegory, the very first conception of such fictions, may be referable to this class of dreams.[131]

Fiction itself may have originated in the desire to enclose a thought, tie down an idea, travel in good order across the space between one mind and another.

We have seen the several stances Dickens has taken concerning the size of his audience: expressing his desire to reach as many readers as possible, confident at times that he could address almost all, fearing at times that many might not understand his art, telling Lewes that he would not italicize, but would leave the reader to understand or fail to do so, all on his own. But the preponderance of his comment falls on the side that favors being as clear as possible for his audience. "My view," he said, "has been to make transparent the design of my writings, and my belief is that by my readers generally I am perfectly understood." Sir Arthur Helps said that "He had a horror of being misunderstood, and grudged no labour to be 'understanded of the people.'" "The more we see of Life and its brevity," he wrote in 1853 to Macready, "and the World and its Varieties, the more we know that no exercise of our abilities in any Art, but the addressing it to the great ocean of humanity in which we are drops, and not to bye-ponds (very stagnant) here and there, ever can or ever will lay the foundation of an enduring retrospect.[132]

A FEAST OF HUMOR

It is predictable that the greatest English comic novelist had little to say about humor; one has to learn about its place in his aesthetic from his art, not his correspondence. That he strove for humor in almost everything he did hardly need be documented: when Forster complained that *A Tale of Two Cities* had not enough, Dickens wrote him that in his next novel, *Great Expectations*, "You will not have to complain of the want of humour as in the *TTC*." In his Prospectus for *Bentley's Miscellany* he declared that "The object of this work will be, to place before the public, once a month, a feast of the richest comic humour . . . provided by the ablest and merriest caterers of the age." And it is clear from several comments that he enjoyed his comic creations every bit as much as his readers. He told Forster, while writing *Dombey and Son*, that ". . . I seem to have such a preposterous sense of the ridiculous . . . as to be constantly requiring to restrain myself from launching into extravagances in the height of my enjoyment." And he said of the encounter between the major and a tax-collector in "Mrs. Lirriper" that "it has in it something--to me at all events--so extraordinarily droll, that though I have been reading it some hundred times in the course of the working, I have never been able to look at it with the least composure but have always roared in the most unblushing manner." When illness forced him to stay in his hotel room one night while on his last reading tour, he asked George Dolby to bring him one of his own novels to read, and was found a few hours later "laughing immoderately" over *The Old Curiosity Shop*; he explained that he laughed not so much at his own work as at the memory of the circumstances under which certain passages were written.[133]

On only one occasion that I have found did Dickens admit to having difficulty in creating humor. Asked by Wills to liven up an issue of *Household Words*, he answered, "I really can't *promise* to be comic. Indeed your note puts me out a little, for I had just sat down to begin, 'It will last my time.' I will shake my head a little, and see if I can shake a more comic substitute out of it." As editor, he sometimes found humor to be misplaced, and removed it, reporting on one occasion to Wills that he had "shorn" a contributor "of his humour. . . ." Butt and Tillotson report that when Dickens himself was "forced to lop and crop" a monthly number of one of his novels in order to reduce it to the required size, he was "accustomed to make his cuts at the expense of the comedy."[134]

The only comment I have found that suggests how Dickens thought humor should be used is the following, in which he sees it as a necessary balance for severity--just as, throughout his novels, he uses it as balance for tears: writing to Collins about his work on *No Name*, he urged that

> great care is needed not to tell the story too severely. In exact proportion as you play around it here and there, and mitigate the severity of your own sticking to it, you will enhance and intensify the power with which Magdalen holds on to her purpose. For this reason I should have given Mr. Pendril some touches of comicality, and should have generally lighted up the house with some such capital touches of whimsicality and humor as those with which you have irradiated the private theatricals.[135]

Of the methods of creating humor, of other uses to which it

should be put--of theory of humor, Dickens says nothing.

ALL WERY CAPITAL

Dickens' few comments on his own writing demonstrate more than a casual speculation about the nature of composition, especially as he himself engaged in that act. He said that he needed deep involvement in his subject before he could write "seriously": ". . . My composition is peculiar; I never can write with effect--especially in the serious way--until I have got my steam up, or in other words until I have become so excited with my subject that I cannot leave off. . . ." When he failed to meet a deadline for his monthly number of *Pickwick Papers*, he wrote to Chapman and Hall that ". . . You would scarcely believe how often I sit down to begin a number, and feeling unequal to the task, do what is far better than writing, under such circumstances--get up, and wait till I am." This was in 1836, at the very beginning of his career, when Dickens was supposed to have been god-like in his inventiveness. What it was that made him equal to the task at one time and unequal at another, Dickens knew no more than anyone does, but he believed that he could only write well when he was capable of feeling deeply. Replying to a query from G. H. Lewes about a passage in *Oliver Twist*, perhaps that in which Oliver, between waking and sleeping, dreams of Fagin and Sykes, and wakes to see them, he said,

> I scarcely know what answer I can give you. I suppose like most authors I look over what I write with exceeding pleasure and think (to use the words of the elder Mr. Weller) "in my innocence that it's all wery capital". I thought that passage a good one *when* I wrote it, certainly, and I felt it strongly (as I do almost every word I put on paper) *while* I wrote it, but how it came I can't tell. It came like all my other ideas, such as they are, ready made to the point of the pen--and down it went. Draw your own conclusion and hug the theory closely.[136]

COMPLETELY IN DIALOGUE

Our study of the Dickensian aesthetic must end by emphasizing once again what has been either overt or implicit in almost everything we have seen: Dickens' firmest conviction about art was that, before all else, it should be dramatic. ". . . Every writer of fiction," he said, ". . . writes, in effect, for the stage. . . ." To Dickens drama was not only a principle: it was the way his literature came into being. Had he speculated further, he might have found in it some answer to the kind of question Lewes asked him about how things came to him. ". . . No man," Forster wrote, "had ever so surprising a faculty as Dickens of becoming himself what he was representing; and of entering into mental phases and processes so absolutely, in conditions of life the most varied, as to reproduce them completely in dialogue without need of an explanatory word. . . ."[137] Little wonder that Dickens was such a success when he read from his novels: he had begun to practice such readings when he began to write the stories. Instead of being his characters, Henry James observed them; perhaps he could have acted them successfully, but he never felt called upon to try.

Yet in a way, James and Dickens agreed about the dramatic nature of the novel; the word *drama* and associated terms are to be found throughout the prefaces in which James explained his theory of fiction. If James did not become what he represented, still he desired to refine the narrator out of existence, leaving the characters on their own as in a play, not so much to be seen acting or heard speaking as in Dickens, but certainly to be seen and heard thinking, presented on a kind of thought-stage upon which we watch the minds of the characters acting and talking. If Dickens did not try to dispense with the narrator, he did, as we have seen, desire the author so to disappear from his fiction that the reader could feel as much in direct contact with the characters as he would with actors upon a stage. Like the drama of which Dickens approved, fiction needed to attract its readers by undertaking that which was new, picturesque, varied, active--interesting. As he understood the

theater, it failed when it did not do these things: its decline
in his time, he believed, was owing to its "persistence in
conventionality when all was changed around it; . . . a dull
grinding of its chariot wheel in the ruts of precedent. . . ."
The conventional was the enemy of both the play and the
novel (as well as of dramatic art); but though Dickens does
not say so, the tone of his commentary sometimes suggests
that the conventional can be fun for the reader who
understands it as kitsch, and may even become good art in
the hands of a writer who knows what to do with it. He
begins in "A Christmas Tree" to show how his favorite genre,
the ghost story, has been reduced to a few trite formulas,
with plots revolving around blood-stained planks in the floor
of a suicide's room, or doors that will not stay open or keep
shut, or haunted sounds from "a spinning-wheel, or a
hammer, or a footstep, or a cry, or a sigh, or a horse's
tramp, or the rattling of a chain"--or a clock that strikes
thirteen when someone is about to die, or a black carriage
waiting for someone--and so on for two more pages.[138]   The
interesting thing is that Dickens finds himself so amused by
the triteness of such stuff that he turns the last four items
on his list (which in itself is inventive in its seeking out and
humorously presenting so many clichés) into little one-
paragraph stories (the last of which consists of forty-eight
lines!), written not so much to show how bad fiction must be
when it depends on the trite as written because Dickens has
been caught up in the comic possibilities of the devices he is
listing.   One of Dickens' critical principles is certainly that
literature must shun the antidramatic dullness of the
conventional; but though he did not enunciate it, another
principle was that, with a little twist from the skilled writer,
the trite could become delightful.

Certainly Dickens was not afraid of employing some
rather conventional devices to arouse interest when he tried
to write drama.   Working with Wilkie Collins on *No
Thoroughfare*, he said,

I have a general idea which I hope will supply the
kind of interest we want.   Let us arrange to
culminate in a wintry flight and pursuit across the

Alps, under lonely circumstances, and against warnings. Let us get into all the horrors and dangers of such an adventure under the most terrific circumstances, either escaping from or trying to overtake (the latter, the latter, I think) some one, on escaping from or overtaking whom the love, prosperity, and Nemesis of the story depend. There we can get Ghostly interest, picturesque interest, breathless interest of time and circumstance, and force the design up to any powerful climax we please.[139]

The chase was not as overworked in 1878 as it is now, when every script writer except Woody Allen (and even he in *Manhattan*) finishes with one, but even then it was hardly new. The conventional is only dull in conventional hands, Dickens seems to feel.

The deeper aesthetic conviction, then, lay not in the material to be used but in the use to which it was put. Rarely trusting in the inherent appeal of a topic to hold the reader, he labored carefully to add interest to anything he worked on. He wrote to his subeditor about "The Doom of English Wills," which they had written together, that "I have endeavored to made it picturesque. . . ." As it was for the play, so the picturesque was a favorite attention-getter for fiction: part of Dickens' praise of Bulwer's *The Lost Tales of Millitus* was for its ability to present "as clear and vivid a picture as if I had looked in at the window. . . ." Variety was also helpful: the same work was praiseworthy for its "amazing variety and wealth. . . ." So was action: a contributor's story was good, but could be improved by "a little more stir and action. . . ."[140]

As editor he was always searching for unusual places and activities with which his writers could attract the reader. But again, he knew that the unusual could be found among the commonplace: in thinking about possible topics for George Augustus Sala, he suggested streets and locales in London where one could find "extraordinary men holding forth on Saturday night about Corn Plaister . . . the most extraordinary things sold, near Whitechapel workhouse--the strangest shows--and the wildest cheap Johns. . . ." His "A Preliminary Word" promised the unusual to readers: "giants, Slaves of the Lamp of Knowledge," in "all their wild, grotesque, and fanciful aspects. . ." but he also said he intended "to show to all, that in all familiar things, even in those which are repellant on the surface, there is Romance enough if we will find it out. . . ." It was the finding out, the eye for the aesthetic potential of the commonplace, even of the dull and trite, that was for Dickens the beginning of art.   Like all of us, he liked that which was different: "Novelty," he wrote in *Pictures from Italy*, "pleasant to most people, is particularly delightful, I think [sic] to me."   But the novelty the artist supplied should come primarily from his or her way of seeing and expressing.   Though he found some verses sent him by a Mrs. Price "very agreeable and womanly," he did not think them publishable because he did not discern in them "any novelty, either of thought or expression, that is likely to attract attention."[141]   He praised some qualities in another would-be poet, Samuel Newton, but wondered "Whether there is sufficient originality in the thoughts themselves, or in the form of their expression, to constitute you a Poet. . . ."   As editor, we remember, he seems to have worked on a sliding scale, the ends of which were interesting topic and interesting treatment: a piece deficient in one must compensate by increasing the percentage of the other.   Thus one paper was rejected because "Nothing can justify such a subject, but some exceedingly vigorous treatment of it--and this is in the last degree flat and poor."[142]

In *Sketches by Boz* Dickens said that the writer's hope of interesting the reader was "founded more upon the nature of the subject, than on any presumptuous confidence in our descriptive powers," but this early profession of reliance on raw material soon gave way to the preference for the artist's process of refinement.   The lesser writer depended largely on sensational material; the better one might also work with a subject of interest, but would not try to get by on that alone: his aim would be to gain acceptance by presenting it well.   That Dickens admired the accomplishing of the difficult, not the easy, is clear: he praised Edmund Yates's

"Land at Last" thus: "I cannot better express what I think of its execution than by saying honestly, that all the things in the book the most difficult to do, are the best done." He rejected a story on the grounds that "something more is wanted in such a narrative, than its literal truth--that it is the very nature of such truths as are treated here, to require to be told artistically, and with great discretion." Of another story he complained, "There is too much in it *about* the subject, and too little of the subject."[143]   Effective execution lent certain interest to writing, especially execution which could create vigor and arouse human feeling. As always, the key to the infusion of interest was the ability to arouse emotion.

The human heart is where Dickens' conception of literature began and ended. For him perhaps all writing, but most certainly fiction, should address the heart, should attract it, move it, teach it something about itself both through the power of seeing what is and the ability to imagine what could be. Literature should make the heart sensitive to the humanity he called tenderness. Like all artists he did not know how some things came to him; like many consummate writers he strove desperately to transcend human limitations in order to express them. But within these limitations, he knew with no iota of uncertainty how fiction was made: the artist used the tools of drama that could attract and move and teach more readers more effectively than any other method available to human skill. He needed to know little more than this.

Notes

Key: frequently-used sources are identified by the following abbreviations:

AN-*American Notes for General Circulation.* Eds. John S. Whitley and Arnold Goldman. Baltimore: Penguin Books, 1972.

AYR-*All the Year Round.* Ed. Charles Dickens.

BC-*Letters of Charles Dickens to the Baroness Burdett-Coutts.* Ed. Charles C. Osborne. London: John Murray, 1931.

BT-Butt, John, and Kathleen Tillotson. *Dickens at Work.* London: Methuen and Co., 1957.

C-Chesterton, G. K. *Charles Dickens.* New York: Schocken Books, 1965. First pub. 1906.

CP-*Collected Papers of Charles Dickens.* Eds. Arthur Waugh, Hugh Walpole, Walter Dexter, and Thomas Hatton. 2 vols. Bloomsbury: Nonesuch Press, 1932.

CS-Dickens, Charles. *Christmas Stories from "Household Words" and "All the Year Round."* London: Chapman and Hall, 1880.

D-*The Dickensian.*

DG-Dolby, George. *Charles Dickens as I Knew Him.* 1885. Repr. London: Everett & Company, 1912.

Diaries-*The Diaries of William Charles Macready.* Ed. William Toynbee. 2 vols. New York, London: Banjamin Blom, 1969. 1st pub. 1912.

DTR-*The Dickens Theatrical Reader.* Eds. Edgar and Eleanor Johnson. Boston: Little, Brown, 1964.

EW-Wilson, Edmund. "Dickens: the Two Scrooges," *The Wound and the Bow.* London: W. H. Allen, 1952. First pub. 1941.

F-Forster, John. *The Life of Charles Dickens.* Intro. by G. K. Chesterton. 2 vols. London: J. M. Dent; New York: E. P. Dutton, 1927. References are to book, chapter, and page, e.g. F:6 (book six), 2 (chapter 2), 226 (page 226).

FN-Frye, Northrop. "Dickens and the Comedy of Humor," *Experience in the Novel.* Ed. Roy Harvey Pierce. New

York and London: Columbia University Press, 1968. Pp. 49-81.

FW-*The Selected Letters of Charles Dickens.* Ed. F. W.
Dupee. New York: Farrar, Straus, and Cudahy, 1960.

GK-Graham, Kenneth. *English Criticism of the Novel, 1865-1900.* Oxford: Clarendon Press, 1965.

GP-Putnam, George. "Four Months with Charles Dickens,
during his First Visit to America (in 1842); By His
Secretary," *Atlantic Monthly*, 26 (1870), repr. IR.

HCD-Johnson, Edgar. *The Heart of Charles Dickens.* Boston:
Little, Brown and Company, 1952.

HD-Dickens, Charles. *A Child's History of England* in *Master
Humphrey's Clock and A Child's History of England.* Intro.
by Derek Hudson. London: Oxford University Press, 1958.

HH-House, Humphrey. *The Dickens World.* London: Oxford
University Press, 1941.

HW-*Household Words.* Ed. Charles Dickens.

IR-*Interviews and Recollections.* Ed. Philip Collins. 2 vols.
London: Macmillan, 1981.

JE-Johnson, Edgar. *Charles Dickens: His Tragedy and
Triumph.* 2 vols. New York: Simon and Schuster, 1952.

JR-Romano, John. *Dickens and Reality.* New York: Columbia
University Press, 1978.

K-Kent, Charles. *Charles Dickens as a Reader.* 1872. Repr.
New York: Haskell House Publishers, 1973.

KA-Kaplan, Fred. *Dickens: a Biography.* New York: William
Morrow, 1988.

L-Lehmann, R. C. *Charles Dickens as Editor.* New York:
Sturgis and Walter, 1912.

LC-*The Letters of Charles Dickens.* Eds. Georgiana Hogarth
and Mary Dickens. 2 vols. 1879.

LD-*The Letters of Charles Dickens.* Pilgrim Edition. Oxford:
Clarendon Press. 6 vols. V. 1, ed. Madeline House and
Graham Storey, 1965. V. 2, ed. Madeline House and
Graham Story, 1969. V. 3, ed. Madeline House, Graham
Storey, and Kathleen Tillotson, 1974. V. 4, ed. Kathleen
Tillotson, 1977. V. 5, eds. Graham Storey and K. J.
Fielding, 1981. V. 6, eds. Graham Storey, Kathleen
Tillotson, and Nina Burgiss, 1988.

LE-Lehr, Dolores. *Charles Dickens and the Arts.* Unpub.
doctoral dissertation, Temple University, 1979. University
Microfilm Reprints, Ann Arbor, Mich., 1979.

MD-Dickens, Mary. *My Father as I Recall Him.* London: the
Roxburge Press, 1896.

ME-Engel, Monroe, "Dickens on Art," *Modern Philology*, 53
(8/1955), 25-38.

MR-*Mr. and Mrs. Charles Dickens: His Letters to Her.* Ed.
Walter Dexter. London: Constable & CO., Ltd., 1935.

NL-*Nonesuch Letters.* The Collected Papers of Charles
Dickens. Ed. Arthur Waugh. 2 vols. Bloomsbury: the
Nonesuch Press, 1937.

P-Phillips, Walter C. *Dickens, Reade, and Collins: Sensation
Novelists.* 1919. Revised, New York: Russell and Russell,
Inc., 1962.

PC-*Charles Dickens: the Public Readings.*   Ed. Phillip Collins.
London: the Clarendon Press, 1975.

PD-*The Poems and Verses of Charles Dickens.* Ed. F. S.
Kitton. New York and London: Harper, 1903.

PI-Dickens, Charles. *Pictures from Italy. Pictures from Italy
and American Notes*, in *The Complete Works of Charles
Dickens.* V. 2. New York: Harper, n.d.

PP-*Charles Dickens: By Pen and Pencil, including Anecdotes
and Reminiscences Collected by his Friends and
Companions.* Ed. Frederic G. Kitton. 1890. Supplement,
1890; repr. in part in IR.

S-Storey, Gladys. *Dickens and Daughter.* London: Frederick
Muller, 1939.

SB-Dickens, Charles. *Sketches by Boz. The Works of
Charles Dickens.* Intro., Critical Comments, and Notes by
Andrew Lang, Charles Dickens the Younger, John Forster,
Adolphus William Ward, and others. New York: P. F.
Collier, 1911.

SD-*Speeches of Charles Dickens.* Ed. K. J. Fielding. Oxford:
Clarendon Press, 1960.

SH-Stone, Harry. *Uncollected Writings from Household
Words.* 2 vols. Bloomington: Indiana University Press,
1968.

ST-Stone, Harry. Dickens and the Invisible World.
Bloomington and London: Indiana University Press, 1979.

TN-Stang, Richard. *The Theory of the Novel in England:*
  1850-1870. New York: Columbia University Press; London:
  Routledge and Kegan Paul, 1959.
UT-*The Uncommercial Traveller,* in *The Uncommercial*
  Traveller and Reprinted Pieces, Etc. London: Oxford
  University Press, 1964.
WA-Wilson, Angus. *The World of Charles Dickens.* New
  York: The Viking Press, 1970.
WC-*Letters of Charles Dickens to Wilkie Collins.* Ed.
  Laurence Hutton. New York: Harper, 1892. Repr. New
  York: Kraus Reprint Co., 1969.
WE-Catherine Van Dyke, "A Talk with Charles Dickens's
  Office Boy, William Edrupt of London," *Bookman* (3/1921),
  repr. IR.

Chapter 1

Criticism: A Nervous Dread

1. "Dickens in Relation to Criticism," *Fortnightly Review*
   (2/72), repr. IR, I, 126. *The Dickens Aesthetic* (New
   York: AMS Press, 1989), 69-9. CP, I:65. "Address"
   announcing the new journal to be called *All the Year*
   Round, CP, II:3. SB, xviii.
2. CP, II:385.
3. LD, II (3/7/40), 38; (10/14/40), 135-36; (11/25/40),
   154.
4. LD, II (11/23/41), 426; V (11/7/47), 190; II (11/15/41),
   421.
5. NL, II (2/27/53), 449. LC, I (6/13/47), 206. LD, V
   (1/9/48), 227-28.
6. "Introduction" to *Art of the Novel,* p. xiii. JE, II:690.
7. TN, p. ix; p. xi; p. 11.
8. LD, V (6/17/48), 341: such status as it had, he
   occasionally suggested in his fiction, was unsavory: Mrs.
   Harris warns Mrs. Gamp to keep her distance from writers,
   for "litterary and artistickle society migh be the ruin of
   you before you was aware, with your best customers. . . ."
   F, VI:i, 8. WA, p. 105.

9. SD (1/27/52), 137. LC, I (4/14/55), 460. LD, V(11/7/47), 191.

10. *Cornhill Magazine* (9/26/46), reprinted in TN, p. 21, and CP, I:98.

11. SD (2/26/44), 54. F, XI:iii, 388. NL, III (9/25/58), 58: the statement was repeated with slight variations in his speech at the farewell dinner before his second trip to the United States: see SD (11/2/67), 371.

12. NL, III (4/10/63), 347. *Christmas Stories: The New Oxford Illustrated Dickens* (London, New York,Toronto: Oxford University Press, 1964), p. 62. "The Martyr Medium," AYR (4/4/63), reprinted in CP, II:38: the book was *Incidents in my Life*, by the spiritualist Daniel Douglas Home. NL, II (7/10/55), 678. Charles and Francis Brookfield, *Mrs. Brookfield and Her Circle* (1905), I, 137, repr. SD, p. 68.

13. LD, V (6/17/48), 341. "Preface" to *Evenings of a Working Man* (1844), repr. CP, I:29. F, XI:iii, 382.

14. LD, V (1/31/48), 241. SD (4/17/48), 93; (5/21/49), 95; pp. 178, 187.

15. SD, p. 176. HCD (3/23/51), 182. LC, I (12/25/50), 273.

16. SD (1/6/53), 156-57; (12/2/40), 5. F, XI:iii, 381; 382.

17. "Threatening Letter to Thomas Hood, from an Ancient Gentleman," *Hood's Magazine and Comic Miscellany* (5/44), reprinted in CP, I:25. CP, I:598: at the same time, Dickens could be more than a little courteous to the nobility: in several letters to the Duke of Devonshire about performances of *Not So Bad as We Seem* at Devonshire House, his politeness in place borders on the obsequious: see e.g. NL, II (6/1/51), 316, and (8/27/52), 378-79. "Insularities," HW (1/19/56), reprinted in CP, I:269. F, VI:vi, 86. SD, p. 98.

18. F, VIII:ii, 203. SD (4/29/58), 264. LC, I (2/28/55), 456.

19. LC, I (10/18/52), 335; (6/7/54), 417. NL, III (6/24/68), 655f.

Chapter 2

Journalism: Indispensable to Civilization

1. WA, p. 220: Wilson should have added "and to his subeditor, Wills," for many important comments are made there. P(hilip) Collins, "Keep HW Imaginative!" D, 52 (6/56), 117.
2. LD, II (8/24/41), 368. LC, I (1/31/52), 318. LD, IV (1/7/46), 466: the Pilgrim Edition editors say no such misinformation about Dickens is to be found in papers of the time. LD, IV (2/2/46), 487.
3. LC, II (4/19/66), 298, see also LD, V (12/2/47), 204. LD, V (12/29/47), 214: perhaps Dickens had in mind the first edition of the *Glasgow Chronicle*, which had an incomplete report. LD, V (12/30/47), 217.
4. HW (9/2/54), repr. CP, I:496-503. "Refreshments for Travellers," UT, pp. 52-53.
5. "Insularities,' HW (1/19/56), reprinted in CP, I:628. "The Tattlesnivel Bleater," HW (12/31/59); CP, II: 17-24.
6. AN, p. 136; p. 287. LC, II (4/1/68), 438: the dinner was on April 18, 1868; George Dolby says it was the "press-men of America" who, "under the presidency of Mr. Horace Greeley," gave him the banquet at Delmonico's: DG, p. 303.
7. SD (11/21/49), 102-104; (5/21/55), 192; (6/1/58), 273; (9/17/67), 366-67. PD, p. 100. SD (4/4/43), 38.
8. SD (5/20/62), 310; 309. SD (5/20/65), 345.
9. SD (5/20/62), 307-308.
10. NL, III (2/19/66/), 460.
11. LD, IV (3/1/44), 57; (6/10/44), 143; (1845), 460-61. SD (1/27/52), 136. LC, II (12/12/68), 466.
12. LD, III:577; III (8/13/43), 540: the theater topics in its August issue must have particularly appealed to him. LD, IV ((1/8/45), 246; II (10/21/41), 405; LD, V (5/3/49), 531.
13. IV (4/23/44), 110. "Perfect Felicity," HW (3/30/50), 36.
14. DTR, p. 11.
15. SD (5/20/65), 348, 348; (4/18/68), 379; p. 342. SH, p. 4. "Dickens' Editorial Method," *Studies in Philology*, 40 (1943), 79.

16. LC, II (6/10/68), 443. John Hatter, *Charles Dickens: The Story of His Life* (New York: Harper, 1870), 107.

17. LC, II (3/9/70), 505-506; (3/11/70), 506.

18. F, XI: iii, 383: curiously, Forster told William Macready "that no one could be a worse editor than Dickens . . ." (*Diaries*, II, 321) but this was said when things were going wrong with the *Daily News*, and doubtless does not reflect his overall opinion. "Dickens as Editor," *Contemporary Review*, 191 (2/1957), 89. F, XI: iii, 385.

19. LD, I (12/12?/36), 211. L (2/28/50), 23; (8/22/51), 67; (7/17/53), 107; (8/31/61), 285.

20. L (6/3/52), 79; (7/27/51), 61; (11/24/55), 188-89.

21. L (11/4/62), 313; (2/4/63), 327; (12/24/52), 93. NL, III (10/9/60), 182. LD, I (11/27?/36), 199.

22. NL, III (12/27/66), 494. L (9/26/57), 236.

23. L (1/8/59), 263; (5/3/59), 268-69.

24. LD, VI (3/29/50), 74. L (12?/2/50, 93: the story was "The Deaf Playmate's Story."

25. NL, III (5/26/53 to 10/19/63), 354 passim to 363. L (7/31/68), 388.

26. L (7/12/55), 166-67. NL, II (7/17/55), 679-80. L (7/22/55), 169.

27. NL II (5/30/57), 849-50; one has to think of Elizabeth Bowen, in "Notes on the Novel": "Nothing is in that does not tell."

28. NL, III (7/6/65), 430; (7/22/69), 731; (8/19/69), 738; (10/21/69), 747.

29. L (2/8/53), 98; (7/22/55), 168; 169.

30. NL, II (8/14/55), 684-85.

31. L (10/24/62), 311; (8/7/54), 136; (7/22/55), 169.

32. L (9/5/55), 171. *Mrs. Lynn-Linton* (1901), reprinted in IR:211: possibly this statement to one outside the editorial staff was owing to Miss Lynn's being a protegee of Landor. L (11/11/62), 315.

33. L (1/5/62), 303. NL, III (12/11/64), 406. L (8/5/53), 113.

34. NL III (8/3/60), 169; (1/23/61), 207; (5/12/61), 218-19; (5/16/61), 221.

35. NL, III (8/28/61), 231; (9/17/61), 236; (11/20/61), 255; (12/18/61), 268.

36. WC (10/14/55), 39-40; (12/12/55), 40. NL II (12/12/55), 714. LC, I (7/8/56), 525.
37. L (2/17/56), 213. HCD (12/9/56), 331; the piece was in HW (12/6/56). L (8/21/58), 244. WC (7/13/56), 56. BC (7/15/56), 168. L (9/24/58), 247; (4/11/59), 264. NL, III (11/14/60), 192.
38. *My Literary Life* (London: 1899), pp. 71-2.
39. LC, I (1/31/50), 250. LD, VI (1/31/50), 22; (2/9/50), 34.
40. L (2/28/50), 23. LD, VI (3/6/50), 55. L (12?/52), 93; (3/6/50), 24. LD, VI (2/27/50), 48; (3/14/50), 65. NL, II (7/3/50), 220.
41. LD, VI (10/6/50), 188. L (12/12/50), 42. LD, VI (12/17/50), 238. NL, I (12/20/50), 255.
42. LD, VI (8/21/50), 153. L (12/12/50), 42: (12/14/50), 43. LD, VI (12/4/51), 549; (3/9/52), 623. NL, II (11/6/52), 428. LC, I (12/17/52), 342; (12/1/52), 340.
43. L (9/25/55), 176. NL, II (4/13/53), 451: *Cranford* was published in nine numbers, from 12/13/51 to 5/21/52, with titles supplied by Dickens. Gaskell collected the sketches under the title *Cranford* in 1853; a tenth sketch, "The Cage at Cranford," was published in *All the Year Round* in 1863. NL, II (1/2/54), 531; (2/18/54), 542.
44. NL, II (6/16/54), 561-62; (6/16-17/ 54), 563.
45. NL, II (7/26/54), 571; (7/31/54), 573; (8/20/54), 582. JE II, 751. NL II (8/20/54), 582: Edwin Chadwick was a social reformer, and friend of Dickens; I do not know what connection he had with any of Gaskell's stories.
46. L (8/24/54), 145; (8/19/54), 141-42; (8/20/54), 142; (8/23/54), 144.
47. L (8/24/54), 145; (9/21/54), 146; (10/14/54), 155.
48. WC (3/24/55), 28. *The Letters of Mrs. Gaskell*, eds. J. A. V. Chapple and Arthur Pollard (Manchester: Manchester University Press, 1966), (1/55), p. 328.
49. Letters (see note 48) (12/17?/54), 323. LC, I (1/27/55), 446. "Dickens as Editor," *Contemp[orary Review*, 191 (2/1957), 90. *Letters* (see note 48) (12/23/59), 595.
50. Elizabeth Gaskell (London: Routeledge and Kegan Paul, 1979), 214-15. *Letters* (see note 48) (12/11/62), 699. NL, III 912/20/59), 139; (11/28/60), 193; (12/16/68), 688.
51. L (11/21/62), 318: for other earlier instances of

controversy which I have been forced by lack of space to
omit, see A. B. Hopkins, *Elizabeth Gaskell: Her Life and
Work* (London: John Lehmann, 1952), pp. 152-57. See also
Gaskell's letter of March 9, 1859, *Letters* (see note 48),
pp. 534-35, and Dickens' letter to her LC, I (12/5/51),
313-14.

52. LD, VI (2/22/50), 43.
53. LD, I (4/10?/37), 247.
54. LD, I (1/29/38), 362; (3/27/39), 534-35.
55. L (7/25/53), 109; (7/14?/15?/54), 132. NL, III (5/26/63),
354.
56. LD, I (12/2/37), 336; (11/21?/38), 458. L (7/11?/51), 58.
57. L (12?/52), 93. NL, II (9/22/50), 236. HCD (8/14/50),
172. 58. L (6/30/68), 385. LC, II (9/15/66), 305. NL, III
(11/19/59), 137; (10/1/69), 743.
59. L (11/?/52), 92. LC, II (4/1/67), 333-34: George
Barrington was an Irish pickpocket who was transported to
Australia, where he wrote Australian history.
60. LD, I (12.27/38), 476. L (10/7/52), 86. NL, II (1/21/50),
200.
61. L (12/20/63), 330. NL, III (9/2/69), 740; II (6/16/54),
561. LC, I (3/17/54), 411.
62. LD, I (3/14/39), 526; (5/37), 255; (12/27/38), 477.
63. LD, I (1838), 485; IV (1/30?/46), 483. NL, III (11/19/59),
137. L (7/12/55), 167.
64. LC, I (4/15/54), 414. NL, II (8/14/55), 684; (8/9/51),
336.
L (3/28/51), 50; (3/29/50), 26; (8/13/51), 65; (8/22/51), 67.
65. L (9/27/51), 70; (1/10/56), 205. NL, II (2/28/52), 380;
III (6/21/60), 165.
66. L (2/17/56), 213. LC, II (2/20/66), 292. NL, II
(7/21/52), 402. LD, I (10/22/38), 442; (11?/38), 464.

Chapter 3

Literary Judgments: Scratches in the Sand

1. Elias Bredsdorff, *Hans Christian Andersen": the Story of
his life and work, 1805-75* (New York: Scribner, 1975), 213.
2. F, IV:i, 275.

3. LD, I (8/31/38), 430; IV (3/25/44), 85. LD, VI (5/30/50), 108. "Night Walker," UT, p. 132: see also SD (6/25/41), 20; (5/17/64), 333.
4. NL, III (1/27/59), 90. F, VIII:iii, 210. PC, p. 154.
5. *A Child's History of England*, HD, p. 436. NL, II (10/23/52), 423. "The Great International Walking Match of February 29, 1868," CP, I:112.
6. SD (6/27/55), 201. See e.g. the allusions to the Old Testament in LD, VI (2/5/50), 29, and SD (2/14/66), 356. LC, II (12/13/58), 96; (10/25/64), 258; (5/28/63), 235; (10/15/68), 456. LC II (1868?), 467. WA, p. 207: for Dickens' use of the Bible in his fiction, see Dean James S. Stevens, "Dickens' Use of the English Bible," D, 21 (1/1925), 32-4; (4/1925), 93-95; (7/1925), 152-57; (10/1925), 214-18.
7. F, VII:v, 166. LC, I (7/5/56), 520. CP, I:416. LD, I (11/3/37), 328; II (3/16/41), 235.
8. LD, V (1/28/47), 20. SB, p. 419.
9. NL, II (6/13/55). LC, I (5/30/54), 416-17. *My Confidences* (1896), repr. IR, I:117. "Some Memories of Charles Dickens," *Atlantic Monthly*, 26 (1870), 238. Philip Collins, "George Russell's Recollections of Dickens," D (Autumn, 1982), 154.
10. LD, IV (10/6?/44), 199; V (3/29/49), 51.
11. LD, V (4/22/48), 289. PC, p. 154. LC, I (4/14/55), 460. LC I (12/26/51), 315; in *The Bastard*, (1728), Savage claimed noble parentage.
12. LD, II (4/21/41), 267. F, VI:iii, 57. SD (8/30/69), 397.
13. AN, p. 107. SH, p. 433. Grace Greenwood (Mrs. Sarah Jane Lippincott, nee Clarke), "Charles Dickens: Recollections of the Great Novelist," New York *Daily Tribune* (7/5/70), repr. IR, II:236. SD (5/2/53), 165.
14. NL, II (10/29/52), 423; (8/4/54), 575; III (10/6/69), 744; (10.24.69), 748.
15. F, II:vii, 125.
16. LD, I (1839), 576. Constance Cross, "Charles Dickens: A Memory," *New Liberal Review* (10/1901), repr. IR, II:345. LD, IV (8/3/44), 164; V (7/13/47), 128.
17. LD, V (3/30/47), 47; (late June, 1848?), 243: the story

became known as "The Tin Soldier." LD, V (6/4/49), 549. NL, II (9/2/57), 876: To Be or Not to Be, a novel, was dedicated to Dickens.

18. F, VII:v, 168. JE, II:612, and LD, V (1/27/47), 15. NL, III (3/2/58), 9. WA, p. 204.

19. My Confidences (1896), repr. IR, I:117. LD, I (1839), 576. HD, p. 416. SD (6/25/41), 12. F, II:ii, 84.

20. Boz Club Papers (1908), repr. IR, II:228. Philip Collins, "George Russell's Recollections of Dickens," D, (Autumn, 1982), 154. Examiner (9/2/38); quoted by K. J. Fielding in "A New Article by Dickens: Scott and his Publishers," D, XLVI (Summer, 1950), 127.

21. Letters and Private Papers, ed. Gordon N. Ray, II, 113; LD III, 492n. SD (3/29/58), 262-63. CP, I:98; 99-100.

22. S, p. 15. Constance Cross, "Charles Dickens: A Memory," New Liberal Review (10/1901), repr. IR, pp. 346-47.

23. Constance Cross, "Charles Dickens: A Memory," New Liberal Review (10/1901), repr. IR, II:347. F, IV:i, 275. NL, III (1/18/58), 3; 4.

24. FW (7/10/59), 253. NL, III (11/14/59), 136. L (5/26/61), 284.

25. LC, I (1/31/50), 250-51. F, VI:iv, 66; VII:ii, 123: the story was probably "Morton Hall."

26. LD, VI (12/20/52), 823-4. WC (10/31/61), 104; (7/22/54), 19: to Georgy, who with her sister Catherine had apparently formed a poor opinion of Collins' novel, he repeated his praise, word for word, preceded by the criticism that "Neither you nor Catherine did justice to Collins's book": LC, I (7/22/54), 420-21.

27. WC (1/7/59), 89; (7/29/60), 96; (1/24/62), 108-109; (9/20/62), 112-13; (10/14/62), 121; (11/1/63), 124.

28. WC (3/19/55), 25; (9/20/62), 113. See e.g. L (4/1/56), 218; and (9/16/56), 221.

29. LC, II (1/18/66), 288. LD, V (8/4/48), 383. SD (4/17/48), 93.

30. LD, III (7/31/42), 297; V (7/23/48), 376: the book was Final Memorial of Charles Lamb (1848), 2 vols. LD, III (10/13/42), 342-43: the book was probably Percival Keene (1842). LD, IV (8/20/46), 608.

31. LD, V (8/11/47), 148; (11/7/47), 190; (5/20/48), 312.
J. T. Fields, "Some Memories of Charles Dickens," *Atlantic Monthly*, 26 (1870).
32. LD, III (5/3/43), 481: one of the books was probably *Cakes and Ale*, 2 vols. (1842); the "opening paper" was "Elizabeth and Victoria" in the *Illuminated Magazine* (5/43). LD, IV (1/23/44), 28: the story referred to was published in the *New Monthly* (9-11/37). LD, IV (5/44), 120.
33. LD, IV (10/6?/44), 198; (5/26/46), 557: the story was printed in the *Illuminated Magazine* (1843-44), and published in 1866. LD, IV (6/29/45), 324; III (11/2/43), 591.
34. "Some Memories of Charles Dickens," *Atlantic Monthly* XXVI (1870), 240. WC (2/20/67), 138. LD, IV (7/5/46), 581; I (2/1 or 2?/39), 505 & n.3.
35. LD, V (7/11/47), 124. F, VI:1, 7.
36. F, VIII:vii, 252. LD, III (5/3/42), 232. HW (12/18/58), quoted by WC, pp. 621ff.
37. LD, V (4/14/48), 279; 4/18/48), 284; 4/22/48), 288-90; Carlyle also liked the book for being "picturesque"; the Pilgrim Edition *Letters* editors say that the italics in the book are "not obtrusively" used.
38. LC, I (4/14/55), 460; II (5/2/60), 131.
39. "Landor's Life," AYR, repr. CP, I:8, 49, 54-5.
40. LD, I (1838), 485. NL, II (5/8/52), 394. "Insularities," HW (1/19/56), repr. CP, I:628. LD, III (12/16/42), 395. LD III (11/10/43), 596. LD IV (1/2/44), 4.
41. MR (10/20/53), 188. LD, IV (1/2/44), 9; (4/13/44), 176; (6/4/44), 139.
42. LD, V (1/27/47), 16; (5/26/47), 72; (7/2/47), 111; (5/3/47), 64.
43. LD, II (12/30/40), 176; (3/5/41), 224: the editors of the Pilgrim Edition *Letters* say the last chapter is "movingly told"; the piece includes jesters and imitations of Shakespeare's clowns. LD, II (8/20/41), 362; 363.
44. LD, II (10/22/41), 407; III (7/15/43), 523; (7/24/43), 526; (8/3/43), 535; (9/5/43), 555; IV (3/21/44), 80.
45. LD, III (6/12/43), 500: the article was in *Quarterly Review*, 72 (5/43), 53-108. LD, I (12/23/38), 475; IV

(3/19/43), 78: syncretic as a philosophical term refers to emphasis on common beliefs underlying differences; a "Syncretic Society" had been formed in 1839, of which Horne was a member. His book defended unacted dramas, a concern of the Society. LD, V (7/1/49), 561; (8/12/49), 592.

46. LD, V (11/11/47), 194; (12/31/49), 687. LC, I (1/3/55), 445.

47. LD, V (6/18/49), 555: Cunningham had included passages from several poets describing places mentioned; the DNB says that all later works on London are indebted to Cunningham. SD (12/30/54), 175.

48. LD, V (9/23/49), 613: the "Letters" were published in *Blackwood's Magazine*, 65 (6/49), 679-96. F, XI:iii, 385. NL, (6/10/66), 474: the book may have been *Kissing the Rod*, *Land at Last*, or *Running the Gauntlet*, all published 1866 to 1867.

49. HCD (95//57), 347. NL, III (12/31/64), 408; (3/3/70), 765.

50. LC, II (11/6/65), 279: probably *Footprints on the Road* (1864), a collection of his essays from *Westminster Review*, Blackwood's, and HW. LC, II (2/2/66), 289: the book was *Charles Lamb: his Friends, his Haunts, and his Books* (1860). NL, III (8/9/58), 37. LC, II (8/13/66), 302.

51. LC, II (1/15/68), 394; (1/1/69), 474.

52. NL, III (2/3/60), 148: *Rocabella* was published in 1859, under the pseudonym Paul Bell.

53. NL, II (1/25/54), 537: the letters were published in *Russian of the South* in the sixth edition of the *Traveller's Library*. LD, II (4/17/41), 262: the *Examiner* favorably reviewed the pamphlet.

Chapter 4

The Practise of Literature: Unicorns and Griffins

1. LD, VI (1/31/50), 24. AN, p. 146. FW (7/8/57), 228.

2. TN, p. 19: if Dickens was not interested in the abstract,

he is not alone: Goethe is reported to have said, "I never thought about the meaning of meaning."

3. LD, VI (8/13/50), 146. "H.W.," HW (4/16/53), repr. SH, p. 468.
4. *Daily News* (1/22/46), copied in Dickens' letter, LD, IV (1/21/46), 477.
5. L (11/15/55), 185. LD, V (10/7/48), 420; (4/22/48), 288.
6. NL, III (5/12/61), 219. L (7/30/51), 64.
7. "Francis More in China," HW (10/14/54); L (9/25/54), 150. LD, IV:xxi.
8. LD, V (8/4/47), 211; (9/19/47), 165. HCD (7/11/56), 322.
9. WC (9/20/62), 113-14. LD, V (4/3/47), 52. NL, III (6/4/68), 652.
10. LC, I (7/27/51), 302. NL II (4/18/52), 387. L (1/2/62), 303. L (7/4/51), 56; (1/28/62), 307. NL, III (7/23/68), 659.
11. SH, p. 38. LC, II (2/20/66), 293. LD, II (2/7?/40), 19; V:561n. BT, p. 20.
12. S, p. 122. LD, IV (10/29?/44), 207; V (8/9/49), 590.
13. LD, V (8/26/49), 599-600. HD, p. ix. L (7/4/51), 56.
14. DG, p. 19. LD, IV (3/16/46), 521: most of his serialized novels begin in March, April, or May; none begins in the summer months; only *David Copperfield* begins in October.
15. James L. Hughes, *Dickens as an Educator* (New York: D. Appleton, 1901), 106. LD, I (6/16/40), 83. BT, pp. 35, 39, 53.
16. LD, V (3/24/47), 42. F, VI:vii, 108. 32. LC, II (1/9/57), 7: the association of hand and heart was repeated in a letter: ". . . Whatever the right hand finds to do must be done with the heart in it, and in a desperate earnest": F, I:iii, 45. F, V:v, 418.
17. F, VII:ii, 123. LC, I (7/5/56), 524. LC, II(6/11/61), 166. LC, II (3/29/64), 252.
18. F, IX:v, 293. F, IX:i, 273. LC, II (3/29/64), 252. Wolf Mankowitz, Dickens of London (New York: Macmillan, 1976), p. 116. SD (9/27/69), 406.
19. LC, II (2/11/68), 413-14. K, p. 22, pp. 243-44. IR, II:123.

20. SD (4/10/69), 388. NL, II (3/11/54), 546; III
    (1/16/61), 206; (8/25/58), 46.
21 LD, II (1/15/41), 186; VI (9/52), 767.
22. *Hogarth and the Dickens Circle* (1957), repr. Ir, I:120.
    Grace Greenwood (Sarah Jane Lippincott, nee Clarke),
    "Charles Dickens: Recollections of the Great Novelist," New
    York Daily News (7/5/70); IR, p. 234. *Yesterdays with
    Authors* (Boston, 1872), repr. IR, II:311. LD, III (9/16/42),
    325; (6/28/43), 516.
23. WE, repr. IR, I:194. LD, II (1/10/40), 5; III (11/10/43),
    595.
24. WE, repr. Ir, I:194. LD, I (6 or 7/39), 558. *Hogarth
    and the Dickens Circle* (1957), repr. IR, I:120. IR, I:123.
    DG, p. 272.
25. LD, II (3/9/40), 41; (4/12/40), 53; V (7/1/49), 561. F,
    XII:iii, 384.
26. F VIII:i, 184-85. L (2/18/53), 98.
27. C, pp. 118-19.
28. AN, p. 111: the chapter was number 4. LD, I (7/11/39),
    561. LC, II (2/20/66), 291, 293: the novel was published in
    weekly numbers.
29. F, IX:iii, 288-89. LD, I (4/7/39), 540. LD II (6/5/40),
    80.
30. See, e.g., p. 130. F, VI:vi, 91; ii, 23.
31. LD, V (12/17/49), 673. F, IX:ii, 281; see also LC, II
    (8/25/59), 115; I (11/1/54), 434.
32. LD, II:176n. F, II:iv, 99: slips was Dickens' word for
    the sheets of paper on which he wrote. LD, V (2/17/47),
    30.
33. F, IV:v, 339f; 338. LD, II (10/4/40), 132.
34. SH (2/21/51), 32. L (1/29/65), 341.
35. SH, p. 30. L (4/13/51), 52.
36. WC (10/9/56), 61. LD, III (9/14/42), 323; II
    (11/6/41), 418; V (1/2/49), 466: twilight refers to the
    description in Chapter 1 of The Haunted Man which is in
    preparation for the appearance of Redlaw's ghostly double.
    To the description of Dickens' process here compare James:
    "The artist's pleasure dwells less, surely, in [what] he can
    smuggle in than in [what] he succeeds in keeping out."
    Art of the Novel, p. 312. SH, p. 30.

37. LD, I (1837-38?) 485-86.

38. F, VII:v, 166. LC, II (2/20/66), 291. S, p. 77.

39. *Dickens and the Trials of the Imagination* (Cambridge, Mass., and London, England: Harvard University Press, 1974), p. 225.

40. SH, P. 33.

41. LD, VI (2/8/50), 32; I (4/25/44), 587.

42. "A Clause for the New Reform Bill," HW (10/9/58); SH, p. 591. LD, V (9/19/47), 165; F, VI:1, 467.

43. LD, V (8/18/48), 394: the riddle was mentioned in *David Copperfield*.

44. LD, V (1/2/49), 466. L (8/5/53), 113; (8/21/58), 244; (3/10/53), 101. WC (1/27/70), 165.

45. *Dickens and the Trials of the Imagination* (Cambridge, Mass., and London, England: Harvard University Press, 1974), p.56. "Our Bore," UT, p. 581ff. "A Few Conventionalities III," HW, IV:313-14: see also "Our Honorable Friend," HW, V:453.

46. LD, III (5/3/43), 482; (5/10/43), 484-85; IV (11/28/44), 232. LC, I (9/7/51), 305. "The Best Authority," HW (6/20/57), repr. CP, I:682. PI, p. 6. SB, p. 258. "Characters--Making a Night of It," SB, p. 258. AN, p. 107.

47. LD, II, 126-27n4. BT, p. 23. HCD, p. 168. F, II:vii, 123. LD, II (3/26/41), 243.

48. LD, II (6/3/41), 294; IV (3/15?/44), 73: the scene has not been identified; the Pilgrim Edition *Letters* editors guess at something in either Chapter 43 or 52, dealing with Pecksniff. LD, IV (11/1-2?/44), 209: (8/7/46), 599: Forster counseled keeping Chapter 4 in the first number. LD, IV (8/13 & 14/46), 602; (10/3/46), 628-29.

49. LD, IV (10/18/46), 637-38; (10/31/46), 650; (11/4/46), 652; (11/7/46), 654; (11/13/46), 656; (11/21/46), 658.

50. LD, V (11/19/47), 197; (12/21/47), 211; (3/25/48), 264.

51. LD, V (12/14/48), 451. F, VI:iii, 503. LD, V (8/22/49), 598.

52. L (3/12/50), 25; (7/12/50), 30; (8/24/54), 145. Diaries, II, 316; partially quoted in LD, IV:457n5.

53. Some recent critics would certainly object to the idea that in his early novels Dickens was "feeling his way":

Garrett Stewart, for example, argues that Dickens is as
accomplished an artist in *Pickwick Papers* as he is
anywhere; see *Dickens and the Trials of the Imagination*,
Ch. 1. F, VI, ii, 27.

54. LD, II (4/5/41), 253: the editors of Pilgrim Edition
Letters add that "Dickens's growing awareness that while
writing he was often a poor judge of what was 'too strong'
is illustrated in Kathleen Tillotson's analysis of the
'consistent and progressive curbing of over-emphatic
expression in his revision of *Oliver*'"; see above note, and
Oliver Twist, ed. Kathleen Tillotson (Oxford: Clarendon
Press, 1966), pp. xxxi, xxxii, xxxvi. LD, IV (11/13/46),
656.

57. DG, p. 389.

Chapter 5

The Idea of Literature: Hug the Theory

1. Essays in Dickens (1970), ed. Michael Slater, p. 219.
ME, p. 29.
2. WA, p. 148. See, e.g., TN, pp. 19, 23, but see also FN,
pp. 79-80. ST, p. 26. HW (3/19/53), repr. SH, p. 459.
3. "Bound for the Great Salt Lake," UT, p. 222. "The Noble
Savage," UT, pp. 467 see also 472. "The Lost Arctic
Voyagers,   Part I," HW, 10 (1854-5), 361-5. WA, p. 234.
4. UT, p. 387. See Lettis, *The Dickens Aesthetic* (New
York: AMS Press, 1989), pp. 201-2. LD, II (2/23/41), 218.
AN, p. 118.   See for example AN, pp. 221ff.
5. HH, p. 194. PK, pp. 126, 130. F, V:ii, 387. LD, I
(7/25/39), 568. SD, p. 24.
6. LD, II:90-91; III (5/3/43), 102. LC, I (16/10/44), 140.
LD, IV (11/1-2?/44), 209; (8/9 & 10)/46), 601: many
passages in *A Child's History of England* express the same
sentiment, e. g. HD, p. 153.
7. PD, p. 97. AN, p. 101.
8. *The Village Coquettes* (1836), repr. CP, II:124.
9. HH, p. 19. F, VIII:ii, 198. LC, II (9/14/60), 144.
Hood's Magazine and Comic Miscellany (5/44), repr. CP,
I:23. FW (2/10/55), 209.

10. P, p. 124. ST, p. 57. "When We Stopped Growing," HW
    (1/1/53), repr. CP, I:416. F, I:i, 12. HW (1/1/59)), repr.
    CP, I:709.
11. "Doctor Dulcamara, M. P.," HW (12/18/50), repr. SH, p.
    622. "Home for the Homeless Women," HW (4/23/53), repr.
    CP, I:432. LD, V (12/1/48), 451.
12. LD, V (10/20/49), 628. PI, p. 50. SD (6/25/41), 10.
    HW, No. 1 (3/30/50), 49.
13. SD (2/28/44), 64. DG, p. 18. LC, I (7/5/56), 520. NL,
    II:768, 550.
14. HH, p. 111. WC (9/9/67), 145. F, IX:i, 278. LD, II
    (3/16/41), 236.
15. Quoted in a review of *The Sense of an Audience*, by
    Janice Carlyle (Athens: University of Georgia Press, 1981)
    in D, 79 (1983), 167. "The Perfect Audience," New York
    Times Book Review (3/28/82), 39. Robert Garis, "Dickens
    Criticism," *Victorian Studies*, 7 (1964), 95: the most famous
    damning of Dickens with the faint praise of popularity is
    probably Leslie Stephen's statement in the DNB that if
    popularity made one great, then Dickens was a great
    novelist, the implication being that it did not, and he was
    not. ME, p. 26.
16. HW, I:49. BT, p. 13; p. 16.
17. Not all of his friends agreed that he could write for
    everybody. When *Master Humphrey's Clock* ran into some
    trouble, the actor Macready wondered "whether or no it
    was too good for so wide a circulation": *Diaries*, II
    (4/9/40), 56. HD, p. 5. WA, p. 12. HW, I (3/30/50), 1.
18. LD, V (6/17/48), 341. F, IX:viii, 315-16. FW (11/3/51),
    191: see also LD, V (12/1/48), 452, and (12/22/49), 677.
19. SD, p. xxii; p. xxiv. WA, p. 261. HW (10/4/51), repr.
    SH, p. 344.
20. SD (4/29/58), 264; (2/1/42), 21. "To the Readers of
    Master Humphrey's Clock,'" notice in 10/41 issue of *Master
    Humphrey's Clock*, repr. BT, p. 88. DG, p. 20.
21. K, p. 93. DG, p. 36; p. 249. L (3/13/52), 78: a story
    revealing the other side of the coin is told by William
    Howard Russell. Dickens was invited to a shooting party,
    but his note declining the invitation did not reach the
    hostess until the party was about to begin. At once she

called to the cook, "Martin, don't roast the ortolans; Mr.
Dickens isn't coming." Thackeray, who was present, "never
felt so small," according to Russell. "There's a test of
popularity for you! No ortolans for Pendennis": LD, VI,
642n.1.

22. SD (6/25/41), 9. HCD (8/23/58), 362-3. SD (2/1/42), 21.
23. HW, I:1. HCD (4/8/60), 370. LD, I (7/14/39), 563-64.
    SH, p. 20.
24. LD, V (9/19/47), 165. BT, p. 23. L (12/25/67), 375:
    as a public reader of his own novels, Dickens felt the same
    sense of obligation; George Dolby tells us that he "held it
    as a maxim that 'No man had a right to break an
    engagement with the public if he were able to be out of
    bed'" DG, p. 227.
25. BT, p. 170.
26. "The Amusements of the People, II" HW (4/13/50), repr.
    DTR, p. 247. JE, I:304.
27. NL, III (5/29/58), 24: in SB (p. 80), Dickens said that
    "the autobiography of a broken-down hackney-coach, would
    surely be as amusing as the autobiography of a broken
    down [sic] hackneyed dramatist. . . ." "An American in
    Europe," *Examiner* (7/21), repr. CP, I:207.
28. L (3/10/53), 101. HCD (8/22/51), 185. L (5/30/54),
    128.
29. NL, III (7/10/67), 536. LC, II (4/1/67), 373. SB, pp.
    177, 178. L (10/13/52), 89.
30. "The Martyr Medium," AYR (4/4/63), repr. CP, I:42.
    "Landor's Life," AYR (7/24/69), repr. CP, II:55. HW, II:99:
    see also NL, II (9/16/50), 233. L (12/29/52), 95.
31. TN, p. 196. *University* (Princeton, N.J.: Winter,
    1965-66), quoted in D, 63 (1967), 329.
32. L (7/22/55), 168.
33. L (2/8/53), 98: to Forster Dickens wrote, probably about
    this article, "I am not sure whether I could have prevailed
    upon myself to present a large audience the terrible
    consideration of hereditary madness, when it was
    reasonably probable that there must be many--or some--
    among them whom it would awfully, because personally,
    address": F, XI:iii, 384. L (10/2/58), 248. LC, II (8/3/69),
    494. L (8/14/50), 33.

34. HCD (2/4/50), 165. NL, II (2/28/53), 449. LD, II (12/30/40), 177.
35. WC (2/20/67), 138; 139. LD, I (12/29/38), 48. LC, II (2/20/66), 292.
36. DS, p. 156. BT, p. 48.
37. "An Enlightened Clergyman," AYR (3/8.62), repr. CP, II:30-31. "Frauds on the Fairies," HW, VIII:97. "Stores for the First of April," HW (3/7/57), repr. CP, I:678.
38. DTR, p. 247. UT, p. 342. SH, p. 625. LD, IV (1/29/44), 35.
39. (New York: Penguin, 1955), tr. David Magarshack, p. 433. SD (2/1/42), 19-20. WC (8/23/67), 144. LE, p. 103. NL, II (8/15/56), 797: Thackeray makes much the same comment in places in *Pendennis*.
40. *Metropolitan Magazine* (3/41), repr. LD, II:xi. S, pp. 113-14. LD, III (10/15/42), 345. TN, p. 26: see e.g. "The Sensational Williams," AYR, 11 (2/13/64), 14-15, and "The Spirit of Fiction," AYR, 18 (7/27/67), 119.
41. TN, p. 199; p. 198. F, IX:viii, 313.
42. LD, I (7/25/39), 567-68. BT, p. 72.
43. ME, p. 28. "The Historical Perspective," *The Arts in a Permissive Society*, ed. Christopher Macy (London: Rationalist Press Association, 1971), p. 33. NL, III (1/24/62), 282; (1/21/70), 761.
44. L (10/12/52), 87. NL, III (12/18/61), 268; (1/7/60), 145: see also NL, III (11/20/61), 255, and SD (1/6/53), 158.
45. Faulkner, Peter, p. 31. FW, p. xiii. Philip Collins, "George Russell's Recollections of Dickens," D (Autumn, 1982), 153: Collins, however, suggests there is little evidence for the intimacy Russell claimed.
46. NL, III (7/29/62), 301. LD, III (5/16/42), 238.
47. NL, III (8/5/63), 359. FW, p. xiii. LD, V (9/22?/49), 610. My Confidences (1896), repr. IR, I:117. NL, III (3/16/58), 12.
48. LD, V (11/1 or 2?/45), 423. WA, p. 24: as we have seen, the similarity extends to Scheherezade's performing before an audience: Kathleen Tillotson says that the serial form of publication gave Dickens "something of the stimulating contact which an actor or a public speaker receives from an audience. Serial publication gives back to

story-telling its original context of performance. . . .":
Novels of the 1840's (Oxford, 1954), 36.

49. F, VIII:ii, 193. JE, II:304. HH, p. 50. LD, III
    (7/25-26/46), 593: to be fair to Dickens, the decision to
    keep Walter a hero seems to have been made on aesthetic
    grounds, as well as for consideration of the reader: see
    e.g. his letter to Forster: LD, IV (11/22 & 23/46), 658.
    Perhaps a clearer example of change made for the reader is
    the well-known instance in Great Expectations. When
    another ur-sales researcher, Bulwer, advised Dickens that a
    change in the ending of the novel would make it more
    appealing to lovers of romance, Dickens promptly changed
    it. WA, p. 180. "A Chat about My Father," *Harper's
    Magazine*, 129 (1914), repr. IR, I:159.

50. LD, III (11/2/43), 590: Dickens had decided to live
    abroad and not write anything else for a year. SD
    (10/5/43), 49. LD, I (6/9?/38), 404.

51. C, p. 106. SD (1/6/53), 158. L (5/20/64), 335. NL,
    III (3/9/60), 152.

52. L (12/6/67), 372. HCD (11/3/61), 372. LC, II (2/24/68),
    419.

53. LD, V (10/7/49), 622. LC, I (5/1/42), 83. SD, p. 166.

54. HCD, p. 250n.: the readings were given 12/27, 29,
    30/51. L (1/28/66), 349.

55. LC, II (8/3/57), 27. "The Spirit of Chivalry," *Douglas
    Jerrold's Shilling Magazine* (8/45), repr. CP, I:35. "Some
    Accounts of an Extraordinary Traveler," HW (4/20/50), 271.

56. LC,I (3/22/42), 73; II (4/4/69), 487. LD, IV (4/3/44), 95.

57. "The Amusements of the People, II, " HW (4/13/50),
    repr. DTR, p. 244.

58. F, IX:viii, 313. Quoted by Harry Stone in "Charles
    Dickens and Harriet Beecher Stowe," *Nineteenth-Century
    Fiction* 12:3 (12/1957), 196-97. "Curious Misprint in the
    Edinburgh Review," HW, 16:97.

59. LD, III (11/12/42), 366; V (10/7/49), 622; (4/25/49),
    527.

60. 97 (1931), repr. IR, II:240. SD (3/14/42), 34. IR, I:44.
    LD, I (7/14/39), 563-64; III (5/26/43), 497.

61. ME, p. 28. SH, p. 64; p. 343. SD (6/25/41), 9-10. F,
    II:vii, 124: the passage is reminiscent of the benefits

Wordsworth claims from nature in "Tintern Abbey." SD
(12/4/58), 286; (12/2/40), 4.

62. DTR, p. 239. AN, pp. 117-18. WA, p. 216.

63. LD, I (4/19/39), 544.

64. See e. g. fairy tales in HW XI, beginning on pp. 49 and
265. *Yesterday with Authors* (Boston, 1872), repr. IR,
II:313. BC, (3/5/57), 181. LD, V (11/6/49), 640: Mary
Tayler had called the show "the game of murder and
profligacy. Satan seemed to possess the Master spirit."

65. SD (6/1/58), 274. DTR, p. 243.

66. SD (4/6/64), 324. ST, p. 3. NL, III (4/17/67), 523. SD
(12/22/55), 209. LC, I (12/12/38), 17-18.

67. Critics differ about the existence of Mercy. SH, p. 5.
SD (4/6/57), 230. AN, p. 238. L (7/27/53),
110. LC, II (4/14/58), 54. F, IV:ii, 301.

68. LC, I (2/21/51), 286. ST, p. 25; p. 38. CP. I:269.

69. DTR, p. 8. EW, p. 7. F, I:ii, 25.

70. "Frauds on the Fairies," HW, 8:97. SH, p. 60; p. 10;
p. 34. Percy Fitzgerald, Memories of Charles Dickens,
repr. SH, p. 34. SH, p. 182.

71. HW (4/16/53), repr. SH, p. 470. LD, VI (9/22/50), 177;
(6/2/52), 689. L, p. 65; (10/9/51), 73.

72. L (12/8/51), 75; (10/17/51), 74.

73. F, IX:i, 273: in Pope it is "self-love to urge, and
reason to restrain." HW (1850), repr. SH, p. 13.
"Address," (5/28/59), repr. CP, I:225, and SH, p. 26.

74. LD, V (10/7/49), 623. F, IX:viii, 312. SD (9/27/69),
406.

75. ST, p. 3. "The English Dickens and *Dombey and Son*,"
Dickens Centennial Essays, eds. Ada Nisbet and Blake
Nevius (Berkeley, Los Angeles, London: University of
California Press, 1971), p. 2. NL, II (9/7/52), 415.

76. FN, p. 81: for a summary of contemporary comments on
imagination and realism in Dickens, see GK, pp. 34-5. FN,
pp. 67-68; p. 49. C, p. 127. TN, p. 156. F, IX:i, 279. NL,
III (1/18/59), 88. LD, IV (3/18/44), 75.

77. LD, III (7/15/42), 271; V (7/28/48), 378. DG, p. 18. AN,
p. 53; p. 56.

78. AN, p. 62; p. 226; pp. 237-38.

79. F, IX:i, 272; LD, II (10?/41), 410: it is interesting

that, in view of this powerful sense of the real in the imagined world, which Lewes considered the effect of halucination ["Dickens in Relation to Criticism," *Fortnightly Review* (February 1872), see LD, II:410n1], Dickens seems not to have believed in visions. Throughout *A Child's History of England* he discredits visions, giving rational explanations for the voices Joan of Arc heard (she spent much time alone, kneeling for hours in gloomy churches, staring at altars; see Dickens' comment on solitude producing imaginative vision in *Robinson Crusoe*, below; also, she was a "moping, fanciful girl," and probably "a little vain, and wishful for noteriety.") Dickens would seem to have wished to keep vision out of history, and save it for literature; perhaps, too, his strong bias against Catholicism was a cause of his rejecting Joan's vision. ST, p. 48. PP, p. 181. CP, I:710.

80. "Characters--The Parlour Orator," SB, pp. 227-28.

81. SD (4/6/57), 230: Tom Thumb was Charles Stratton, Barnum's midget, known as General Tom Thumb. SD (12/3/58), 284. BC (9/6/50), 103.

82. LD, III (9/1/43), 550: psychologists have learned that no one dreams of what he or sees on television, perhaps for the reason Dickens gives. LD, V (1/18/47), 9; IV (10/29?/44), 207.

83. S, p. 93. LD, III (2?/43), 441.

84. The Dickens Aesthetic, p. 197. LD, V (1/27/47), 13. AN, p. 153. LC, I (7/11/51), 296. CP, I:419.

85. SH, p. 59. "Nurse's Stories," UT, p. 149. F, VIII:ii, 194; 196. L (6/6/67Z), 358. AN, p. 259.

86. TN, p. 155. LD, V (7/11/49), 570. TN, pp. 23-28. Letter to Forster (Victoria and Albert Museum), quoted by ST, p. 52.

87. *Christmas Stories, The New Oxford Illustrated Dickens* (London, New, York, Toronto: Oxford University Press, 1964,) pp. 29-39. CP, I:564. ST, p. 62.

88. Kathleen Tillotson has located the story Dickens had in mind: see "Steerforth's Old Nursery Tale," D, 79 (Spring 1983), 31-34. A modern version of the story may be found in Maurice Sendak's "Pierre."

89. WA, p. 14. See *The Dickens Aesthetic*, pp. 72-8.

90. LD, I (4/19/39), 544; V:466: the chemist is Redlaw, and the dark shadow is his doppelganger.
91. F, IX:viii, 313. BT, p. 20. LD, IV (8/30/46), 612.
92. F, VIII:i, 182; IX:1, 272; v, 293.
93. JR, p. 106.
94. "The Seven Poor Travellers," extra Christmas Number of HW for 1854, quoted in SH, p. 469. F, VII:i, 121.
95. SD (2/6/50), 107-109. The Old Curiosity Shop, Ch. 1. JR, p. 113.
96. LD, I (7/37), 289: apparently Clarke had offered further information for Dickens' use; another motive for Dickens' refusal here was, as the letter suggests, his fear that after his death it might be claimed that he was not the "sole author" of *Pickwick Papers*. LD, II (6/3/41), 296: Dickens repeated the remark to John Cay (7/21/41), 337. LD, II (11/17/41), 423. FN, p. 67.
97. WA, p. 27. UT, p. 77: see also his comment on Nicholas Nickleby, quoted earlier, in LD, I (12/29/38), 481. "The Household Narrative," HW, I:49.
98. "North American Slavery," HW (9/18/52).
99. LD, III (1/31/42), 43; (11/1/43), 587; V (12/47), 205. See e.g. NL, II (3/20/51), 283; (4/28/51), 303; (1/10/60), 146; (9/29/61), 241. LD, V (10/7/49), 622.
100. L (9/24/58), 247. NL, III (1/21/64), 378. ME, p. 48.
101. ME, p. 30. *Examiner* (2/9/48), repr. CP, I:178-81. WA, p. 29. NL, II (2/1/50), 203.
102. AN, p. 289. F, VIII:ii, 200. "Charles Dickens, A Memory," *New Liberal Review* (October, 1901), repr. IR, II:348: note this is the opposite of Frye's assessment, above.
103. "A Clause for the New Reform Bill," probably by Dickens, HW 10/9/58); SH, p. 588.
104. Letter to Collins about "A House to Let," Christmas Number for HW, 1858, quoted in SH, p. 588; the statement was to be the theme of the proposed story.
105. HD, p. 109. SD, p. xxiii. LD, V (1/2/49), 466.
106. F, II:iii, 89' III:ii, 185. WC (12/25/67), 158. LD, V (9/6/47), 160; the *Westminster Review* rejected Dickens' defense of *Our Mutual Friend*, on the grounds that it was true to life, with a similar argument: ". . . How does that

affect the matter? Truth is not always probable. And it is probability which is required in a novel." GK, p. 45. But Dickens of course sees "grace," not probability, as the test of good fiction.

107. F, VII:v, 175. NL, II (2/7/53), 446-47. F, IX:ii, 282.
108. LD, IV (11/12/44), 217. HCD (11/16-17/54), 279.
109. LD, V (11/27/48), 448.
110. J. T. Fields, "Some Memories of Charles Dickens," *Atlantic Monthly*, 26 (1870), 238.
111. IR, I:47. P, p. 132. TN, p. 100. F, VI:iii, 57.
112. F, IX:v, 295; IX:ii, 282; IX:i, 281; V:i, 374.
113. ME, p. 33. FW (7/10/59), 254. IR, I:44.
114. FW (7/10/59), 254. L (4/13/55), 160-61. LD, VI (Summer, 1851), 453.
115. LD, IV (7/5/46), 581; III (91/43), 550. F, II:i, 70-71. IR, I:46: Samuel Longfellow, however, said that Dickens told him that Daniel Quilp "was entirely a creature of his imagination. . . ." IR, I:54. "Mr. Marcus Stone, R. A., and Charles Dickens," D, VIII (1912; Ir, II:188. "Charles Dickens: Recollections of the Great Novelist," New York *Tribune* (7/5/70), repr. IR, p. 235.
116. NL, III (1/18/59), 88.
117. LD, V (1/49), 483. FN, p. 49. GK, p. 22.
118. WA, p. 96.
119. LD, I (9/27/39), 587-88. NL, III (11/19/57), 138.
120. "Doctor Dulcamara, M.P.," HW (12/18/58), repr. SH, p. 623. WC (1/24/62), 110. LD, I (12/29?/35), 113; III (9/1/42), 318.
121. LD, II (4/12/40), 53. LC, II (7/27/64), 254. F, VII:i, 115. LD, IV (1/2/44), 5: see also his preface to the 1844 edition of Martin Chuzzlewit: "All the Pecksniff family upon earth are quite agreed, I believe, that no such character as Mr. Pecksniff ever existed. . . .

"But, although Mr. Pecksniff will by no means concede to me, that Mr Pecksniff is real, I am consoled by finding him keenly susceptible of the truthfulness of Mrs. Gamp." Dickens would indeed have been troubled by Frye's assertion that his characters are not real.
122. "Out of the Season," UT, p. 456.

123. LD, IV (8/30/46), 612.
124. LD, V (11/7/47), 190. P, p. 130. LC, II (2/20/66), 292. NL, III (11/19/59), 137; II, (2/9/55), 624.
125. TN, p. 99: see NL, II, 624, 685, and III, 138, 461. L (1/2/62), 303. SD (4/10/69), 387.
126. L (10/2/58), 248. F, VI:i, 522-23.
127. NL, III (9/12/67), 547-48.
128. LD, II (3/16/41), 235: Lady De Lancey's husband was killed while talking to Wellington. Emma was Lady De Lancey's maid. General Dundas was a friend of the husband. The Prussian officer had tried to interfere with the wife's getting to her dying husband. James T. Fields, "Some Memories of Charles Dickens," *Atlantic Monthly*, 26 (1870), 238; see repr. in IR, II:311. "Reminiscences of my Father," *Windsor Magazine* (Christmas Supplement), 1934, repr. IR, I:120-21. F, IX:i, 271; VIII:ii, 194.
129. MD, pp. 13-14: "Plorn" was the nickname for Dickens' youngest son, Edward. F, II:i, 170. HCD (8/23/50), 173. F, VII:1, 115.
130. Quoted from *University* (Winter, 1965-66), in D, LXIII (1967); IR, p. 328: I treat this idea in relation to Dickens' illustrations and his dramatic readings in The Dickens Aesthetic, Chs. 1 and 4.
131. NL, II (6/10/57), 856; (3/2/53), 451. FW (2/2/51), 178.
132. From *University* (Princeton, N. J.: Winter 1965-66), quoted in D, 63 (1967), repr. IR, II:329. "In Memoriam," *Macmillan's Magazine*, XXII (1870), repr. IR, II:334. LC, I (1/14/53), 351.
133. F, IX:111, 285. LD, I:682; IV (8/30/46), 612. F, IX:i, 278. DG, pp. 34-49.
134. L (3/29/50), 26; (8/14/50), 33. BT, p. 22.
135. WC (1/24/62), 109-10.
136. LD, I (36), 97; (11/1/36), 189; (6/9?/38), 403.
137. J. W. T. Ley, *The Dickens Circle* (London, 1919), p. 75. F, VII:i, 116.
138. HW (10/4/51), repr. SH, p. 344; 1st Christmas Number, 850.
139. LD, IV (10/24/46), 647. HW (9/28); 10/5; 11/2, 16, 23; L (9/8/50), 39. NL, III (1/10/66), 454; p. 455; II (4/1/57), 843.

140. L (9/27/51), 70-71. No. 1, Saturday (3/30/50), 1. PI, p. 31. LD, V (3/31/48), 269: the only instance I have found of a dislike of novelty in Dickens is in a letter to Bulwer, in which he expressed "a certain inadaptible obstinacy as to novelties in tacit rhythm," which obliged him "to separate some ideas of some friends of ours from the mechanism with which they are associated . . . and to express the thoughts to my thoughts in my own manner." NL, III (1/10/66), 454. This, it should be noted, is novelty of form, not of content.
141. LD, V (1/1/48), 270. L (3/28/51), 50; (10/9/51), 72.
142. SB, p. 190. NL, III (3/7/66), 464.; II (9/22/50), 236.
143. NL, III (1/16/61), 206; II (8/14/55), 684. TN, p. 22. NL, II (7/17/55), 679. HW, No. 1, Saturday (3/30/50), 49.

Index

A

Ackland, John (character in Lytton's "The Disappearance of John Ackland"), 54

"Actor, The," 26

Adam Bede, by Eliot, 74-5, 165, 216, 217

Adams, H. G., 3

Addison, Joseph, 68, 175

Ahab (character in Melville's *Moby Dick*), 182

Ainsworth, Harrison, 80

Alice (character in Carrol's *Alice in Wonderland*), 187

Allen, Woody, 239

All the Year Round, 22, 24, 25 26, 27, 30, 32, 35, 37, 38, 48, 49, 53, 75, 78, 93, 111, 114, 148, 151, 153, 154, 155, 170, 186, 223, 226, 227

Andersen, Hans Christian, 59, 71

"An Experience," by Emily Jolly, 32-3

Antaeus, 181

Arabian Nights, 110, 130, 136, 167, 180-1

Archer, W. B., 116

Aristotle, 174

Arle, Mr., by Emily Jolly, 30

"Art in Fiction," by Bulwer, 7

Artist's Benevolent Society, 9

Art of the Novel, The, by James, 3

Athenaeum, 59

Atlantic Monthly, 70

"At the Bar," 111

Austen, Jane, 72

Austin, Henry, 52, 94

"Autobiography of a Small Boy," by Percy Fitzgerald, 53

Autogryph (in traveling letters by Brooks), 94

B

Balzac, Honoré de, 152, 159

Barlow, Mr. (character in Day's *Sandford and Merton*), 157, 177, 198

Barrington (a criminal), 54

Barthes, Roland, 201

Basil: A Story of Modern Life, by Collins, 76, 79

Beauclerc, Topham, 83

Beadnell, George, 204

Beadnell, Maria, 135

Bell, Mr. (character in Gaskell's North and South), 47

Bells (characters in Chorley's *Rocabella*), 93-4

Bentley, Richard, 27, 72, 114

Bentley's Miscellany, 25, 27, 50, 52, 55, 57, 114, 234

Bernstein, Carl, 184

Bible, The, 53, 62-5, 132

Birmingham and Midland Institute, 20, 104, 186

Birmingham Journal, The, 20

AMS Studies in the Nineteenth Century, No. 8
ISSN 0196-657X